Charting

the Book of Mormon

FARMS Publications

Charting

the Book of Mormon

Visual Aids for Personal Study and Teaching

by John W. Welch and J. Gregory Welch

Foundation for Ancient Research and Mormon Studies
Provo, Utah

Cover Design: Yvette Jones

The Foundation for Ancient Research
and Mormon Studies (FARMS)
at Brigham Young University
P.O. Box 7113
University Station
Provo, Utah 84602

07 06 05 04 03 02 01 00   6 5 4 3

Library of Congress Cataloging-in-Publication Data

Welch, John W. (John Woodland)
    Charting the Book of Mormon : visual aids for personal study and teaching / John W. Welch and
J. Gregory Welch.
        p.   cm.
    Includes bibliographical references and index.
    ISBN 0–934893–40–3 (pbk.: alk. paper)
    1. Book of Mormon Charts, diagrams, etc.   I. Welch, J. Gregory, 1979–   . II. Title.
BX8627.A2W47   1999
289.3'22'0223—dc21   99–38847
                                                                        CIP

*With special thanks
to Jeannie,
devoted wife and mother,
caring teacher and friend*

Table of Charts

Section 4: Jesus Christ in the Book of Mormon

Section 5: Teachings of the Book of Mormon

Section 6: Messages of the Book of Mormon

Section 7: Comparative Studies of the Book of Mormon

Section 8: Money in the Book of Mormon

Section 9: Law in the Book of Mormon

Section 10: Word Studies of the Book of Mormon

Section 11: War in the Book of Mormon

Section 12: Cycles in the Book of Mormon

Section 13: Geography in the Book of Mormon

Section 14: The First Edition of the Book of Mormon

Section 15: Invitations of the Book of Mormon

Scripture Index

Subject Index

Preface

The Book of Mormon is full of facts, ranging from eternal truths to mundane details. This collection charts many of those facts in clear and convenient graphs and visuals.

This newly reformatted and enhanced collection of 177 visual aids aims to serve multiple purposes. Students and teachers will find here helpful guides for personal study, as well as masters for making handouts or projectable classroom images.

The idea for this book first began to take shape a decade ago. One of my responsibilities on the board for Macmillan's *Encyclopedia of Mormonism* was to gather or create the five hundred maps, charts, and photographs that accompany its thirteen hundred articles. Personal experiences in working with several people in collecting and selecting those graphic images and, similarly, in using such visuals in illustrating many subsequent publications and lectures have convinced me of the value of charts in communicating important gospel information.

In 1996 my research focused on Book of Mormon visuals. Morgan A. Ashton, serving as a BYU intern under my supervision, worked to locate as many previously circulated Book of Mormon charts, graphs, and maps as possible. From his findings, certain recurring themes were identified and composite charts were created. In addition, many new charts were conceived. All of these schematics were then refined and shaped on the computer by my son, Gregory Welch, who devoted the summers of 1997 and 1998 to the graphic and conceptual development of this project.

A preliminary packet containing samples of about half of these charts was distributed by the Foundation for Ancient Research and Mormon Studies in 1997. Feedback and additions from many people have improved this new publication, and they are acknowledged with much appreciation.

In order to enhance understandability, a brief narrative explanation was then added to each chart. Because each chart is by nature an incomplete abstraction of much more complicated data, these brief explanatory notes quickly orient the viewer to the contents and purposes of each chart. A fuller discussion of each topic can be found in the bibliographic sources given. Amy K. Bingham, Don L. Brugger, and Eden N. Rasmussen at FARMS superbly shared much of the load in writing or editing those comments, as well as in designing the layout of this book, checking sources, and finalizing the graphic presentation of each chart.

This collection is by no means complete. Many more charts could easily be added, and other excellent schematics can be found in other publications. Readers may want to make new charts on their own, as well as add further details to the charts created so far.

I am deeply grateful to all who have helped transform the vision of this book into a concrete reality. We hope that these visuals will open new vistas of insight for Book of Mormon students everywhere.

John W. Welch
Provo, Utah, July 1999

The Coming Forth

of the Book of Mormon

Chart 1

Joseph Smith on the Correctness and Importance of the Book of Mormon

Explanation In one of the most famous declarations ever made about the Book of Mormon, the Prophet Joseph Smith declares this sacred record to be the keystone of the restored gospel of Jesus Christ and the best guide available for drawing nearer to God. This statement implies that the Book of Mormon is not only doctrinally but also historically correct. The Book of Mormon brings people closer to God by testifying of Jesus Christ, teaching the importance of obeying the commandments, explaining the plan of salvation, and revealing many other truths conducive to personal righteousness.

Sources Introduction to the Book of Mormon, 1981 edition. See Joseph Smith, *Teachings of the Prophet Joseph Smith,* comp. Joseph Fielding Smith (Salt Lake City: Deseret Book, 1976), 194.

I told the brethren that the Book of Mormon was the most correct of any book on earth, and the keystone of our religion, and a man would get nearer to God by abiding by its precepts, than by any other book.

— *Joseph Smith, 1841*

Chart 1

Chart 2

The Keystone of Our Religion

Explanation Just as a keystone holds an arch in place, knowing that the Book of Mormon is true holds together the edifice of faith built on the sturdy foundation of apostles, prophets, and the Lord Jesus Christ. For example, one cannot fully accept the Book of Mormon without also accepting the means by which it came forth—the Prophet Joseph Smith. In this chart, the archway stones representing the restored priesthood and living prophets are similarly reinforced by the keystone truth, as are the stones representing the reality of Christ's redemptive mission. In addition, the Book of Mormon ties together the New and Old Testaments by overtly explaining how the law of Moses was fulfilled in Christ, and it further upholds and complements the Bible by serving as another divinely inspired covenantal testament of Jesus Christ.

The Keystone of Our Religion

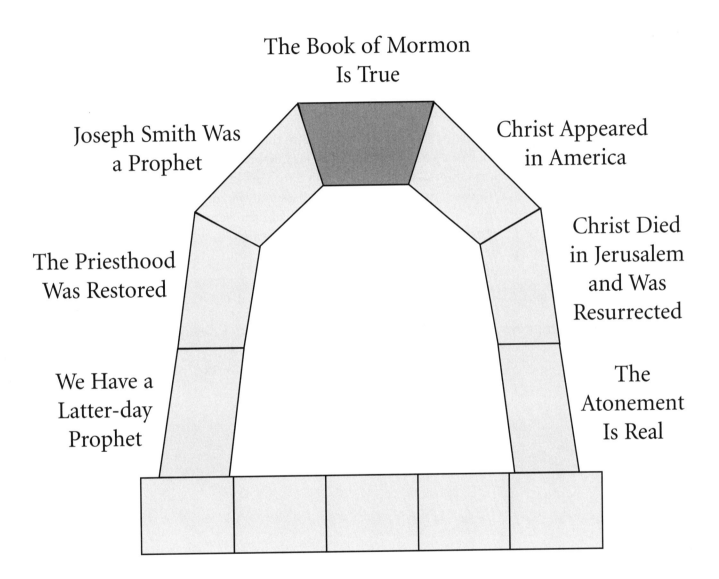

The Book of Mormon Is True

Joseph Smith Was a Prophet

Christ Appeared in America

The Priesthood Was Restored

Christ Died in Jerusalem and Was Resurrected

We Have a Latter-day Prophet

The Atonement Is Real

"Built upon the foundation of the apostles and prophets, Jesus Christ himself being the chief corner stone" (Ephesians 2:20).

Chart 2

Chart 3

Joseph Smith on How the Book of Mormon Will Prove Him a True Prophet

Explanation Although proof alone does not create testimonies or convince souls that the Book of Mormon is true, circumstantial evidence does support Joseph Smith's claim that the Book of Mormon is an ancient record written by former inhabitants of the Americas. In this editorial comment, Joseph Smith explained that the Book of Mormon would stand as circumstantial evidence of the validity of his prophetic calling. As Moses and Elijah were proved to be prophets through miracles they performed, so will Joseph Smith be vindicated through evidences for the authenticity of the Book of Mormon.

Sources Joseph Smith, *Teachings of the Prophet Joseph Smith,* comp. Joseph Fielding Smith (Salt Lake City: Deseret Book, 1976), 267; excerpt first printed in *Times and Seasons* 3 (15 Sept. 1842): 922.

We can not but think the Lord has a hand in bringing to pass his strange act, and proving the Book of Mormon true in the eyes of all the people. . . . It will be as it ever has been, the world will prove Joseph Smith a true prophet by circumstantial evidence, in experiments, as they did Moses and Elijah.

— *Joseph Smith, 1842*

Chart 3

Chart 4

Emma Smith on the Book of Mormon Translation Process, Quote 1

Explanation   In an interview conducted by her son Joseph Smith III in 1879, Emma Smith, wife of the Prophet Joseph Smith, expressed her faith in the restored Church of Christ, which was established in 1830 after the Prophet had translated the Book of Mormon and published it to the world. As a firsthand witness of the translation process when she acted as his scribe, Emma could testify that her husband had no notes, drafts, or books with him while he translated that ancient record. She, like the Three and Eight Witnesses of the Book of Mormon, never wavered in her testimony of the book's authenticity.

Sources   Joseph Smith III, "Last Testimony of Sister Emma," *Saints' Advocate* 2 (Oct. 1879): 51. For additional source information and related discussion, see John W. Welch and Tim Rathbone, "The Translation of the Book of Mormon: Basic Historical Information" (FARMS, 1986), 14–15.

Q. *What is the truth of Mormonism?*

A. I know Mormonism to be the truth; and believe the church to have been established by divine direction. I have complete faith in it. In writing for your father I frequently wrote day after day, often sitting at the table close by him, he sitting with his face buried in his hat, with the stone in it, and dictating hour after hour with nothing between us.

Q. *Had he not a book or manuscript from which he read, or dictated to you?*

A. He had neither manuscript or book to read from.

Q. *Could he not have had, and you not know it?*

A. If he had anything of the kind he could not have concealed it from me.

— *Emma Smith, 1879*

Chart 4

Chart 5

Emma Smith on the Book of Mormon Translation Process, Quote 2

Explanation Answering a question posed by her son Joseph Smith III in 1879, Emma Smith indicated that the Prophet Joseph Smith could not have been the author of the Book of Mormon, for he had neither the writing abilities nor adequate knowledge of ancient Israel. In fact, so limited was Joseph's knowledge when he translated the plates that he feared he had found an error when he read from the plates of Nephi that the city of Jerusalem was surrounded by a wall.

Sources Joseph Smith III, "Last Testimony of Sister Emma," *Saints' Advocate* 2 (Oct. 1879): 51; Edmund C. Briggs, "Interview with David Whitmer," *Saints' Herald* 31 (21 June 1884): 396–97. For additional sources and related discussion, see John W. Welch and Tim Rathbone, "The Translation of the Book of Mormon: Basic Historical Information" (FARMS, 1986), 8–9, 15.

Q. *Could not father have dictated the Book of Mormon to you, Oliver Cowdery and the others who wrote for him, after having first written it, or having first read it out of some book?*

A. Joseph Smith could neither write nor dictate a coherent and well-worded letter; let alone dictating a book like the Book of Mormon. And, though I was an active participant in the scenes that transpired, . . . it is marvelous to me, "a marvel and a wonder," as much so as to any one else.

— *Emma Smith, 1879*

Chart 5

Chart 6

Emma Smith on the Physical Characteristics of the Book of Mormon Plates

Explanation In an 1879 interview, Emma Smith described the plates of Mormon, which she had once felt beneath the linen cloth that covered them. She recalled that they were pliable like thick paper but rustled with a metallic sound when they were moved. Though Emma did not directly see the plates, she stands as yet another witness verifying the Book of Mormon's authentic origin.

Sources Joseph Smith III, "Last Testimony of Sister Emma," *Saints' Advocate* 2 (Oct. 1879): 51. For additional source information and related discussion, see John W. Welch and Tim Rathbone, "The Translation of the Book of Mormon: Basic Historical Information" (FARMS, 1986), 14–15.

Q. *Are you sure that he had the plates at the time you were writing for him?*

A. The plates often lay on the table without any attempt at concealment, wrapped in a small linen table cloth, which I had given him to fold them in. I once felt of the plates, as they thus lay on the table, tracing their outline and shape. They seemed to be pliable like thick paper, and would rustle with a metallic sound when the edges were moved by the thumb.

— *Emma Smith, 1879*

Chart 6

Chart 7

Elder B. H. Roberts on the Holy Spirit and Scholarly Evidence

Key Scripture   Moroni 10:3–5

Explanation   This is one of the plainest statements ever made about the roles of the Spirit and scholarly evidence in knowing and stating the truthfulness of the Book of Mormon. As Elder B. H. Roberts stated, secondary evidences can help make truth more clear and complete, thereby creating an atmosphere in which the Holy Ghost may more easily testify of it.

Source   B. H. Roberts, *New Witnesses for God* (Salt Lake City: Deseret News Press, 1909), 2:vi–vii, viii.

This [the Holy Ghost] must ever be the chief source of evidence for the truth of the Book of Mormon. All other evidence is secondary to this, the primary and infallible. No arrangement of evidence, however skillfully ordered; no argument, however adroitly made, can ever take its place. . . .

To be known, the truth must be stated and the clearer and more complete the statement is, the better opportunity will the Holy Spirit have for testifying to the souls of men that the work is true. . . .

Secondary evidences in support of truth, like secondary causes in natural phenomena, may be of firstrate importance, and mighty factors in the achievement of God's purposes.

— *Elder B. H. Roberts, 1909*

Chart 7

Chart 8

Austin Farrer on Rational Argument and Belief

Key Scripture   Moroni 10:3–5

Explanation   Elder Neal A. Maxwell once quoted philosopher Austin Farrer, who stated that although rational argument—that is, reasoning based on careful study of relevant evidence—does not necessarily create belief, it fosters an atmosphere conducive to it. Research in scientific, archaeological, and linguistic fields often elucidates ancient texts, the Book of Mormon included. Scholars who argue in favor of the ancient origins and character of the Book of Mormon maintain a climate in which people may take that book seriously as a historical record, helping them to embrace and receive it.

Sources   Quoted by Neal A. Maxwell in "Discipleship and Scholarship," *BYU Studies* 32/3 (1992): 5. The statement also appears in Austin Farrer, "The Christian Apologist," in *Light on C. S. Lewis*, ed. Jocelyn Gibb (New York: Harcourt, Brace and World, 1965).

Though argument does not create conviction, the lack of it destroys belief. What seems to be proved may not be embraced; but what no one shows the ability to defend is quickly abandoned. Rational argument does not create belief, but it maintains a climate in which belief may flourish.

— *Austin Farrer, 1965*

Chart 8

Events Surrounding the Translation of the Book of Mormon, 1827–1828

Key Scripture   Joseph Smith—History 1:59–65

Explanation   After Joseph Smith obtained the gold plates in September 1827, opposition threatened to stop the work of translation. Several attempts were made to steal the plates, and mounting persecution forced Joseph and Emma to move to Harmony, Pennsylvania. In early 1828 Professor Charles Anthon in New York certified in writing that the characters copied from the plates and Joseph's translation of them were correct, but he tore up the certificate upon hearing that an angel had told Joseph where the plates lay buried. June 1828 saw the death of Joseph and Emma's newborn first child. Another setback occurred when Martin Harris lost 116 pages that Joseph had translated from the Book of Lehi and, as a result, the Lord chastened Joseph and suspended his translation privilege for a season. While on a business trip to Palmyra in December 1828, David Whitmer met Oliver Cowdery, who would become Joseph's chief scribe. Although the years 1827 and 1828 presented obstacles to the translation effort, the stage was being set for Oliver's arrival in Harmony in April 1829.

Sources   *History of the Church,* 1:18–28. For additional sources and related discussion, see John W. Welch and Tim Rathbone, "The Translation of the Book of Mormon: Basic Historical Information" (FARMS, 1986), 3–15; and John W. Welch and Tim Rathbone, "How Long Did It Take to Translate the Book of Mormon?" in *Reexploring the Book of Mormon,* ed. John W. Welch (Salt Lake City: Deseret Book and FARMS, 1992), 1–8.

Events Surrounding the Translation of the Book of Mormon, 1827–1828

1827   Sept. — Joseph obtains the plates from the angel Moroni

Oct. —

Nov. —

Dec. — Joseph and Emma move to Harmony, Pennsylvania

1828   Jan. — Joseph translates some characters from the plates

Feb. — Martin Harris takes sample of characters and Joseph's accompanying translation to Charles Anthon

Mar. —

Apr. — Book of Lehi translated (April 12–June 14)

May —

June — Joseph and Emma's first child is born and dies
Martin Harris loses 116 pages

July — Joseph travels to Manchester, New York
Interpreters and plates are taken away from Joseph

Aug. —

Sept. — Joseph reobtains interpreters and plates

Oct. —

Nov. —

Dec. — David Whitmer makes business trip to Palmyra, where he meets Oliver Cowdery

Chart 9

Chart 10

Events Surrounding the Translation of the Book of Mormon, 1829–1830

Key Scripture   Joseph Smith—History 1:66–67

Explanation   This chart, highlighting some of the events of 1829 and 1830, illustrates the sacrifices of those who were instrumental in helping bring forth the Book of Mormon in a miraculously short period of time. Oliver Cowdery spent the two months of April and May 1829, in Harmony, Pennsylvania, assisting the Prophet Joseph Smith as scribe for most of the Book of Mormon translation. Prejudice against the Prophet made it difficult for him to find a willing printer for the controversial "gold bible." Fortunately, Martin Harris gave much support to this cause, mortgaging his farm to secure payment for the cost of printing five thousand copies of the first edition of the Book of Mormon. Despite such challenges, in March 1830 the ancient Nephite record was published, opening the way for the organization and growth of the restored Church of Christ.

Sources   *History of the Church*, 1:28–33, 71–80. For additional sources and related discussion, see John W. Welch and Tim Rathbone, "The Translation of the Book of Mormon: Basic Historical Information" (FARMS, 1986), 16–32.

Events Surrounding the Translation of the Book of Mormon, 1829–1830

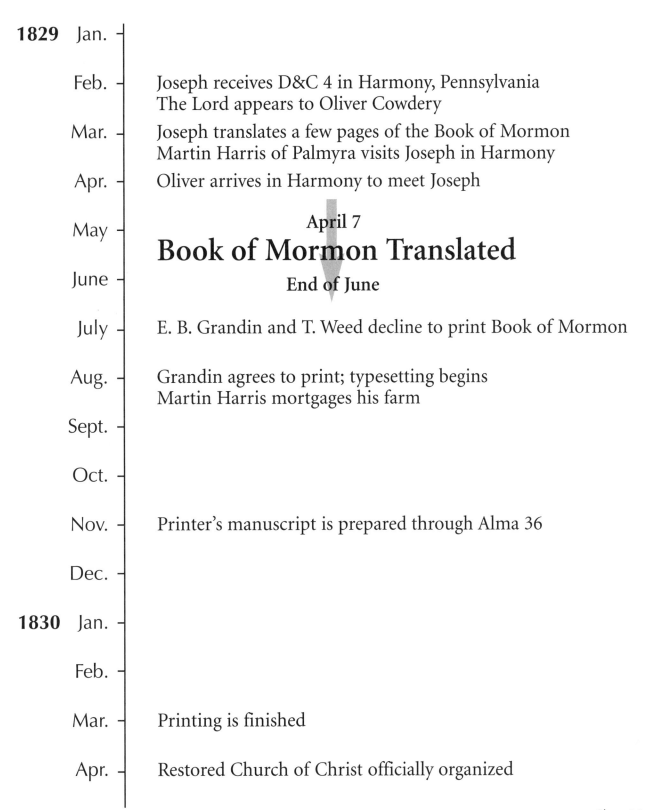

1829 Jan.

Feb. — Joseph receives D&C 4 in Harmony, Pennsylvania
The Lord appears to Oliver Cowdery

Mar. — Joseph translates a few pages of the Book of Mormon
Martin Harris of Palmyra visits Joseph in Harmony

Apr. — Oliver arrives in Harmony to meet Joseph

April 7
Book of Mormon Translated
End of June

May

June —

July — E. B. Grandin and T. Weed decline to print Book of Mormon

Aug. — Grandin agrees to print; typesetting begins
Martin Harris mortgages his farm

Sept. —

Oct. —

Nov. — Printer's manuscript is prepared through Alma 36

Dec. —

1830 Jan. —

Feb. —

Mar. — Printing is finished

Apr. — Restored Church of Christ officially organized

Chart 10

Chart 11

Church History Sites
near Palmyra, New York, 1820–1831

Explanation   This map shows historical sites connected with the Book of Mormon, such as the Hill Cumorah, where Joseph Smith received the gold plates from the angel Moroni; the Joseph Smith farm, where Joseph and Emma lived for nearly a year after their marriage in January 1827 and where the plates were concealed in various places to safeguard them from ransackers; the Martin Harris farm, which was mortgaged and later sold to cover the expense of printing the Book of Mormon; and the Grandin print shop, where the Book of Mormon was printed in 1830.

Source   John W. Welch and Jeff Bird, "History of the Church," in Daniel H. Ludlow, ed., *Encyclopedia of Mormonism,* 5 vols. (1992), 2:599.

Church History Sites
near Palmyra, New York, 1820–1831

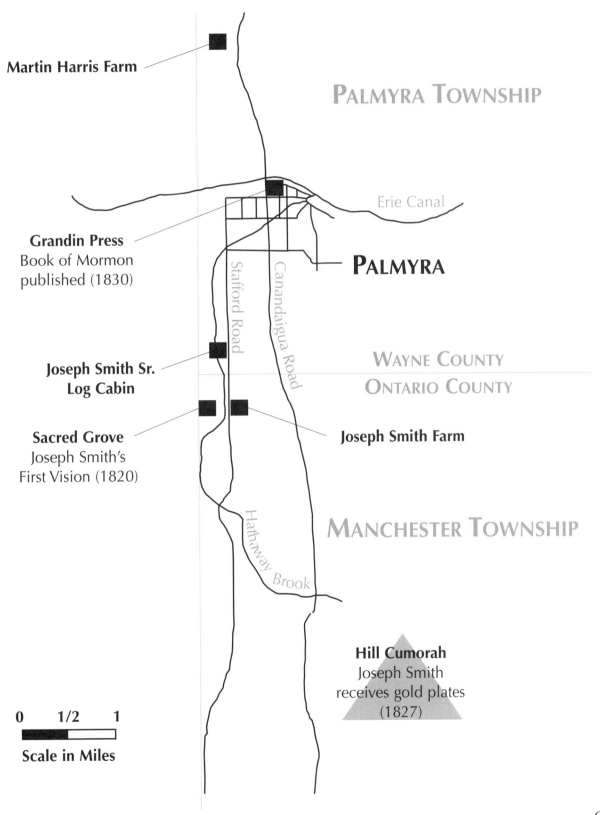

Martin Harris Farm

PALMYRA TOWNSHIP

Erie Canal

Grandin Press
Book of Mormon
published (1830)

PALMYRA

Stafford Road

Canandaigua Road

Joseph Smith Sr.
Log Cabin

WAYNE COUNTY
ONTARIO COUNTY

Sacred Grove
Joseph Smith's
First Vision (1820)

Joseph Smith Farm

MANCHESTER TOWNSHIP

Hathaway Brook

Hill Cumorah
Joseph Smith
receives gold plates
(1827)

0   1/2   1
Scale in Miles

Chart 11

Chart 12

Church History Sites in Western New York, 1820–1831

Explanation   This area map of New York and Pennsylvania highlights locations linked to the Book of Mormon and the establishment of the restored church. Fleeing persecution in Manchester, New York, in December 1827, Joseph and Emma Hale Smith settled in Harmony, Pennsylvania, where Joseph would translate most of the plates. In June 1829 Joseph (and probably Emma) moved about one hundred miles to Fayette, New York, where that same month the Three Witnesses were shown the plates (a few days later the Eight Witnesses saw the plates in Manchester) and, in the Peter Whitmer home, the translation was completed. It was in the Whitmer home that the church was organized on 6 April 1830. Other church history sites in southern New York include South Bainbridge, where Joseph and Emma were married on 18 January 1827; Seneca Lake, where several people were baptized during the early years of the restoration; and Colesville, where the church's first branch was formed in October 1830.

Source   John W. Welch and Jeff Bird, "History of the Church," in Daniel H. Ludlow, ed., *Encyclopedia of Mormonism*, 5 vols. (1992), 2:599.

Church History Sites
in Western New York, 1820–1831

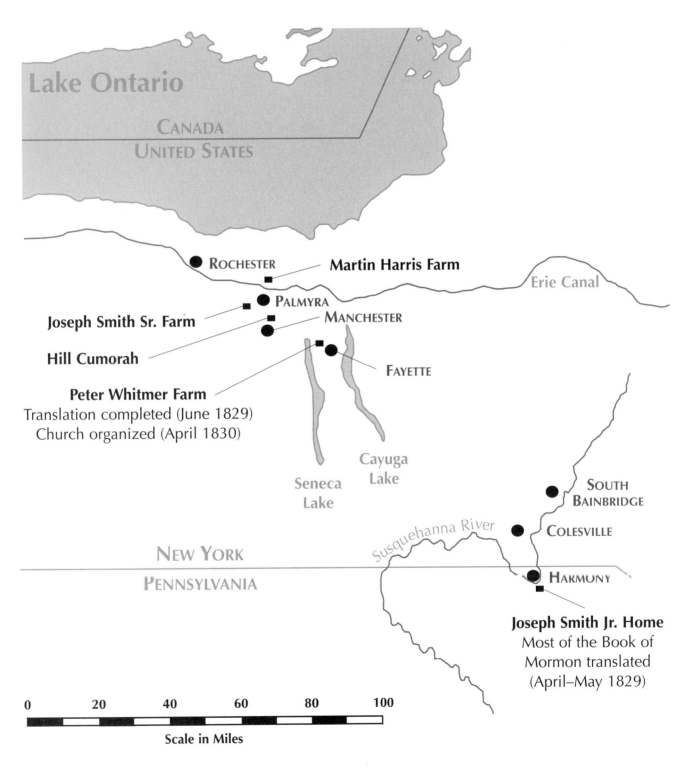

Lake Ontario

CANADA

UNITED STATES

Erie Canal

● ROCHESTER ■ **Martin Harris Farm**

■ ● PALMYRA

Joseph Smith Sr. Farm ■ ■ **MANCHESTER**

Hill Cumorah ●

■ ● **FAYETTE**

Peter Whitmer Farm
Translation completed (June 1829)
Church organized (April 1830)

Cayuga
Lake

Seneca
Lake

Susquehanna River

● **SOUTH
BAINBRIDGE**

● **COLESVILLE**

NEW YORK

PENNSYLVANIA

● ■ **HARMONY**

Joseph Smith Jr. Home
Most of the Book of
Mormon translated
(April–May 1829)

0   20   40   60   80   100

Scale in Miles

Chart 12

The Structure

of the Book of Mormon

Chart 13

Book of Mormon Plates and Records

Key Scripture   Words of Mormon 1:3–11

Explanation   Many ancient documents such as King Benjamin's speech or the plates of brass were quoted or abridged by the ancient authors who compiled the books found on the small and large plates of Nephi. The abridgments, quotations, and original writings of those Book of Mormon historians are displayed on the left-hand and middle columns of this chart and are then shown in relation to the new set of plates produced by Mormon and Moroni that was delivered to Joseph Smith by the angel Moroni. Joseph dictated the original manuscript of the Book of Mormon from the plates of Mormon. Copying that original manuscript, parts of which survive today, Oliver Cowdery prepared a printer's manuscript (owned by the RLDS Church). The first edition of the Book of Mormon was typeset from that printer's manuscript.

Source   Grant R. Hardy and Robert E. Parsons, "Book of Mormon Plates and Records," in Daniel H. Ludlow, ed., *Encyclopedia of Mormonism*, 5 vols. (1992), 1:196.

Book of Mormon Plates and Records

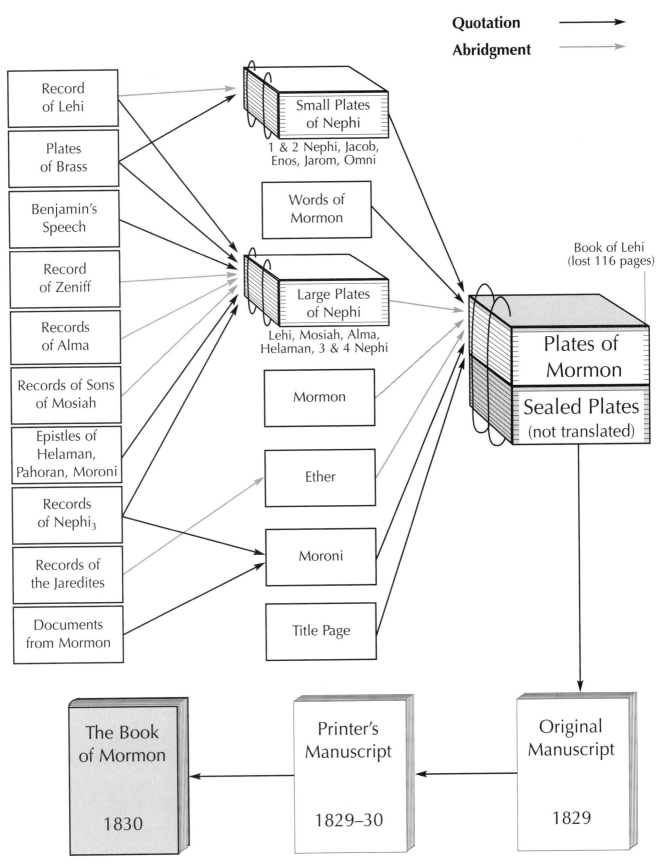

Quotation ⟶
Abridgment ⟶

Record of Lehi

Plates of Brass

Benjamin's Speech

Record of Zeniff

Records of Alma

Records of Sons of Mosiah

Epistles of Helaman, Pahoran, Moroni

Records of Nephi₃

Records of the Jaredites

Documents from Mormon

Small Plates of Nephi
1 & 2 Nephi, Jacob, Enos, Jarom, Omni

Words of Mormon

Large Plates of Nephi
Lehi, Mosiah, Alma, Helaman, 3 & 4 Nephi

Mormon

Ether

Moroni

Title Page

Book of Lehi (lost 116 pages)

Plates of Mormon

Sealed Plates (not translated)

The Book of Mormon
1830

Printer's Manuscript
1829–30

Original Manuscript
1829

Chart 13

Chart 14

Contents of the Plates of Brass

Key Scripture   1 Nephi 5:11–14

Explanation   The plates of brass contained a copy of the Law (five books of Moses), a history of the Jews, Lehi's genealogy, and the writings of many prophets. Some of these records were comparable to certain books now found in the Old Testament, but others did not find their way into the Bible. Nephi's summary of these contents, found in 1 Nephi 5:11–14, is graphically displayed here, along with sample references illustrating the profound influence of these records elsewhere in the Book of Mormon.

Source   Expanded from the work of Paul Bankhead, student of John W. Welch, Book of Mormon 121H, Brigham Young University, fall 1997.

Contents of the Plates of Brass
Listed in 1 Nephi 5:11–14

1 Nephi 5:11	**Five Books of Moses**	
	creation of the world	2 Nephi 2:15
	account of Adam and Eve	2 Nephi 2:18–19
	law of Moses	2 Nephi 5:10
1 Nephi 5:12	**A Record of the Jews to the Reign of Zedekiah**	Jacob 2:23
1 Nephi 5:13	**Prophecies of the Holy Prophets**	
Isaiah	coming of Christ	2 Nephi 19:1–8
	scattering of Israel	2 Nephi 19:11–21
	day of the Gentiles	1 Nephi 20
	victory of God	1 Nephi 21
Zenos	burial of Christ	1 Nephi 19:10
	allegory of the olive tree	Jacob 5
	hymn on prayer	Alma 33:4–11
Zenock	crucifixion of Christ	1 Nephi 19:10
Neum	crucifixion of Christ	1 Nephi 19:10
Joseph	concerning his posterity	2 Nephi 4:2
Jeremiah	many prophecies	Helaman 8:20
1 Nephi 5:14	**Genealogy of Lehi's Fathers**	Alma 10:3

Chart 14

Chart 15

Sources behind the Book of Ether

Key Scripture   Ether 1:1–5

Explanation   What we now know as the book of Ether originated from early Jaredite records and Ether's writings, which Ether combined to produce his twenty-four gold plates near the end of the Jaredite civilization. The people of Limhi later found these plates while searching for the city of Zarahemla, and King Mosiah translated them around 120 B.C. Moroni later abridged the translated plates and, together with his commentary, included them in his record, thus producing the final form of the book of Ether. The seams between the insertions of Moroni's comments into the final text of this book are clearly discernible, with the underlying text resuming flawlessly after each interruption.

Source   John W. Welch, "Sources behind the Book of Ether" (FARMS, 1986).

Sources behind the Book of Ether

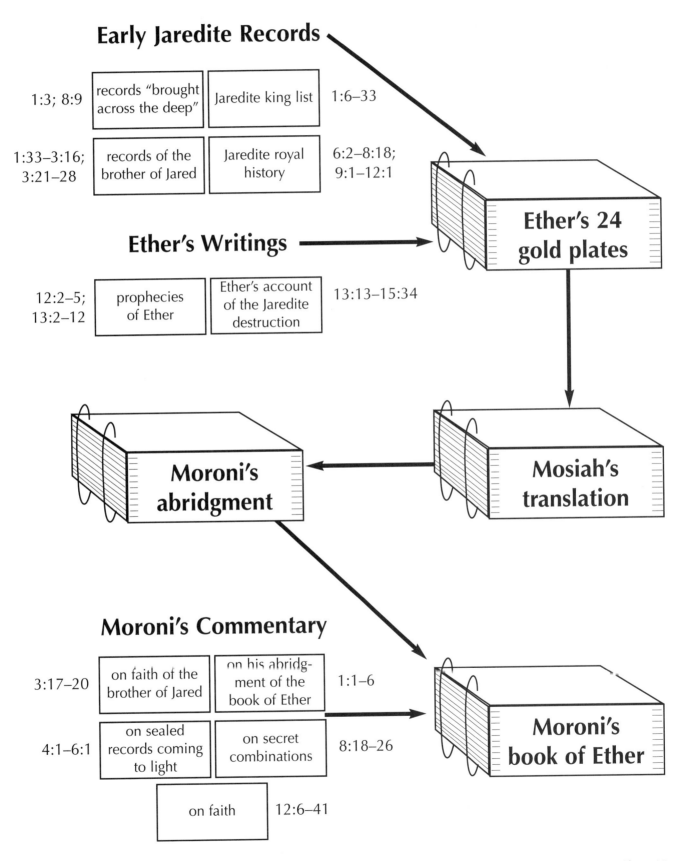

Early Jaredite Records

1:3; 8:9	records "brought across the deep"	Jaredite king list	1:6–33
1:33–3:16; 3:21–28	records of the brother of Jared	Jaredite royal history	6:2–8:18; 9:1–12:1

Ether's Writings

12:2–5; 13:2–12	prophecies of Ether	Ether's account of the Jaredite destruction	13:13–15:34

Ether's 24 gold plates

Mosiah's translation

Moroni's abridgment

Moroni's Commentary

3:17–20	on faith of the brother of Jared	on his abridgment of the book of Ether	1:1–6
4:1–6:1	on sealed records coming to light	on secret combinations	8:18–26
	on faith	12:6–41	

Moroni's book of Ether

Chart 15

Chart 16

Who Kept the Records in the Book of Mormon? (Overview)

Key Scripture Mormon 9:30–37

Explanation Genealogical, historical, legal, and prophetic records of the Nephites were handed down in sacred trust, usually from father to son. Only four Nephite families kept the plates: Lehi's posterity mainly through Jacob, Mosiah's family, Alma and his long line of descendants, and Mormon and his son Moroni. As anthropologist John L. Sorenson has pointed out, the Book of Mormon is structured as a "lineage history."

Who Kept the Records in the Book of Mormon?

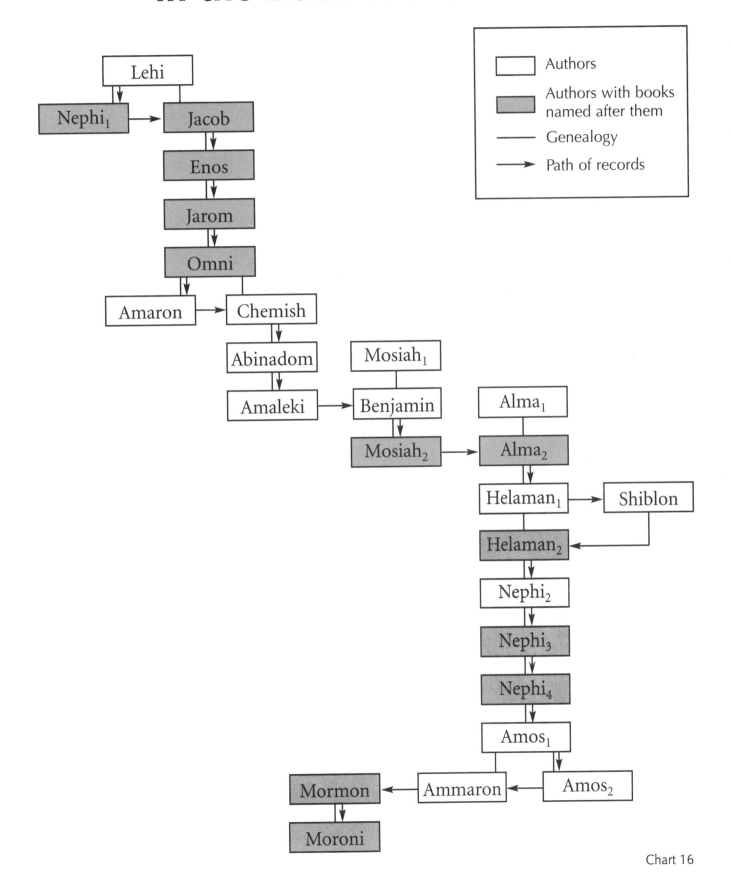

Authors

Authors with books named after them

Genealogy

Path of records

Chart 16

Chart 17

Who Kept the Records in the Book of Mormon? (By Lineages)

Key Scripture   Mormon 9:30–37

Explanation   The four families of Nephite record keepers of the Book of Mormon are listed chronologically here, along with their approximate dates of birth and other important information. If a date is not found in or tied directly to a specific verse, then the information has been deduced from general historical information. This list is similar to chart 16 and can be used to document and explain the relationships between keepers of the plates of Nephi.

Source   John W. Welch, "Longevity of Book of Mormon People and the 'Age of Man,'" *Journal of Collegium Aesculapium* 3 (1985): 34–45.

Who Kept the Records in the Book of Mormon?

Lineage of Lehi

Record Keeper	Dates*	Comments	Reference
Nephi₁	615 B.C.	born in Jerusalem	1 Nephi 1:4
	600 B.C.	begins record when about 15 years old	1 Nephi 1:1
	540 B.C.	dies about 75 years old	
Jacob	592 B.C.	born son of Lehi, brother of Nephi₁	1 Nephi 18:7
	544 B.C.	becomes record keeper	Jacob 1:1
	495 B.C.	dies about 97 years old	Jacob 7:27
Enos	515 B.C.	born son of Jacob	Jacob 7:27
	420 B.C.	about to die	Enos 1:25
	417 B.C.	dies about 98 years old	
Jarom	440 B.C.	born son of Enos	Jarom 1:1
	420 B.C.	becomes record keeper	Jarom 1:1
	361 B.C.	gives plates to Omni	Jarom 1:15
	355 B.C.	dies about 85 years old	
Omni	390 B.C.	born son of Jarom	Omni 1:1
	361 B.C.	becomes record keeper	Jarom 1:15
	317 B.C.	writes 3 verses on plates in 44 years	Omni 1:1–3
	315 B.C.	dies about 75 years old	Omni 1:3
Amaron	350 B.C.	born son of Omni	Omni 1:4
	317 B.C.	becomes record keeper	Omni 1:4
	277 B.C.	dies about 73 years old	Omni 1:8
Chemish	330 B.C.	born son of Omni, brother of Amaron	Omni 1:9
	279 B.C.	becomes record keeper	Omni 1:9
	250 B.C.	dies about 80 years old	Omni 1:9
Abinadom	270 B.C.	born son of Chemish	Omni 1:10
	180 B.C.	dies about 90 years old	Omni 1:10
Amaleki	210 B.C.	born son of Abinadom	Omni 1:12
	150 B.C.	Nephites move to Zarahemla	Omni 1:13
	138 B.C.	dies about 72 years old	Omni 1:30

* dates are approximate

Chart 17

Benjamin and Mosiah

Benjamin	190 B.C. born son of Mosiah$_1$	Omni 1:23
	140 B.C. becomes record keeper	Omni 1:25
	121 B.C. dies 69 years old	Mosiah 6:5
Mosiah$_2$	154 B.C. born son of Benjamin	Mosiah 6:4
	91 B.C. dies about 63 years old	Mosiah 29:46

Lineage of Alma$_1$

Alma$_1$	174 B.C. born a descendant of Nephi	Mosiah 17:2
	149 B.C. "young man" 25 years old; Abinadi martyred	Mosiah 17:2, 20
	120 B.C. becomes high priest over church in Zarahemla	Mosiah 23:16
	91 B.C. dies about 83 years old	Mosiah 29:47
Alma$_2$	126 B.C. born son of Alma$_1$	Mosiah 27:8
	91 B.C. becomes record keeper	Mosiah 29:42
	73 B.C. departs out of land; assumed to have been translated	Alma 45:18, 19
Helaman$_1$	97 B.C. born son of Alma$_2$	Alma 36:3
	73 B.C. becomes high priest	Alma 45:20
	64 B.C. leads 2,000 Ammonite warriors; 33 years old	Alma 53:22
	57 B.C. dies about 40 years old	Alma 62:52
Shiblon	95 B.C. born son of Alma$_2$, brother of Helaman$_1$	Alma 63:1
	57 B.C. becomes record keeper	Alma 63:1
	53 B.C. dies about 42 years old	Alma 63:13
Helaman$_2$	76 B.C. born son of Helaman$_1$	Helaman 2:2
	53 B.C. becomes record keeper	Helaman 2:2
	39 B.C. dies about 37 years old	Helaman 3:37
Nephi$_2$	54 B.C. born son of Helaman$_2$	Helaman 3:37
	A.D. 1 departs out of land	3 Nephi 1:3
	A.D. 13 dies about 67 years old	

Chart 17

Nephi₃	30 B.C.	born son of Nephi₂	3 Nephi 1:1
	A.D. 1	becomes record keeper	3 Nephi 1:1
	A.D. 34	one of 12 disciples	3 Nephi 12:1
	A.D. 60	dies about 90 years old	
	A.D. 100	all but 3 disciples have passed away	4 Nephi 1:14
Nephi₄	A.D. 50	born son of Nephi₃	
Amos₁	A.D. 90	born son of Nephi₄	
	A.D. 110	becomes record keeper for 84 years	4 Nephi 1:19
	A.D. 194	dies about 104 years old	4 Nephi 1:21
Amos₂	A.D. 174	born son of Amos₁	
	A.D. 194	becomes record keeper	4 Nephi 1:21
	A.D. 305	dies about 131 years old	4 Nephi 1:47
Ammaron	A.D. 190	born son of Amos, brother of Amos₂	
	A.D. 305	becomes record keeper	4 Nephi 1:48
	A.D. 320	dies about 130 years old	Mormon 1:5

Mormon and Moroni

Mormon	A.D. 311	born	Mormon 1:2
	A.D. 321	told by Ammaron that at age 24 he would become record keeper	Mormon 1:2
	A.D. 326	visited by Lord; leads Nephite armies	Mormon 1:15
	A.D. 335	becomes record keeper	Mormon 2:18
	A.D. 385	delivered plates to Moroni; buried others in hill Cumorah	Mormon 8:1
	A.D. 401	dies about 90 years old at hands of Lamanites	Mormon 8:3
Moroni	A.D. 360	born son of Mormon₂	Mormon 8:1
	A.D. 385	becomes record keeper	Mormon 8:1
	A.D. 421	"soon go to rest," about 61 years old	Moroni 10:34

Chart 17

Chart 18

Whose Words Are Found in the Book of Mormon?

Key Scripture Omni 1:9

Explanation Although four families kept the main Nephite records (see chart 16), the words of many other authors are included in the Book of Mormon as well. The writings or speeches of Jesus Christ, Isaiah, Captain Moroni, and Zenos, for example, all add significantly to the Book of Mormon, even though these authors did not actually write upon the plates themselves. This chart adds to chart 16 some of the additional writers or speakers who are quoted in the Book of Mormon.

Whose Words Are Found in the Book of Mormon?

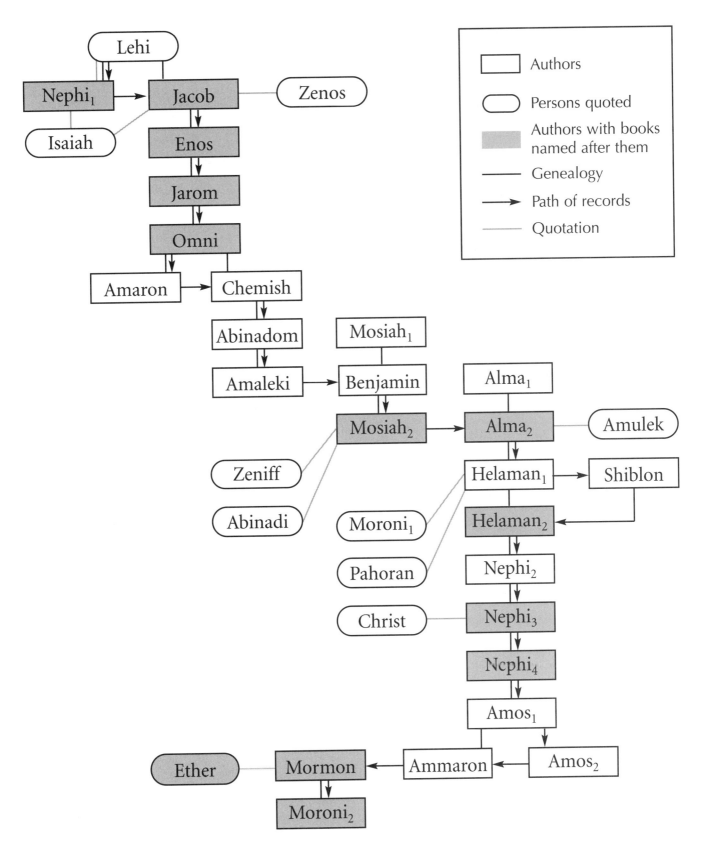

Chart 18

Chart 19

Writings of Lehi

Key Scripture   2 Nephi 1:1–4:11

Explanation   Although the 116 pages of translation lost by Martin Harris in 1828 contained writings from the Book of Lehi, not all of Lehi's words are lost to us. Lehi's prophecies, visions, and teachings were often quoted or paraphrased by his sons Nephi and Jacob in their own writing and preaching. S. Kent Brown, professor of ancient scripture at Brigham Young University, suggests that this is evidence that Nephi and Jacob used the personal record of Lehi as a primary source in writing about the new land of promise, Jesus Christ, Israel, marriage, and other important topics. This chart indicates where in the small plates of Nephi the words of Lehi, originally written from about 600 to 570 B.C., are found today.

Source   S. Kent Brown, "Lehi's Personal Record: Quest for a Missing Source," *BYU Studies* 24/1 (1984): 19–42.

Writings of Lehi
Quoted or Paraphrased by Nephi and Jacob

1 Nephi 1:4–15	Lehi's calling as a prophet
1 Nephi 5:17–19	prophecies regarding brass plates
1 Nephi 8:2–28	dream of the tree of life
1 Nephi 10:1–16	prophecies about Christ and Israel
2 Nephi 1:1–12	prophecies about the New World
2 Nephi 1:13–32	blessing to Laman, Lemuel, Sam, sons of Ishmael, Nephi, Zoram
2 Nephi 2:1–30	blessing to Jacob
2 Nephi 3:1–25	blessing to Joseph
2 Nephi 4:3–7	blessing to the children of Laman
2 Nephi 4:8–9	blessing to the children of Lemuel
2 Nephi 4:11	blessing to Sam
Jacob 2:23–34	fidelity in marriage

Chart 19

Chart 20

Writings of Mormon

Key Scriptures   Words of Mormon; Helaman 12; Mormon 1:1–7:10; Moroni 7–9

Explanation   Mormon, the chief abridger and editor of the full Book of Mormon, also added comments of his own to many of the books in that record, besides writing two books within the Book of Mormon that also bear his name (the Words of Mormon and the book of Mormon). As this chart demonstrates, his editorial commentaries, skillfully woven into the text of the primary authors, provide important explanations of human nature, the gathering of Israel, the Book of Mormon in the latter days, and the Savior's visit to the Americas. His own writings include, among other things (not all of which are listed on this chart), an autobiography and important sermons or letters on good works and infant baptism.

Writings of Mormon

Reference	Description of Text	Date Written*
W of M 1:1–2	on delivering plates to Moroni	A.D. 385
W of M 1:3–11	on abridging the plates of Nephi	A.D. 340
W of M 1:12–18	account of Benjamin	A.D. 340
Helaman 3:13–17	on record keeping	A.D. 340
Helaman 12	on human nature	A.D. 341
3 Nephi 5:8–26	on record keeping	A.D. 341
3 Nephi 10:11–19	on searching the scriptures	A.D. 341
3 Nephi 26:8–21	on Christ's visit to Americas	A.D. 341
3 Nephi 28:24–30:2	on Three Nephites and gathering of Israel	A.D. 341
4 Nephi	four generations of history	A.D. 342
Mormon 1:1–6:15	autobiography	A.D. 384
Mormon 6:16–7:10	lament over people and testimony to latter-day remnant	
Moroni 7	sermon on good works	A.D. 334
Moroni 8	epistle on baptism	A.D. 337
Moroni 9	farewell epistle to Moroni	A.D. 385

* dates are approximate

Chart 20

Chart 21

Writings of Moroni

Key Scriptures   Mormon 8–9; Ether 12; Moroni 10

Explanation   Sometime after A.D. 385, Moroni was left alone to "write the sad tale of the destruction" of the Nephite people (Mormon 8:3). His writings appear within the last three books of the Book of Mormon. Moroni recounted the final battle at Cumorah and abridged the record of the Jaredites. He also testified of Jesus Christ and preserved gospel ordinances for use in future generations. For example, Moroni's record of the Nephite sacrament prayers is the historical source from which Joseph Smith received the prayers that are used today in administering the sacrament.

Writings of Moroni

Reference	Description of Text
Mormon 8–9	concerning nonbelievers; call to repentance; coming forth of the Book of Mormon
Ether 1:1–6	on abridging the book of Ether
Ether 1:6–3:28	early Jaredite history (Moroni frequently relies on Ether's texts here, although only by memory; see Ether 5:1)
Ether 4–5	on the coming forth of sacred records
Ether 6:1–12:5	Jaredite history (Moroni again recites history by memory; see Ether 5:1)
Ether 12:6–41	on faith and overcoming weakness
Ether 13–15	final Jaredite history (again by memory)
Moroni 1	on his inclusion of the book of Moroni
Moroni 2	on ordination of apostles
Moroni 3	on ordination of priests and teachers
Moroni 4–5	on administration of the sacrament
Moroni 6	on baptism and church membership
Moroni 10	exhortation to the Lamanites and others
Title Page	contents of the Book of Mormon

Chart 21

Chart 22

Number of Pages in Books
of the Book of Mormon

Key Scripture   Words of Mormon 1:9

Explanation   The individual books that compose the Book of Mormon vary
significantly in length. The overall record concentrates on three
periods: the founding of the Nephite civilization (sixth century
B.C.), its flourishing (150 B.C.–A.D. 50), and its final years (fourth
century A.D.).

Number of Pages in Books of the Book of Mormon

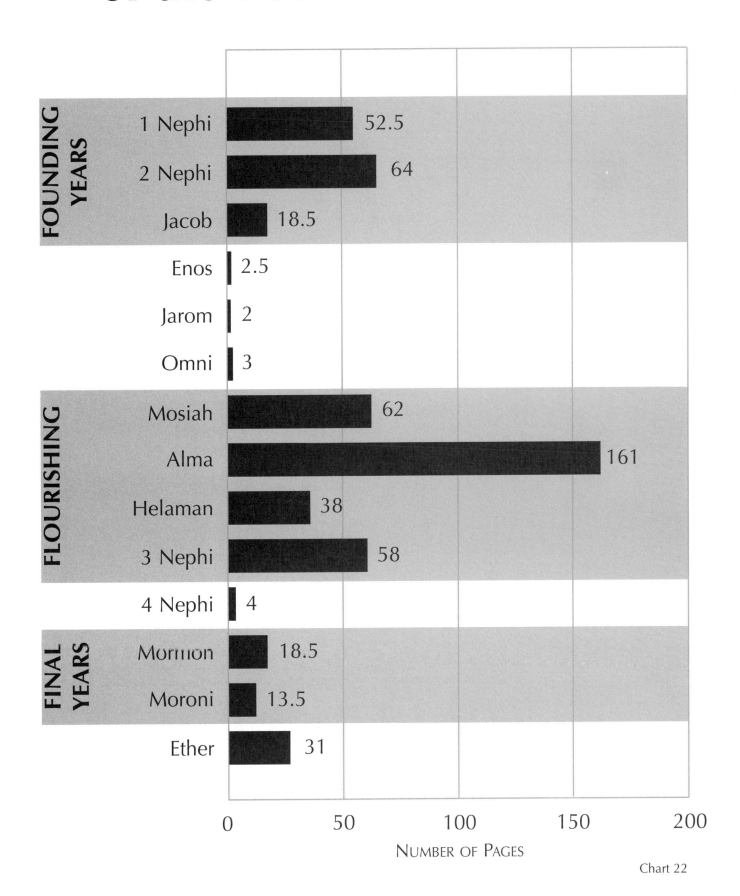

FOUNDING YEARS	1 Nephi 52.5
	2 Nephi 64
	Jacob 18.5
	Enos 2.5
	Jarom 2
	Omni 3
FLOURISHING	Mosiah 62
	Alma 161
	Helaman 38
	3 Nephi 58
	4 Nephi 4
FINAL YEARS	Mormon 18.5
	Moroni 13.5
	Ether 31

0   50   100   150   200

NUMBER OF PAGES

Chart 22

Chart 23

Average Number of Pages Covering One Nephite Year

Key Scripture   Words of Mormon 1:9

Explanation   This chart adds a time factor to chart 22. The number of pages in the Book of Mormon given to each year of Nephite history varies significantly. Some shorter books cover long periods of time, and longer books document relatively few years. For example, the book of Jacob on the average documents a year in one-third of a page, while the book of Alma averages about four pages per year. This suggests that Mormon most likely abridged some records more extensively than others or had less underlying text to work with in certain eras. The data used for this chart is listed below.

Nephite Book	Approximate Years Covered	Total Years Covered	Number of Pages
1 Nephi	600–588 B.C.	13	52.5
2 Nephi	587–545 B.C.	43	64
Jacob	544–482 B.C.	63	18.5
Enos	481–420 B.C.	62	2.5
Jarom	419–361 B.C.	59	2
Omni	360–131 B.C.	230	3
Mosiah	130–91 B.C.	40	62
Alma	91–53 B.C.	39	161
Helaman	52–1 B.C.	52	38
3 Nephi	A.D. 1–35	35	58
4 Nephi	A.D. 36–321	286	4
Mormon	A.D. 322–400	79	18.5
Moroni	A.D. 401–421	21	13.5

Average Number of Pages Covering One Nephite Year
for Books in the Book of Mormon

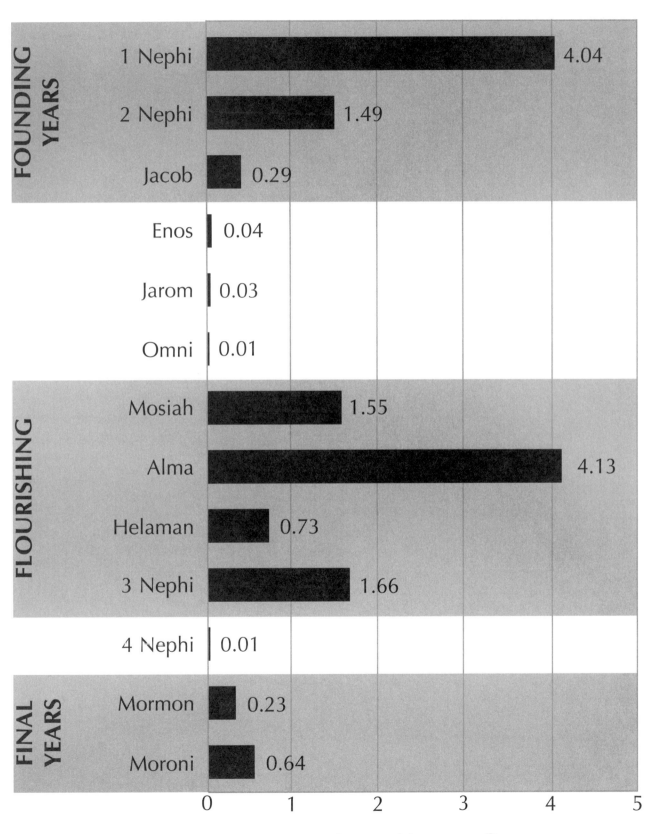

AVERAGE NUMBER OF PAGES

Chart 23

Chart 24

Nephite Books Compared by Length and Years Covered

Key Scripture 3 Nephi 5:8

Explanation This chart highlights the relationship between pages written and years recorded for individual books in the Book of Mormon. In this divided bar graph, each band spans three columns representing, from left to right, a percentage of the total number of pages of Nephite history a particular book includes, the name of the book (the book of Ether excepted because it covers Jaredite, not Nephite, history), and a percentage of the total number of years of Nephite civilization that the book covers. For example, while 4 Nephi is only a few pages long and represents 0.8 percent of the total number of Book of Mormon pages that record Nephite history, it is the record of four generations of people and covers 28 percent of the years in which the Nephite civilization existed. This chart consolidates information also found in charts 22 and 23.

Source Richard O. Cowan, "Historians of the Book of Mormon," *Instructor,* December 1962, 444 and inside back cover. See also chart by Scott Haycock and Robert Turner, Springfield, Virginia.

Nephite Books Compared by Length and Years Covered

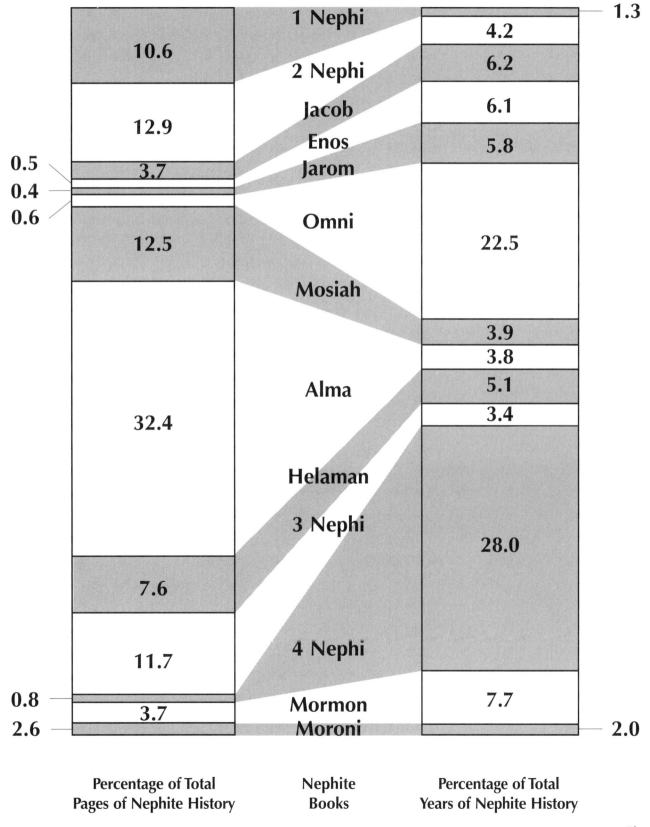

Percentage of Total Pages of Nephite History | Nephite Books | Percentage of Total Years of Nephite History

Chart 24

Chart 25

Nephite Books
Listed Chronologically

Key Scripture Words of Mormon 1:5

Explanation The Nephites lived in the Americas from approximately 600 B.C. to A.D. 385, a period of about one thousand years. Moroni survived his people and buried the plates around A.D. 421. Throughout their history, the Nephites kept historical and doctrinal records. This graph shows which centuries each Nephite book covers, presenting Nephite chronology as a whole. Three periods of Nephite civilization receive the greatest attention: the founding (sixth century B.C.), the flourishing (150 B.C.–A.D. 50), and the final years (fourth century A.D.).

Nephite Books
Listed Chronologically

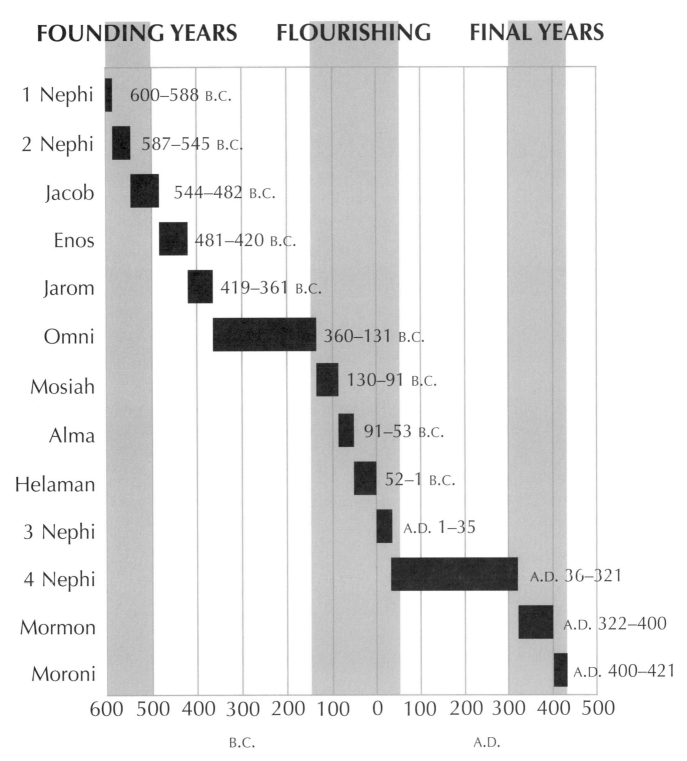

FOUNDING YEARS   FLOURISHING   FINAL YEARS

1 Nephi — 600–588 B.C.

2 Nephi — 587–545 B.C.

Jacob — 544–482 B.C.

Enos — 481–420 B.C.

Jarom — 419–361 B.C.

Omni — 360–131 B.C.

Mosiah — 130–91 B.C.

Alma — 91–53 B.C.

Helaman — 52–1 B.C.

3 Nephi — A.D. 1–35

4 Nephi — A.D. 36–321

Mormon — A.D. 322–400

Moroni — A.D. 400–421

600 500 400 300 200 100 0 100 200 300 400 500

B.C.   A.D.

Chart 25

Chronology

of the Book of Mormon

Chart 26

Life Spans of Lehi's Lineage

Key Scripture   1 Nephi–Omni

Explanation   This chart shows the lineage of Lehi and approximate life spans of him and his descendants, from Nephi to Amaleki, who were responsible for keeping the historical and doctrinal records of their people. Each bar on the chart represents an individual record keeper's life. Although the Book of Mormon does not give the date of Nephi's death, it makes good sense to assume that he was approximately seventy-five years old when he died.

Source   John W. Welch, "Longevity of Book of Mormon People and the 'Age of Man,'" *Journal of Collegium Aesculapium* 3 (1985): 34–45.

Life Spans of Lehi's Lineage

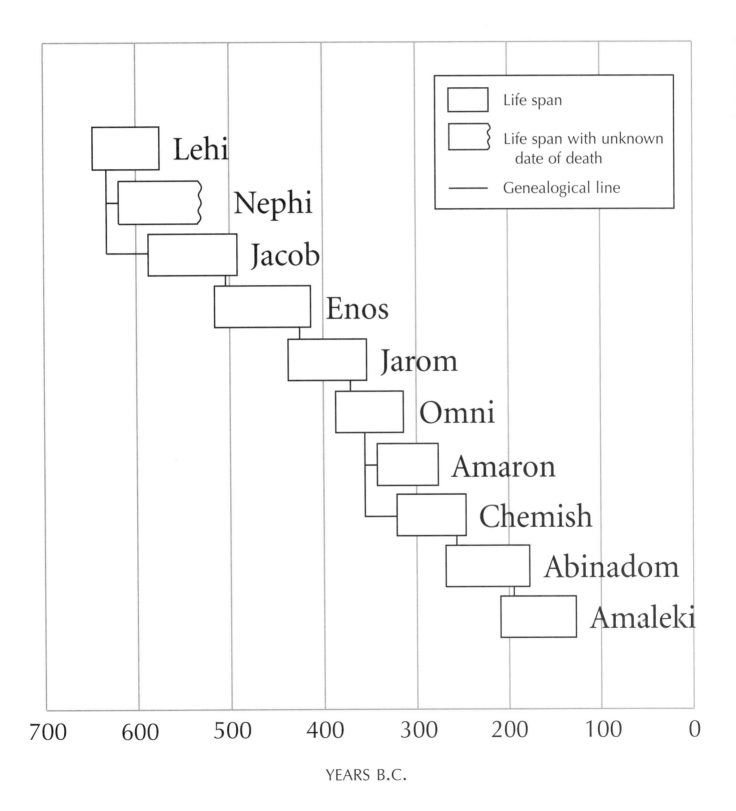

YEARS B.C.

Chart 26

Chart 27

Life Spans of Mosiah's Lineage

Key Scripture   Omni–Alma 27

Explanation   Mosiah and his lineage did much to bring people to Jesus Christ. After being instructed by the Lord to lead the people of Nephi out of the land of Nephi, Mosiah preserved their lives and brought to the people of Zarahemla the brass plates and the Nephite records. He also taught the people of Zarahemla the gospel and the language of the Nephites, and he was made king over both Nephites and Mulekites. His example of righteousness was emulated by his son Benjamin and Benjamin's son Mosiah. In addition to safeguarding the brass plates and the Nephite records, Benjamin and Mosiah admonished the people to have faith in Christ and to renew their covenants with the Lord. Mosiah's four sons, while rebellious in their youth, were instrumental in converting thousands of Lamanites to the gospel of Christ.

Source   John W. Welch, "Longevity of Book of Mormon People and the 'Age of Man,'" *Journal of Collegium Aesculapium* 3 (1985): 34–45.

Life Spans of Mosiah's Lineage

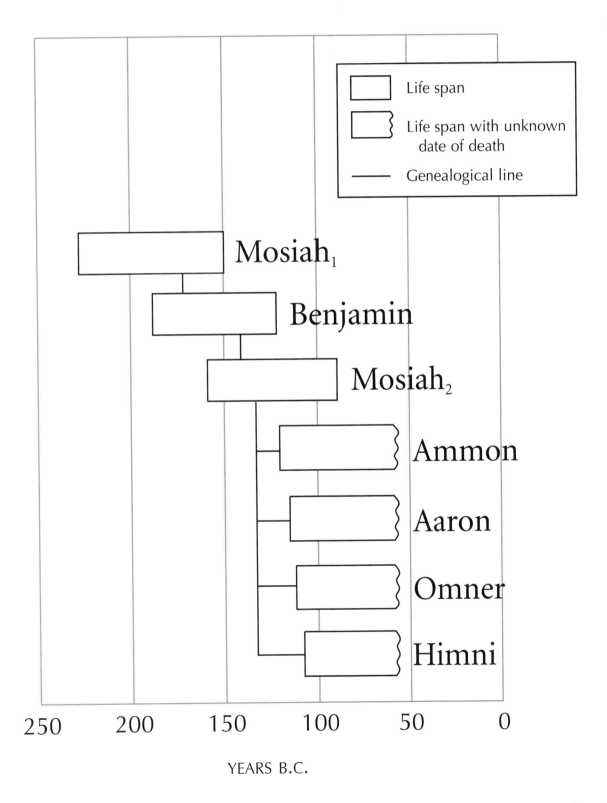

YEARS B.C.

Chart 27

Chart 28

Life Spans of Alma's Lineage

Key Scripture   Mosiah 17–Mormon 1

Explanation   This chart shows the lineage of Alma and approximate life spans of him and his descendants mentioned in the Book of Mormon. Alma's conversion while listening to Abinadi (see Mosiah 18:1) and Alma's baptism at the Waters of Mormon (see Mosiah 18:14) were important events for himself and for the Nephite civilization. Not only were Alma's descendants able to receive the blessings of the gospel, but for over four hundred years many of them were key prophets and principal keepers of the plates of Nephi who in turn spread the gospel to the general population.

Source   John W. Welch, "Longevity of Book of Mormon People and the 'Age of Man,'" *Journal of Collegium Aesculapium* 3 (1985): 34–45.

Life Spans of Alma's Lineage

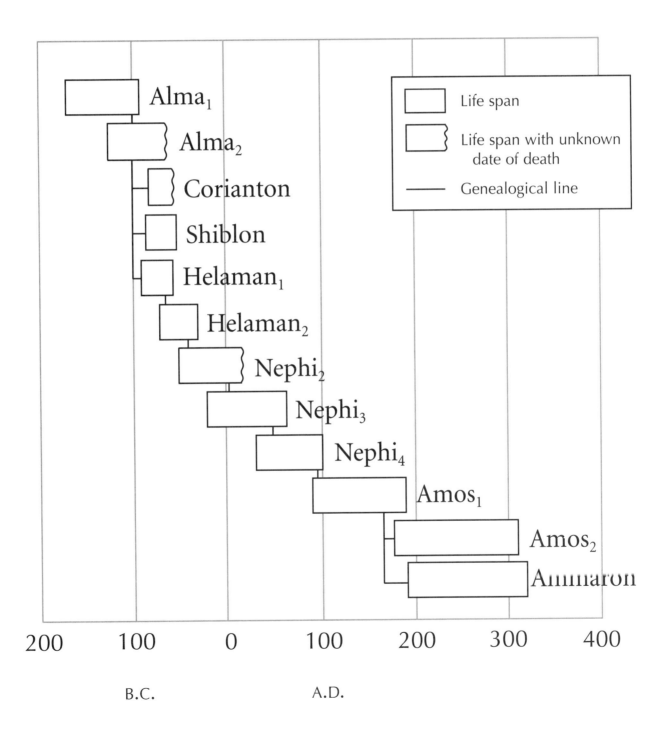

Chart 28

Chart 29

Flashbacks in the Book of Mosiah

Key Scripture   Mosiah 9–24

Explanation   The narratives in the book of Mosiah do not always follow in strict chronological order. The two major flashbacks, Zeniff's and Alma's accounts, illustrate that the book of Mosiah was put together by use of historical records of several authors. These flashbacks also attest to the historicity of the Book of Mormon, because it would have been difficult for the Prophet Joseph Smith to dictate these historically complex flashbacks and still keep his facts straight. In this chart the bars represent the narrative content and flow of the books of Omni and Mosiah over time, while the two flashback episodes are shown in relation to their placement in the book of Mosiah and to the time spans they cover, which predate the time of Mosiah$_1$.

Flashbacks in the Book of Mosiah

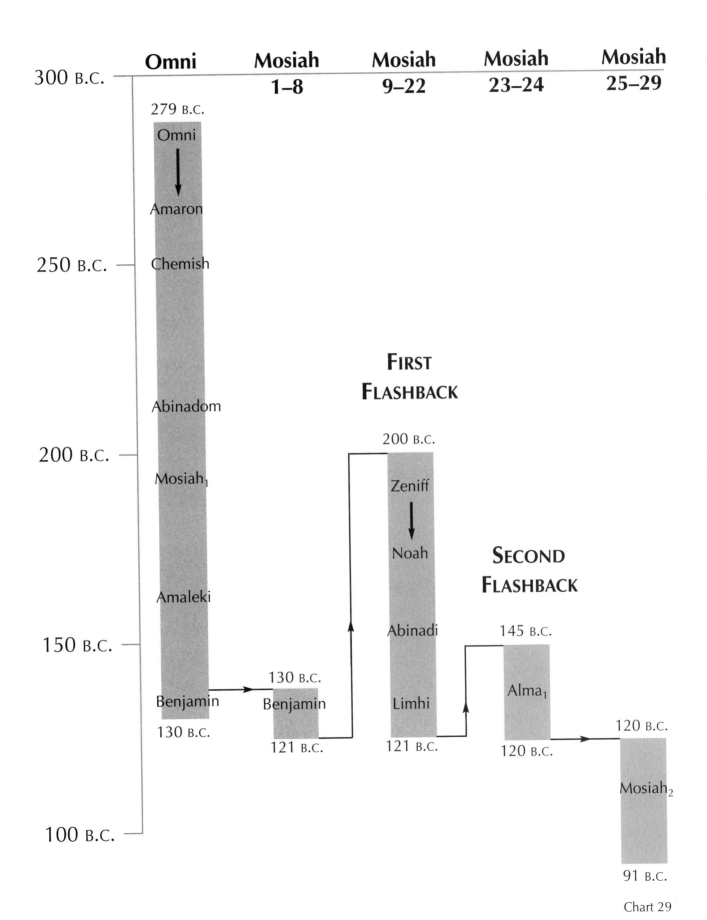

Chart 29

Chart 30

Flashbacks in the Book of Alma

Key Scripture Alma 17–28

Explanation As in the book of Mosiah, there are two significant flashbacks in the first part of the book of Alma. They highlight successful episodes in the missionary work of the sons of Mosiah among the Lamanites. The text in Alma 1–16 covers events in the land of Zarahemla through the fourteenth year of the reign of the judges. In Alma 17 the narrative reverts back to the first year of the judges and then covers events in the lands of Ishmael and Nephi those same fourteen years (see Alma 17:4). The first flashback recounts Ammon's ministry to the people of Lamoni (see Alma 17–20), and the second records how Lamoni's father and his household were converted through the preaching of Aaron, resulting in the conversion of thousands throughout the land (see Alma 21–23). Approximate dates are listed both by standard configuration (B.C.) and Nephite time (reign of the judges, or R.J.). These flashbacks are yet another evidence of the complexity of the Book of Mormon. It is quite remarkable how these historical accounts fit so neatly together, all coming together again with the Lamanite attacks in the eleventh (16:2 = 25:2) and fourteenth (16:12 = 28:2) years. In addition, another flashback (not shown on this chart) is found in Alma 56:1 and 56:9, which returns from the thirteenth year to the twenty-sixth to pick up the story of Helaman's stripling warriors.

Flashbacks in the Book of Alma

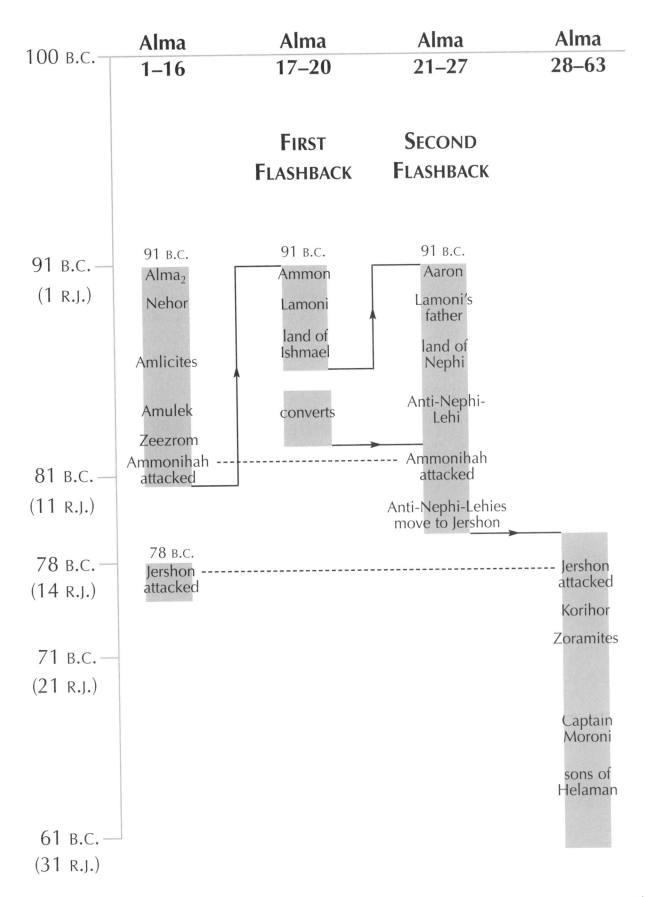

	Alma 1–16	Alma 17–20	Alma 21–27	Alma 28–63
		FIRST FLASHBACK	**SECOND FLASHBACK**	

100 B.C.

91 B.C.
(1 R.J.)

91 B.C.
Alma₂
Nehor

Amlicites

Amulek
Zeezrom
Ammonihah
attacked

91 B.C.
Ammon
Lamoni
land of
Ishmael

converts

91 B.C.
Aaron
Lamoni's
father
land of
Nephi

Anti-Nephi-
Lehi

Ammonihah
attacked

Anti-Nephi-Lehies
move to Jershon

81 B.C.
(11 R.J.)

78 B.C.
(14 R.J.)

78 B.C.
Jershon
attacked

Jershon
attacked

Korihor

Zoramites

71 B.C.
(21 R.J.)

Captain
Moroni

sons of
Helaman

61 B.C.
(31 R.J.)

Chart 30

Chart 31

Jaredite Kings

Key Scripture Ether 1; 7–15

Explanation This chart shows the chronology of Jaredite kings referred to in the book of Ether, their familial ties to each other, and whether they were righteous, unrighteous, or in captivity all of their days (in which case their moral character went unremarked). Mosiah attested to the ability of a king to influence his people for good or evil. Referring specifically to King Noah, he stated, "How much iniquity doth one wicked king cause to be committed, yea, and what great destruction!" (Mosiah 29:17). The main column on this chart gives the genealogy of Ether, the son of Coriantor (see Ether 11:23), which runs back to Jared (see Ether 1:6–32). This king list contains thirty names, from the Jaredite founder down to the prophet Ether, who was not a king but whose name is on the book in the Book of Mormon telling the history of the Jaredites. Conflicts with others who asserted powers as kings are also listed.

Source Expanded from the work of Lee Prince, student of John W. Welch, Book of Mormon 121H, Brigham Young University, fall 1997.

Jaredite Kings

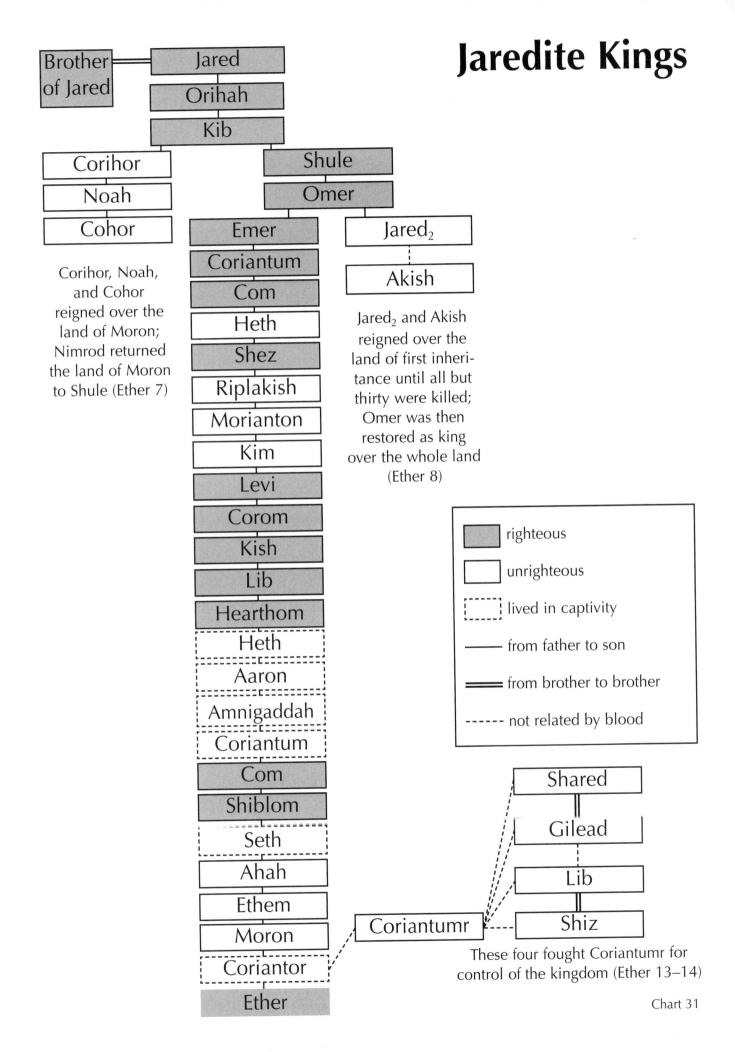

Brother of Jared ═══ Jared

Jared → Orihah → Kib

Kib → Corihor → Noah → Cohor

Corihor, Noah, and Cohor reigned over the land of Moron; Nimrod returned the land of Moron to Shule (Ether 7)

Kib → Shule → Omer

Omer → Emer → Coriantum → Com → Heth → Shez → Riplakish → Morianton → Kim → Levi → Corom → Kish → Lib → Hearthom → Heth → Aaron → Amnigaddah → Coriantum → Com → Shiblom → Seth → Ahah → Ethem → Moron → Coriantor → Ether

Omer → Jared₂ → Akish

Jared₂ and Akish reigned over the land of first inheritance until all but thirty were killed; Omer was then restored as king over the whole land (Ether 8)

Shared ═══ Gilead → Lib → Shiz

Coriantumr

These four fought Coriantumr for control of the kingdom (Ether 13–14)

Legend

- ▓ righteous
- ☐ unrighteous
- ⌈ ⌋ lived in captivity
- ——— from father to son
- ═══ from brother to brother
- - - - - not related by blood

Chart 31

Chart 32

Nephite and Lamanite Kings

Key Scriptures   Omni 1:12–25; Words of Mormon 1:10–18; Mosiah 1–22; Alma 17–22

Explanation   This chart highlights prominent Nephite and Lamanite kings from 200–77 B.C. These men are described in great detail in the Book of Mormon, showing especially the great effect a leader can have on his people. Mosiah$_1$, Zeniff, and King Laman were contemporaries. Benjamin was beginning his reign when Noah was at the height of his power. Limhi's reign ended when he and his people returned to Zarahemla near the beginning of Mosiah$_2$'s reign. Lamoni's father, who may have been a descendant of King Laman, was converted by Aaron about 82 B.C. Lamoni himself was converted a little earlier by Ammon. Lamoni and King Anti-Nephi-Lehi were brothers (see Alma 24:5).

Nephite and Lamanite Kings

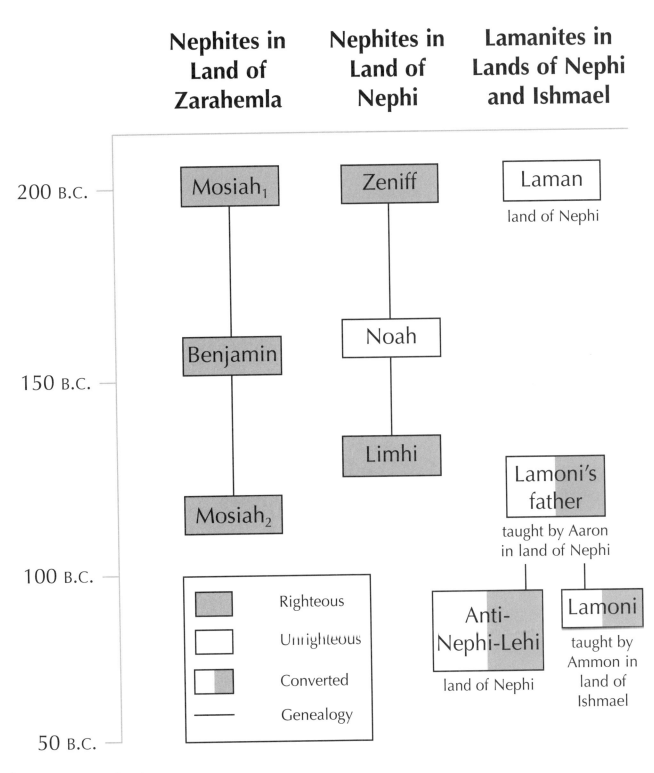

Nephites in Land of Zarahemla	Nephites in Land of Nephi	Lamanites in Lands of Nephi and Ishmael

200 B.C.

150 B.C.

100 B.C.

50 B.C.

Mosiah₁

Benjamin

Mosiah₂

Zeniff

Noah

Limhi

Laman
land of Nephi

Lamoni's father
taught by Aaron in land of Nephi

Anti-Nephi-Lehi
land of Nephi

Lamoni
taught by Ammon in land of Ishmael

Righteous
Unrighteous
Converted
Genealogy

dates are approximate

Chart 32

Chart 33

The Nephite Judges

Key Scripture   Mosiah 29–3 Nephi 7:14

Explanation   From about 91 B.C. to A.D. 30, the Nephite civilization was governed by chief judges. Each judge's name, known church role, tenure, cause of termination, and relation to his predecessors are represented on this chart. Of the thirteen Nephite judges charted, nearly half were assassinated, indicating serious governmental turmoil during the reign of the judges.

The Nephite Judges

Judge	Relation to Predecessors	Church Role	Approximate Tenure	Cause of Termination
Alma$_2$	no data	prophet	91–83 B.C.	resigned
Nephihah	nominated by Alma$_2$	elder	83–67 B.C.	died
Pahoran$_1$	son of Nephihah	no data	67–53 B.C.	died
Pahoran$_2$	son of Pahoran$_1$	no data	52 B.C.	assassinated
Pacumeni	son of Pahoran$_2$	no data	52–51 B.C.	killed by invaders
Helaman$_2$	grandson of Alma$_2$	leader	50–39 B.C.	died
Nephi$_3$	son of Helaman$_2$	prophet	39–30 B.C.	resigned
Cezoram	nominated by Nephi$_3$	no data	30–26 B.C.	assassinated
no data	Son of Cezoram	no data	26 B.C.	assassinated
Seezoram	no data	no data	26–20 B.C.	assassinated
no data	no data	no data	20–A.D. 1	no data
Lachoneus$_1$	no data	prophet	A.D. 1–30	no data
Lachoneus$_2$	son of Lachoneus$_1$	no data	A.D. 30	assassinated

Chart 33

Chart 34

Alma as Chief Judge
Years 1–8 of the Reign of the Judges

Key Scripture Mosiah 29:42–Alma 4:20

Explanation As chief judge during the first years of the reign of the judges, Alma the Younger addressed difficulties such as the execution of Nehor, the revolt of Amlici, and a postwar economic slump. In the eighth year of his term, Alma resigned from office and devoted all of his energy to preaching the gospel to his people, "to stir them up in remembrance of their duty, and . . . pull down, by the word of God, all the pride and craftiness and all the contentions which were among his people" (Alma 4:19). Although Alma resigned from the office of chief judge, he retained the office of high priest, thereby separating the political and religious spheres of influence. This chart outlines the main events for years 1–8 of the reign of the judges (91–83 B.C.).

Alma as Chief Judge
Years 1–8 of the Reign of the Judges

REFERENCES	YEAR	
Alma 1	1	Nehor is executed, but priestcrafts continue Church members are persecuted The church prohibits persecution
Alma 1	2	Pride and contention increase in the church Some are excommunicated or withdraw from the church
Alma 1	3	Church members regroup Preachers and workers are equal Church members prosper
Alma 1	4	Prosperity abounds Wickedness increases outside the church
Alma 2–3	5	Amlici revolts and is killed by Alma$_2$ Alma$_2$ is wounded in battle Lamanites invade again but are defeated
Alma 4	6	Postwar economic problems stimulate religious renewal
Alma 4	7	3,500 people are converted and baptized
Alma 4	8	Pride and contention increase in the church Alma turns the judgeship over to Nephihah

Chart 34

Chart 35

Alma as High Priest
Years 9–19 of the Reign of the Judges

Key Scripture   Alma 5–45

Explanation   Alma the Younger served as the high priest of the church during the first nineteen years of the reign of the judges. He served a dual role of high priest and chief judge for the first eight years but afterwards resigned from serving as chief judge in order to concentrate on improving the spirituality of his people. This chart illustrates some of the more important events that took place during years 9–19 of the reign of the judges (83–73 B.C.). Among other things, Alma assisted in the conversion of Zeezrom, preached to the city of Ammonihah, contended with Korihor, and led missionary activities to Antionum. After this period of faithful labor, Alma journeyed toward the land of Melek and was not seen again. Some supposed that he was taken up by the Spirit and received by the Lord (see Alma 45:19).

Alma as High Priest
Years 9–19 of the Reign of the Judges

References	Year	
Alma 4 Alma 5; 7	9	Nephihah becomes chief judge Alma$_2$ preaches in Zarahemla and Gideon
Alma 8; 9; 15 Alma 10; 15 Alma 14	10	Alma$_2$ preaches in Melek, Ammonihah, Sidom Amulek and Zeezrom are converted Women, children suffer death by fire in Ammonihah
Alma 16	11	Ammonihah is destroyed Peace
Alma 16:16	12	Peace; no inequality exists among Nephites
Alma 16:21	13	Peace; the church is established
Alma 27 Alma 16:12	14	Ammonites possess the land of Jershon Lamanites invade
Alma 28:3	15	Lamanite attack ends
Alma 30	16	Peace
Alma 30 Alma 31–35	17	Korihor contends with Alma$_2$, dies in Antionum Some Zoramites are converted and granted refuge in Jershon, leaving apostate Zoramites angry
Alma 36–43 Alma 43 Alma 43–44	18	Alma$_2$ blesses his sons; they preach in every city Zoramites and Lamanites invade Jershon, Manti Zerahemnah is defeated
Alma 45	19	Alma$_2$ passes the mantle to his son Helaman Alma$_2$ goes as if to Melek and is not seen again Helaman and his brethren preach in every city

Chart 35

Chart 36

Nephihah as Chief Judge
Years 19–24 of the Reign of the Judges

Key Scripture Alma 4:20–50:37

Explanation Nephihah served as chief judge for sixteen years, from the ninth to the twenty-fourth years of the reign of the judges (83–68 B.C.). Although he served a long time, little is known about him. He was largely overshadowed by the activities of Alma$_2$, Amulek, the four sons of Mosiah, Helaman$_1$, Captain Moroni, and other Nephite leaders. For a more complete listing of events during the first ten years of his reign, see chart 35. Nephihah seems to have been a weak ruler. He was the judge at the time of the serious troubles with Korihor and Amalickiah, but he played little role in handling those cases, as far as we know. Due largely to the strength of others around him, his final years were known as the happiest times in all of Nephite history.

Nephihah as Chief Judge
Years 19–24 of the Reign of the Judges

References	Year	
Alma 4:20	9	Alma₂ delivers the judgment seat to Nephihah
Alma 30	17	Korihor appears before the chief judge and Alma
Alma 45 Alma 46–49	19	Helaman reestablishes the church throughout the land Amalickiah desires to be king, rebels, and is expelled by Captain Moroni but becomes king of the Lamanites, who attack Nephite fortifications but are repulsed
Alma 50	20	Peace and rejoicing in the church Extensive work on fortifications
Alma 50	21	Peace and rejoicing in the church Prosperity and never a happier time
Alma 50	22	Peace
Alma 50	23	Peace
Alma 50	24	Captain Moroni stops the people of Morianton, who were trying to leave for the land northward Nephihah dies

Chart 36

Chart 37

Pahoran as Chief Judge
Years 25–39 of the Reign of the Judges

Key Scripture   Alma 50:40–Helaman 1:2

Explanation   War ravaged half of the very eventful fifteen years during which
Pahoran served as chief judge (67–53 B.C.). He tried, often unsuc-
cessfully, to hold the Nephite capital together. With wars dragging
on for seven years in the north and to the south, Pahoran was
unable to effectively administer justice and preserve unity among
the people. He was plagued with rebellions at home and held several king-men in prison for the duration of the conflict. After the
war, governmental offices and church functions were reestablished
and the Nephites began to prosper. Within a short time of each
other, however, four very influential Nephite leaders, including
Pahoran, all died, leaving the Nephites very weak on leadership.

Pahoran as Chief Judge
Years 25–39 of the Reign of the Judges

REFERENCES	YEAR	
Alma 51	25	King-men seek to depose Pahoran as chief judge but are vanquished by Captain Moroni Teancum repels Lamanites attacking on the east and slays Amalickiah
Alma 52 Alma 56:9	26	Lamanites retreat to Mulek; Ammoron continues the war on the west Helaman leads stripling warriors to Judea to assist Antipus
Alma 52 Alma 56	27	Teancum's and Moroni's forces unite in Bountiful, prepare to retake Mulek Helaman and Antipus defeat larger Lamanite armies
Alma 52 Alma 53 Alma 57	28	Moroni retakes Mulek Nephite dissensions enable Lamanites to capture Nephite cities Helaman retakes Antiparah without bloodshed
Alma 54–55 Alma 57–58	29	Ammoron, Moroni negotiate; Moroni frees Nephite prisoners Striplings win at Cumeni and Manti
Alma 56–59:3 Alma 59:3–61 Alma 62	30	Helaman sends epistle to Moroni (56:1), who asks Pahoran for aid (59:3) Moroni and Pahoran exchange epistles; Lamanites take Nephihah Moroni and Pahoran join forces and retake Zarahemla from king-men
Alma 62 Alma 62	31	Moroni sends provisions, reinforcements to Helaman, Lehi, Teancum Nephites retake Nephihah Teancum is killed after slaying Ammoron; Lamanites driven out of land
Alma 62	32–34	Moroni fortifies border cities, yields command to Moronihah Pahoran returns to judgment seat; Helaman and others build up church
Alma 62	35	Helaman dies
Alma 63	36	Shiblon keeps records; Moroni dies
Alma 63	37–38	Many Nephites migrate northward
Alma 63 Helaman 1	39	Shiblon dies Pahoran dies

Chart 37

Chart 38

Helaman as Chief Judge
Years 42–53 of the Reign of the Judges

Key Scripture   Helaman 2:1–3:37

Explanation   Helaman, the son of the Helaman who led the stripling Ammonite warriors, served as chief judge for twelve years, from the forty-second to the fifty-third years of the reign of the judges (50–39 B.C.). After an assassination attempt against him in his inaugural year, his reign was the most peaceful of any Nephite chief judge. He saw no wars, and nine of his years were marked as times of peace. He was centrally noted for his "justice and equity" (Helaman 3:20). Most significantly, the forty-ninth and fiftieth years of the reign of the judges appear to have been jubilee years. The forty-ninth year would have been the seventh sabbatical year (a reasonable time for great celebration and rejoicing) and the fiftieth year the jubilee itself (a time of continual peace and great joy). The jubilee laws under the law of Moses are found in Leviticus 25–26. The forty-ninth and fiftieth years are mentioned in Leviticus 25:8–10.

Helaman as Chief Judge
Years 42–53 of the Reign of the Judges

REFERENCES	YEAR	
Helaman 2:1–12	42	Peace achieved with the Lamanites Kishkumen killed attempting to assassinate Helaman Gadianton flees and becomes robber leader
3:1	43	No contention among the Nephites, but a little pride
3:2	44	No contention
3:2	45	No contention
3:3	46	Much contention and many dissensions Many migrate into the land northward
3:19	47	Great contention continues
3:19, 22	48	Contentions eventually diminish
3:23–25	49	Peace, prosperity, very dramtic church growth Continual rejoicing all year long Gadianton robbers secretly infiltrate settled lands
3:32	50	Continual peace and great joy
3:33–35	51	Peace and sanctification Rising pride among church members
3:36	52	Peace prevails despite increasing pride
3:37	53	Helaman$_2$ dies in office

Chart 38

Chart 39

Nephi as Chief Judge
Years 53–62 of the Reign of the Judges

Key Scripture   Helaman 3:37–5:1

Explanation   Nephi$_2$, the son of Helaman$_2$, served as chief judge for ten years, from the fifty-third to the sixty-second years of the reign of the judges (39–30 B.C.). His time was disastrous for the Nephites. Civil war, pride, wickedness, and weakness led to the loss of the city of Zarahemla and many other lands, even half of all the Nephites' possessions (see Helaman 4:5–10). Like Alma the Younger, his great-grandfather, Nephi$_2$ resigned the judgeship to attempt to improve this situation by preaching the word of God.

Nephi as Chief Judge
Years 53–62 of the Reign of the Judges

REFERENCES	YEAR	
Helaman 3:37	53	Nephi becomes chief judge
4:1–2	54	Dissensions within the church lead to bloodshed, civil war, and banishment of rebels, who go over to the Lamanites
	55	
4:4	56	Dissenters stir up the Lamanites, who prepare for war
4:5	57	Dissenters and Lamanites attack Nephites
4:5	58	Zarahemla and much Nephite territory fall to the Lamanites and dissenters
	59	
4:9	60	Nephites regain many cities
4:10 4:18–26	61	Nephites regain half of their original lands Weakened by transgression and unbelief, Nephites fail to regain more lands
5:1–4	62	Nephi resigns judgeship to preach the gospel with his brother Lehi, first to the Nephites in the land of Zarahemla and then to the Lamanites in Nephi

Chart 39

Chart 40

Nephite and Mesoamerican History

Key Scripture   2 Nephi 5:33

Explanation   Archaeologist John L. Sorenson has found interesting correlations between Book of Mormon events and pre-Columbian American history in Mesoamerica (central and southern Mexico and northern Central America). As depicted in this chart (which, like other archaeological time lines, is oriented with the most recent date at the top), Sorenson suggests that Olmec and Jaredite civilizations correspond historically, while the civilization existing in the Mexican state of Chiapas in highland Guatemala can roughly represent the Nephite and Lamanite peoples. In addition, the dates of Izapan influences spreading northward correspond with the people of Nephi finding the land of Zarahemla and joining with the Mulekites. Because the peak Izapan development occurred between the second century B.C. and the fourth century A.D., Izapans are believed to have been Nephites, although the exact association is unclear. While the Teotihuacans were not related to the Lamanites directly, existing probably as a remnant group of the Jaredites, they are believed to have allied themselves culturally and possibly militarily with the Lamanites near the end of Nephite civilization. These chronological and geographic correlations offer secondary evidence supporting the ancient origin of the Book of Mormon.

Sources   John L. Sorenson, *An Ancient American Setting for the Book of Mormon* (Salt Lake City: Deseret Book, 1985), 135; and John L. Sorenson, *Images of Ancient America: Visualizing Book of Mormon Life* (Provo, Utah: Research Press, 1998), 193.

Nephite and Mesoamerican History

	Book of Mormon		Mesoamerica		
	Land Northward	**Land Southward**	**North of Isthmus of Tehuantepec**	**South of Isthmus of Tehuantepec**	

	Various States	"Classic Maya"	LATE CLASSIC PERIOD
A.D. 600	Prophetic view: wars, "abominations"		
		Teotihuacan influence declines	
		Maya stelae cease	
500			
400	Wars continue among non-Nephites	Teotihuacan groups spread widely	EARLY CLASSIC PERIOD
		Militarism increasing; cults abound	
	Nephites exterminated	Chiapas	
	Nephites retreat north	abandoned	
300	War, turmoil spread	Peak in cultural creativity	
	Widespread trade	Priests flourish	
	Cults, priests flourish	Surge in class symbols, trade	
	Dynamic, prosperous society		
200	Classes reappear		
		Stable socioeconomic growth	PROTO-CLASSIC PERIOD
100	Classless, theocratic-led society		
		Hesitation in growth	
		Volcanic action	
A.D. 1	Great natural, social catastrophe	Precursors of Classic at Tikal,	
	Class distinctions, state rule	Monte Alban, Cuicuilco, etc.	
	Migrations northward		
	Expansion of Nephite and Lamanite	Izapan influences go north	
	lineages and influence		
100 B.C.			LATE PRE-CLASSIC PERIOD
200			
300			
400	Small tribes	Small sociopolitical chiefdoms	
500			MIDDLE PRE-CLASSIC PERIOD
600	Approximate extermination of Jaredite lineages	Approximate end of Olmec civilization	

Chart 40

Jesus Christ

in the Book of Mormon

Chart 41

People to Whom Jesus Christ or the Angel of the Lord Appeared

Key Scripture 1 Nephi 1:9

Explanation We know for certain that Jesus Christ appeared personally to prophets such as Lehi, Nephi, Jacob, Mormon, and Moroni and to the people gathered at Bountiful after his resurrection. These personal visitations are listed in the first part of this chart. But Christ probably appeared to additional prophets as well. The second part of this chart lists those who recorded having seen "an angel of the Lord" (Amulek and Samuel) or "the angel of the Lord" (Benjamin and Alma the Younger). Because it is difficult to distinguish between "the angel of the Lord" and Jehovah in Genesis 16:7–11, Exodus 3:2, and Judges 2:1–4, Nephites who recorded seeing "the angel of the Lord" might have been indirectly writing about the Lord himself. It is therefore possible that prophets such as Alma also saw the Savior and conversed with him (see Mosiah 27:25, "And the Lord said unto me").

Source John W. Welch, "Ten Testimonies of Jesus Christ from the Book of Mormon," in *Doctrines of the Book of Mormon: The 1991 Sperry Symposium*, ed. Bruce A. Van Orden and Brent L. Top (Salt Lake City: Deseret Book, 1992), 223–42.

People to Whom Jesus Christ Appeared

1	Lehi	1 Nephi 1:9
2	Nephi$_1$	2 Nephi 11:2
3	Jacob	2 Nephi 2:4; 11:3
4	Lamoni	Alma 19:13
5	the gatherings at Bountiful	3 Nephi 11–26
6	the twelve Nephite disciples	3 Nephi 27:2
7	the brother of Jared	Ether 3:14
8	Mormon	Mormon 1:15
9	Moroni	Ether 12:39
10	Benjamin	Mosiah 4:1
11	Alma$_2$ with the sons of Mosiah$_2$	Mosiah 27:11

People Who Saw an Angel of the Lord

12	Laman, Lemuel, and Sam	1 Nephi 3:29
13	Amulek	Alma 10:7
14	Samuel the Lamanite	Helaman 13:7

Chart 41

Chart 42

Nephite Declaration of Faith

Key Scripture   Alma 33:22

Explanation   All the prophets of the world, including those in the ancient Americas, have testified "more or less" (Mosiah 13:33; Jacob 4:5) concerning the coming and atonement of Jesus Christ. In Alma 32 the prophet Alma tells how to plant and nourish the seed of true faith. In verses 22 and 23 he discloses what the seed is that people should plant in their hearts and that will sprout and grow into a tree of everlasting life. That seed is a declaration of faith. It has seven parts, as this chart shows. One may well imagine that Alma and his followers could have personally recited this declaration in explaining their faith, in much the same way as members of the church today use the Articles of Faith in stating the fundamental elements of their faith.

Nephite Declaration of Faith

1   We "believe in the Son of God,

2   that he will come to redeem his people,

3   and that he shall suffer and die

4   to atone for their sins;

5   and that he shall rise again from the dead,

6   which shall bring to pass the resurrection,

7   that all men shall stand before him,
        to be judged"

—Alma 33:22

Chart 42

Chart 43

Consistent Elements
in Nephite Declarations of Faith

Key Scriptures   Alma 33:22; 1 Nephi 11:31–33; 19:9–10; 2 Nephi 9:4–15; 25:12–13;
Mosiah 3:5–10; 15:5–9, 20; 16:10; Alma 11:39–41; Mormon 9:1–14

Explanation   Alma 33:22 is not the only place in the Book of Mormon where its
seven principles of Nephite faith in Jesus Christ are revealed. Eight
other important compact doctrinal passages list many, if not all, of
these seven principles. Each of these passages is shown in the left-
hand columns of this chart. To the right, check marks indicate
which principles each passage includes. The consistency of expres-
sion found in these scriptures suggests that the seven principles in
Alma's formulation may have constituted a widely taught and
adopted declaration of faith established among the Nephites.

Source   John W. Welch, "Ten Testimonies of Jesus Christ from the Book of
Mormon," in *Doctrines of the Book of Mormon: The 1991 Sperry
Symposium*, ed. Bruce A. Van Orden and Brent L. Top (Salt Lake
City: Deseret Book, 1992), 223–42.

Consistent Elements
in Nephite Declarations of Faith

Speaker	Reference	Believe in the Son of God	He will come to redeem his people	He shall suffer and die	He will atone for their sins	He shall rise again from the dead	He will bring to pass the resurrection	He shall judge all men
Nephi₁	1 Nephi 11:31–33		✓	✓	✓			
Nephi₁	1 Nephi 19:9–10		✓	✓	✓	✓	✓	
Jacob	2 Nephi 9:4–15	✓	✓	✓	✓	✓	✓	✓
Nephi₁	2 Nephi 25:12–13	✓	✓	✓	✓	✓	✓	
Benjamin	Mosiah 3:5–10	✓	✓	✓	✓	✓		✓
Abinadi	Mosiah 15:5–9, 20; 16:10	✓	✓	✓	✓	✓	✓	✓
Amulek	Alma 11:39–41	✓	✓		✓		✓	✓
Alma₂	Alma 33:22	✓	✓	✓	✓	✓	✓	✓
Moroni	Mormon 9:1–14	✓	✓	✓	✓		✓	✓

Chart 43

Chart 44

Names Used for Christ
by Major Book of Mormon Authors

Key Scripture Mosiah 3:5–27

Explanation Major Book of Mormon authors used sixty-seven different names to refer to Jesus Christ. Of these names, many were used exclusively by one author, while others were used almost universally. This may be because the Lord was to them, as he is to each of us, both the same and different: his atonement is universal, but each of us also has a relationship with him that is entirely personal. For example, King Benjamin is the only prophet in the Book of Mormon who calls Jesus the "Heavenly King" or the "Lord Omnipotent." This could be in part because Benjamin himself was a king, identified with Christ on that level, and recognized the true authority and power of the Son of God. This table shows the names for Christ that appear in the Book of Mormon and the frequency with which its major authors used them. Names for Christ that are unique to certain authors appear in boldface type. The data below show which texts are used to represent each major author.

Lehi: 1 Nephi 1; 8; 10; 2 Nephi 1–4
Nephi$_1$: 1 Nephi 11–22; 2 Nephi 25–33
Jacob: 2 Nephi 6–10; Jacob 2–4; 6
Abinadi: Mosiah 12–16
Benjamin: Mosiah 1–6
Alma$_2$: Alma 5; 7; 12–13; 32–33; 36–42
Amulek: Alma 9–11; 34
Samuel: Helaman 13–15
Mormon: Helaman 12; 3 Nephi 5; Mormon 1–7; Moroni 7–9
Moroni: Mormon 8–9; Ether 4–5; 12:6–41; Moroni 1–10

Source John W. Welch, "Ten Testimonies of Jesus Christ from the Book of Mormon," in *Doctrines of the Book of Mormon: The 1991 Sperry Symposium*, ed. Bruce A. Van Orden and Brent L. Top (Salt Lake City: Deseret Book, 1992), 223–42.

Names Used for Christ
by Major Book of Mormon Authors

	Lehi	Nephi$_1$	Jacob	Abinadi	Benjamin	Alma$_2$	Amulek	Samuel	Mormon	Moroni
A Messiah	2	1								
A Son of God					1					
All-Powerful Creator			1							
Beloved Son		1								
Christ		40	12	8	12	12	8	2	43	46
Christ Jesus						1				
Christ the Lord				1	1					
Christ the Son						1			1	1
Creator			3	1	1		1			
Eternal Father		2		2		2		1		5
Eternal God		2	1			2				1
Father		18	3	5	2	1	1		13	22
Father of Heaven and Earth		1		1	1	1	1			
Father and Son				1						
First-Fruits	1									
God	41	135	87	44	57	201	29	9	76	72
God of Abr., Isaac, Jacob		1			2					1
Good Shepherd						7				
Great Creator			3							
Great and Eternal Head								1		
Great Mediator	2									
Great and True Shepherd								1		
Heavenly King					1					
His Son Jesus Christ									1	

Chart 44

	Lehi	Nephi₁	Jacob	Abinadi	Benjamin	Alma₂	Amulek	Samuel	Mormon	Moroni
Holy Being										1
Holy Child									1	
Holy Messiah	2									
Holy One	1	1	1		2			1		1
Holy One of Israel	2	14	17							
Holy One of Jacob		1								
Jehovah										1
Jesus		4	2					9		6
Jesus Christ		4		3	3	1	1	7		17
King of Heaven		1			1					
Lamb		29			1	1				1
Lamb of God	1	31			1					2
Lord	64	175	46	49	32	54	29	47	53	54
Lord God	8	38	18		6	8	1	1	1	1
Lord God Almighty	1	1	1							
Lord God of Hosts		2								
Lord God Omnipotent				2						
Lord of Hosts		9	7					3		
Lord Jesus										1
Lord Jesus Christ				1	3		1	3		2
Lord Omnipotent				4						
Maker		2								
Messiah	13	12	2	1						
Mighty God		1								

Chart 44

	Lehi	Nephi₁	Jacob	Abinadi	Benjamin	Alma₂	Amulek	Samuel	Mormon	Moroni
Mighty One of Israel		1								
Mighty One of Jacob		1	1							
Only Begotten of the Father		1			2	1				
Only Begotten Son			2		3					
Prophet	1									
Redeemer	5	12	3		3		1	2		
Savior	1	4	1	1					4	1
Shepherd		2			11		1	1		
Son		8		6	12	1		2		8
Son of the Eternal Father		2								
Son of the Everlasting God		1								
Son of the Most High God		1								
Son of Righteousnes		1								
The Christ		1								
The Son of God	2	5		1	2	10	8	3	3	3
The Very Christ		1						1		
The Very God								1		
True Messiah	2	1								
Very God of Israel		1								
TOTALS										
References to Christ	148	565	215	119	126	339	86	74	224	247
Names used unique to author	4	10	4	1	3	3	0	2	3	3
Different names used by author	17	38	22	11	15	20	14	15	20	21
Percent names unique to author	24	26	18	9	20	15	0	13	15	14

Chart 44

Chart 45

Names and Concepts Associated with Christ by Major Book of Mormon Authors

Key Scripture 2 Nephi 10:3

Explanation The writings of major Book of Mormon authors reflect a personalized understanding and testimony of Jesus Christ. This is evident in part by the unique names that they used to describe him. This chart highlights the names for Christ that are unique to each author. For example, Lehi is the only author who refers to Christ as "a prophet" (1 Nephi 10:4), while his son Nephi alone uses the name "Beloved Son" (2 Nephi 31:11) when quoting the words of God the Father. It may be that Lehi's calling as a prophet allowed him to identify personally with Christ on that level and that Nephi's position as a "beloved son" of Lehi helped him to readily understand Christ's sonship. This chart also includes a column showing some of the major topics each author emphasizes in his discourses. Those topics are usually consonant with the names each author uses for Christ.

Source John W. Welch, "Ten Testimonies of Jesus Christ from the Book of Mormon," in *Doctrines of the Book of Mormon: The 1991 Sperry Symposium,* ed. Bruce A. Van Orden and Brent L. Top (Salt Lake City: Deseret Book, 1992), 223–42.

Names and Concepts Associated with Christ
by Major Book of Mormon Authors

Author	Distinctive Name(s) for Christ	Topics Emphasized
Lehi	A Messiah, First-Fruits, Great Mediator, Holy Messiah, Lord God Almighty, Prophet	mercy, redemption
Nephi$_1$	Son of the Most High God, Son of the Everlasting Father, Son of Righteousness, The Christ, Beloved Son, Very God of Israel, Mighty One of Israel	obedience and law, covenants to the house of Israel
Jacob	Mighty God, Maker, All-Powerful Creator, Great Creator	temple and priestly functions
Abinadi	Father, Son	innocent suffering, fatherhood and sonship
Benjamin	Heavenly King, Lord Omnipotent, Lord God Omnipotent	ceremonial and royal functions, atonement, blood
Alma$_2$	Good Shepherd, Shepherd, Christ Jesus	mercy, conversion, judgment, joy, equity
Amulek	Christ the Son	atonement, arms of safety, sacrifice
Samuel	Great and Eternal Head, Lord of Hosts	destruction of evil
Mormon	His Son Jesus Christ, Holy Child, The Very God	God's love for his children
Moroni	Holy Being, Jehovah, Jesus	personal witness of Christ

Chart 45

Chart 46

Number of Names Used for Christ by Major Book of Mormon Authors

Key Scripture Mosiah 3:5–27

Explanation This chart illustrates the penchant of Book of Mormon authors to use multiple names for the Lord Jesus Christ. Nephi$_1$ was especially creative in this regard, though all of these authors demonstrate an intimate, impressive understanding of the Lord's redemptive mission and many divine attributes. Indeed, the Book of Mormon makes clear that these prophets learned of Christ through the scriptures and divine revelation. For example, King Benjamin was a dedicated student of the scriptures, and his stirring words regarding Christ's saving mission were delivered to him by an angel (see Mosiah 3:2–4:1). The particular names that Book of Mormon authors used as they bore witness of the Savior are documented in chart 40.

Source John W. Welch, "Ten Testimonies of Jesus Christ from the Book of Mormon," in *Doctrines of the Book of Mormon: The 1991 Sperry Symposium,* ed. Bruce A. Van Orden and Brent L. Top (Salt Lake City: Deseret Book, 1992), 223–42.

Number of Names Used for Christ by Major Book of Mormon Authors

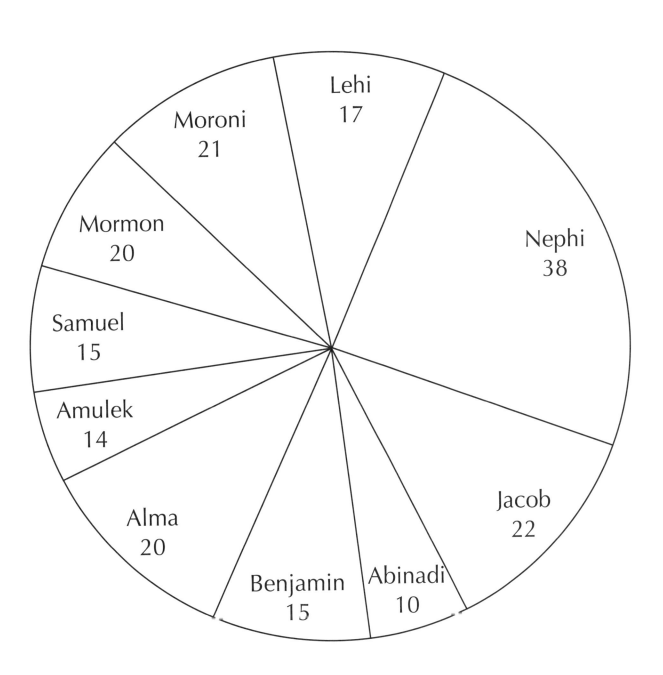

Chart 46

Chart 47

Number of Names for Christ
Used Exclusively by Individual Authors

Key Scripture   Mosiah 3:5–27

Explanation   Of the sixty-seven names for Jesus Christ employed by major Book of Mormon authors, nearly half are used exclusively by individual authors. For example, of the thirty-eight names that Nephi$_1$ used for Christ, ten were used exclusively by him; of the twenty-two names Jacob used, four were unique to him; and so on. These figures suggest the originality and rich gospel perspectives and testimonies of the prophets and record keepers who contributed to the Book of Mormon record—an aspect preserved by Mormon's abridging and Joseph Smith's translating.

Source   John W. Welch, "Ten Testimonies of Jesus Christ from the Book of Mormon," in *Doctrines of the Book of Mormon: The 1991 Sperry Symposium,* ed. Bruce A. Van Orden and Brent L. Top (Salt Lake City: Deseret Book, 1992), 223–42.

Number of Names for Christ
Used Exclusively by Individual Authors

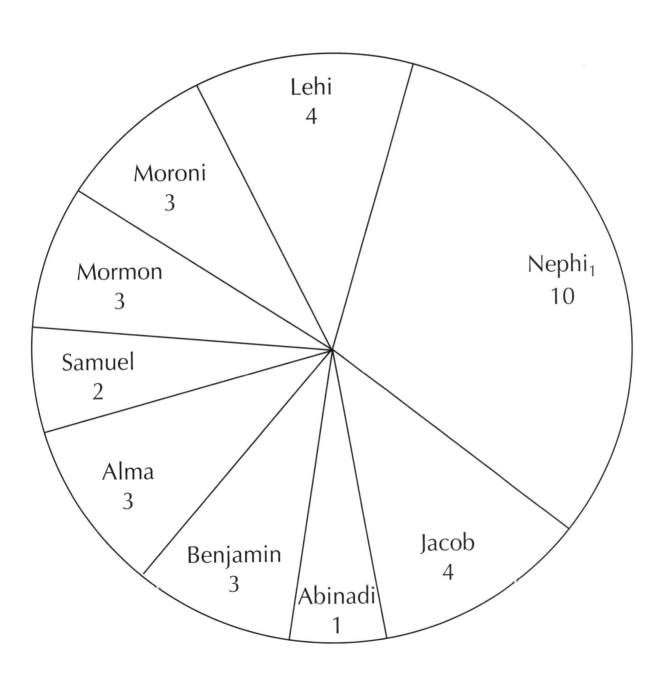

Lehi
4

Moroni
3

Mormon
3

Samuel
2

Alma
3

Benjamin
3

Abinadi
1

Jacob
4

Nephi$_1$
10

Chart 47

Chart 48

Samuel the Lamanite's Prophecies

Key Scripture   Helaman 14

Explanation   As the time neared for Samuel the Lamanite's prophecies to be fulfilled, Nephi$_3$ witnessed the growing skepticism of the people concerning the predicted earthly advent of Jesus Christ. This skepticism led to the persecution of those who believed in Christ's coming by those who felt the time of his birth had already passed. These skeptics threatened to kill the believers unless the sign of Christ's birth appeared before a certain date. Possibly because the very lives of the believers depended on the fulfillment of those prophecies, Nephi paid careful attention to documenting their exact fulfillment. Nephi also tracked Samuel's prophecies concerning Christ's death and their fulfillment.

Samuel the Lamanite's Prophecies

Concerning Christ's Birth	Reference	Fulfillment
Christ will be born in 5 years	Helaman 14:2	3 Nephi 1:13
No darkness for 2 days, 1 night	Helaman 14:3–4	3 Nephi 1:15
A new star will arise	Helaman 14:5	3 Nephi 1:21
There will be signs and wonders	Helaman 14:6	3 Nephi 2:1
People will fall to the earth	Helaman 14:7	3 Nephi 1:16–17

Concerning Christ's Death	Reference	Fulfillment
No light for 3 days	Helaman 14:20, 27	3 Nephi 8:19–23
Thunderings and lightnings	Helaman 14:21	3 Nephi 8:6–7
Earth will shake, tremble, and be broken up	Helaman 14:21–22	3 Nephi 8:12, 17–18
Mountains will be laid low and valleys raised	Helaman 14:23	3 Nephi 8:10, 13; 9:8
Resurrected people will appear to many	Helaman 14:25	3 Nephi 23:9–14

Chart 48

Chart 49

Destructions at the Death of Christ

Key Scripture   3 Nephi 8–9

Explanation   Many wicked cities in the Americas were obliterated during the three-day period of destruction following the death of Jesus Christ. This chart lists the cities that were destroyed and the various elements that destroyed them. The mediums of destruction correspond well with what were known anciently as the four elements of the world—earth, air, fire, and water—showing that the entire cosmos, as the ancients typically understood it, was disrupted and beset the wicked as a result of the Savior's death.

Source   Shawn Rice, student of John W. Welch, Book of Mormon 121H, Brigham Young University, fall 1997.

Destructions at the Death of Christ

Element of Destruction	City Destroyed	Reference
Earth	Moronihah	3 Nephi 8:10; 9:5
	Gilgal	3 Nephi 9:6
	Gadiomnah	3 Nephi 9:8
	Gadiandi	3 Nephi 9:8
	Jacob	3 Nephi 9:8
	Gimgimno	3 Nephi 9:8
Air	some people were carried away in the whirlwind	3 Nephi 8:16
Fire	Zarahemla	3 Nephi 8:8; 9:3
	Jacobugath	3 Nephi 9:9
	Laman	3 Nephi 9:10
	Gad	3 Nephi 9:10
	Josh	3 Nephi 9:10
	Kishkumen	3 Nephi 9:10
Water	Moroni	3 Nephi 8:9; 9:4
	Onihah	3 Nephi 9:7
	Jerusalem	3 Nephi 9:7
	Mocum	3 Nephi 9:7

Chart 49

Chart 50

Old Testament Passages Quoted by Jesus Christ in 3 Nephi

Key Scriptures   3 Nephi 16; 20–22; 24–25

Explanation   Jesus Christ spoke of his life and atonement as fulfillments of ancient prophecy. During his visit to the Americas, he quoted several Old Testament passages, all of which the children of Lehi apparently knew, to show how he fulfilled prophecy—and to explain to them their role as children of the covenant. For example, Jesus identified Lehi's descendants as those who, in the last days, will go among the Gentiles "as a lion among the beasts of the forest" (Micah 5:8–9; 3 Nephi 20:16–17). In this chart the Old Testament passages quoted by Jesus are listed in the left column, with corresponding Book of Mormon references listed on the right-hand side.

Source   Royal Skousen, "Textual Variants in the Isaiah Quotations in the Book of Mormon," in *Isaiah in the Book of Mormon,* ed. Donald W. Parry and John W. Welch (Provo, Utah: FARMS, 1998), 369–71.

Old Testament Passages
Quoted by Jesus in 3 Nephi

Passage	Quotation
Isaiah 52:8–10	3 Nephi 16:18–20
Micah 5:8–9	3 Nephi 20:16–17
Micah 4:12–13	3 Nephi 20:18–19
Deuteronomy 18:15–19	3 Nephi 20:23
Genesis 12:3	3 Nephi 20:25, 27
Isaiah 52:8	3 Nephi 20:23
Isaiah 52:9–10	3 Nephi 20:34–35
Isaiah 52:1–3	3 Nephi 20:36–38
Isaiah 52:6–7	3 Nephi 20:39–40
Isaiah 52:11–15	3 Nephi 20:41–45
Isaiah 52:15	3 Nephi 21:8
Isaiah 29:14	3 Nephi 21:9
Habakkuk 1:5	3 Nephi 21:9
Deuteronomy 18:19	3 Nephi 21:11 (allusion)
Micah 5:8–15	3 Nephi 21:12–18, 21
Deuteronomy 18:19	3 Nephi 21:20 (allusion)
Isaiah 52:12	3 Nephi 21:29
Isaiah 54:1–17	3 Nephi 22:1–17
Malachi 3:1–4:6	3 Nephi 24:1–25:6

Chart 50

Chart 51

The Coming of Christ to the Nephites
A Pattern for His Second Coming

Key Scripture   Helaman 14–3 Nephi 9

Explanation   The recorded conditions that prevailed on the American continent preceding Jesus Christ's visitation to the Nephites and Lamanites can be compared to the prophesied conditions of the world before his second coming. As in the Americas two thousand years ago, there will be increased skepticism concerning Christ's coming, great signs in heaven and on earth, secret combinations that destroy society and the government, and great natural disasters preceding the second coming of Jesus Christ. In addition, as before, the Lord has issued warnings to the Saints in this dispensation concerning pride, hypocrisy, and other forms of wickedness—lest church members "become as the Nephites of old" (D&C 38:39). Such warnings signal potential problems that may exist in the church prior to the second coming. This table lists the conditions that correspond to both the first and second comings of Christ, as well as scriptural references documenting each relevant prophecy or event.

The Coming of Christ to the Nephites
A Pattern for His Second Coming

First Coming to the Americas	Events	Second Coming
	I. Signs	
1. Hel. 14:2–6, 20–27; 3 Ne. 8:2–23	Great signs in heaven and earth	D&C 29:14; 45:39–42; JS—M 1:33
2. Hel. 14:28–31	Purpose of signs: to save mankind, to leave all without excuse	D&C 29:11, 14–17; 39:23–24; 45:16, 31–39, 49–50; 63:6–7; 68:9–11
3. Hel. 16:12–23; 3 Ne. 7:15–26; 8:4	Increased skepticism concerning Christ's coming	D&C 45:26; 2 Pet. 3:3–4
	II. Wickedness	
4. Hel. 13:21–23; 3 Ne. 6:11–13	Pride is the basis of wickedness	D&C 29:9; 38:39; 64:24
5. 3 Ne. 6:17–18; 7:7	People willfully rebel	D&C 64:34–36; 112:24–26
6. 3 Ne. 6:23; 7:14	People reject the prophets	D&C 1:14; 133:71–72; 135:1–7; 136:35–36
7. 3 Ne. 6:11–14	Pride and evil in the church	D&C 38:39; 41:1; 50:2–4, 6–9; 63:63; 98:19–22
	III. Destruction	
8. 3 Ne. 8:23–24; 10:8	Great mourning and weeping	D&C 29:15; 45:53; 87:6; 112:24
9. Hel. 11:1; 3 Ne. 3:4	Wars and rumors of wars	D&C 45:26, 68; 63:32–33
10. Hel. 10:18; 11:4	People kill one another	D&C 45:26, 68; 63:32–33
11. Hel. 13:13–14	People saved or destroyed based on whether they received or rejected the righteous	D&C 84:92–97; 99:4; 109:39–41

Chart 51

12. Hel. 10:6; 12:3	Plagues, pestilence, famine	D&C 29:18–19; 43:25; 45:31; 84:96–97; 87:6; JS—M 1:29
13. 3 Ne. 6:25–30; 7:7–9; 9:9	Secret combinations destroy society and government	Morm. 8:34–40; Ether 8:20–25; D&C 38:28; 42:64; 123:13–14
14. Hel. 14:23, 26; 3 Ne. 8:5–6; 10:14	Tempest, great storms, thundering, lightnings	D&C 43:20–25; 87:6; 88:88–91
15. 3 Ne. 8:6–19	Earthquakes and great disturbances	D&C 29:13; 43:18, 25; 45:26, 33, 48; 49:23; 88:88–89
16. 3 Ne. 8:20–23; 10:13–14	Vapor of smoke and darkness	D&C 29:14; 34:9; 45:40–42
17. Hel. 14:21–23; 3 Ne. 8:23; 9:8	Mountains made low, valleys become great mountains	D&C 49:23; 109:74
18. Hel. 14:24; 15:1; 3 Ne. 8:8–14; 10:7	Cities destroyed, houses left desolate	D&C 84:114–117
19. 3 Ne. 8:1–18; 9:1–12	Wicked destroyed at his coming	D&C 29:9; 63:34; 87:6–8; 136:33–36

IV. Righteousness

20. Hel. 3:24–30; 10:14–17; 3 Ne. 2:10	Gospel preached to all people	D&C 1:1–14; 58:64–65; 112:28–30; 133:37; JS—M 1:31
21. Hel. 6:1–5; 3 Ne. 2:14–16	Lamanites become righteous	D&C 49:24
22. 3 Ne. 3:22–26; 4:4–16	Righteous to gather together	D&C 29:7–8; 43:23–30; 45:43, 68–69; 49:25; 115:6
23. 3 Ne. 4:30–33	Righteous are divinely protected	D&C 45:70–71; 62:6
24. Alma 1:25–28; 3 Ne. 6:12–13	Righteous are persecuted	D&C 99:1; 101:32–38; 123:1–10
25. 3 Ne. 1:4–8; 8:3	Righteous look to signs of Savior's coming with faith	D&C 39:23–24; 45:39–40, 43, 57; 68:9–11; 106:4–5; JS—M 1:29

V. The Living Prophet

26. 3 Ne. 8:25; 9:10; 10:12	Receiving or rejecting living prophets a matter of life or death	D&C 1:14, 36–38; 45:32; 133:57–71
27. Hel. 16:14; 3 Ne. 7:18	Angels minister to prophets	D&C 20:6, 10, 35; 27:16; 43:25; 136:37
28. 3 Ne. 8:23–25; 9:10–13; 10:12–14	The righteous are prepared for Christ's coming by following the prophets	D&C 1:11–39; 21:4–6, 9; 84:36–38; 124:45–46

VI. Coming and Ministry of Christ

29. 3 Ne. 8:2–5, 24–25; 10:2; 11:1–10	Christ comes as a thief in the night	D&C 39:21; 61:38; 106:4–5
30. 3 Ne. 11:8	Christ comes down from heaven in glory	D&C 5:19; 29:11; 133:42–49
31. 3 Ne. 9:13; 10:12–19	Only the righteous are preserved	D&C 29:11; 35:21; 45:56–57; 63:34–35, 54; Moses 7:61
32. 3 Ne. 11:1–11	Christ appears at the temple	D&C 36:8; 42:36; 133:2
33. 3 Ne. 11:14–17	Christ displays the wounds of his body	Zechariah 13:6; D&C 45:51–52
34. 3 Ne. 11:8–12	Christ appears as a man	D&C 130:1–2
35. Hel. 14:25; 3 Ne. 23:9–10	The righteous are resurrected at Christ's coming	D&C 43:18; 45:44–45; 63:49; 88:95–102; 133:56
36. 3 Nephi 11:9–11	Christ testifies of his atoning sacrifice	D&C 133:50–51
37. 4 Nephi 1:1–5, 15–17	People become children of Christ, Satan has no power	D&C 45:55–59
38. 4 Nephi 1:7–10, 23	Righteous who are saved increase and prosper	D&C 45:58
39. 3 Nephi 10:18–19; 11–28	The Lord is in their midst and is their lawgiver	D&C 38:22; 45:59; 133:25

Chart 51

Chart 52

Does Christ Have a Body?

Key Scriptures 3 Nephi 11:8–10, 14–15; Ether 3:9, 15–17; Doctrine and Covenants 76:23; 110:1–4; 130:22; Joseph Smith—History 1:17

Explanation Mainstream Christian doctrine teaches that God does not have a body. The Book of Mormon, however, sheds light on this subject by referring to the premortal, mortal, or resurrected body of Jesus Christ more than two hundred times. This chart lists the parts of Christ's body referred to in the Book of Mormon, along with applicable scriptural references.

Source Susan Easton Black, *Finding Christ through the Book of Mormon* (Salt Lake City: Deseret Book, 1987), 52–56.

Does Christ Have a Body?

Ear
2 Ne. 7:5; 8:4; 15:9; 21:3

Cheek
2 Ne. 7:6

Lips
2 Ne. 21:4; 30:9

Mouth
1 Ne. 13:41; 2 Ne. 3:21;
9:17; 29:2; 30:9; 33:14;
Mosiah 14:7; 15:6; 3 Ne.
14:1; Ether 2:24; Moro.
7:23, 25; 10:28

Hand
1 Ne. 5:14; 2 Ne. 1:5–6, 10;
3:15, 17; 5:12; 7:11; 8:16;
25:17; 28:6; 29:1; 30:6; Jacob
4:10; 6:2; Omni 1:16; Mosiah
1:2, 5, 16; 2:11; 5:9–10, 12;
14:10; 28:15; 29:25; Alma
2:28; 9:9, 22–23; 10:23;
28:12; 37:4; 45:19; 46:7,
24; Hel. 3:30; 3 Ne. 3:2;
12:1; 18:36; 29:4, 9;
4 Ne. 1:16; Morm. 6:6;
8:8; 8:26; Ether 2:6; 3:6;
12:4; Moro. 7:27; 9:14

Finger
Alma 10:2; 3 Ne. 28:12; Ether
3:4, 6, 8, 9, 19; 12:20, 21

Bowels
Mosiah 15:9; Alma 7:12;
26:37; 34:15, 3 Ne.
17:6–7

Loins
2 Ne. 21:5; 30:11

Feet
1 Ne. 11:24; 3 Ne. 11:15,
17, 19; 17:10

Face
2 Ne. 9:38; 18:17; 33:11;
3 Ne. 9:5, 11

Eye
1 Ne. 21:5; 2 Ne. 3:8;
9:44; 10:8; 13:8; Jacob
2:10, 15

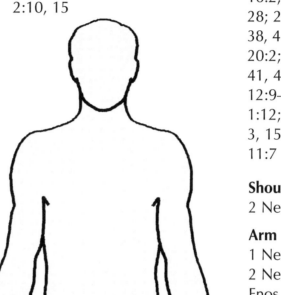

Voice
1 Ne. 16:9, 25, 26, 39;
17:7, 45; 18:5; 19:7, 11;
22:2; 2 Ne. 16:8; 31:12,
14; Jacob 7:5; Enos 1:5, 10;
Omni 1:12–13; Mosiah
16:2; 24:13, 16; 26:14, 21,
28; 27:11, 15; Alma 5:16,
38, 41, 57, 60; 9:21; 13:22;
20:2; 38:7; Hel. 5:29–33,
41, 42, 46, 48; 7:18;
12:9–12, 23; 13:3; 3 Ne.
1:12; 7:15; 9:1; 10:3; 16:2,
3, 15; Morm. 3:14; Ether
11:7

Shoulder
2 Ne. 19:6

Arm
1 Ne. 20:14; 22:10, 11;
2 Ne. 1:15; 8:9; Jacob 6:5;
Enos 1:13; Omni 1:13;
Mosiah 1:14; 12:24; 14:1;
15:31; 16:12; Alma 5:33;
19:36; 29:10; 34:16; 3 Ne.
9:14; 16:20; 20:35; Morm.
5:11; 6:17

Back
2 Ne. 7:6

Side
3 Ne. 11:14, 15

Flesh
Mosiah 15:2, 3; Alma
7:12, 13; 3 Ne. 18:28–30;
Ether 3:8–9; Moroni 4:1

Blood
1 Ne. 12:10, 11; Mosiah
3:11, 15, 18; 4:2; Alma
5:21, 27; 13:11; 21:9;
3 Ne. 18:11, 28–30; 20:8;
27:19; Morm. 9:6; Ether
3:6, 8–9; 13:10; Moro.
4:1; 5:2; 10:33

Chart 52

Teachings

of the Book of Mormon

Chart 53

Key Doctrinal Chapters
1 Nephi–Omni

Key Scripture 1 Nephi–Enos

Explanation This chart features chapters of doctrinal significance from the small plates of Nephi (which comprised 1 Nephi through Omni) along with short descriptions of their contents. These chapters include Lehi's vision of the tree of life, the psalm of Nephi, and various discourses on the atonement of Jesus Christ. Just as readers of the Book of Mormon find it useful to memorize key scriptures, it is also helpful to become familiar with key chapters in order to remember the overall contents of the book and to remember and to utilize its teachings better.

Key Doctrinal Chapters
1 Nephi–Omni

1 Nephi 1	The calling of a prophet
1 Nephi 8	Lehi's dream
1 Nephi 11	The condescension of God
1 Nephi 19	Prophecies of Christ
2 Nephi 2	Opposition, choice, and the purpose of life
2 Nephi 4	Psalm of Nephi
2 Nephi 9	Salvation and the infinite atonement
2 Nephi 25	Belief in Christ
2 Nephi 28	The ways of the devil
2 Nephi 30	The millennial era
2 Nephi 31	Repentance and baptism
2 Nephi 32	The Holy Ghost
Jacob 2	Chastity and consecration
Jacob 5	The allegory of the olive tree
Enos	Prayer

Chart 53

Chart 54

Key Doctrinal Chapters
Mosiah–Alma

Key Scripture   Mosiah 2–Alma 42

Explanation   Part of the large plates of Nephi, the books of Mosiah and Alma
contain many chapters rich in doctrinal significance. As in the
small plates of Nephi, the atonement of Jesus Christ is the center
of doctrine in this material, with service, humility, covenants, and
government forming important parts of the supporting discussion.

Key Doctrinal Chapters
Mosiah–Alma

Mosiah 2	Serving and thanking God
Mosiah 3	The atonement
Mosiah 4	Giving to the poor
Mosiah 5	Covenant making
Mosiah 14	The suffering Messiah
Mosiah 18	The covenant of baptism
Mosiah 27	Conversion of Alma
Mosiah 29	Good government
Alma 5	Remaining born again
Alma 7	The atonement
Alma 12	Adam and Eve, first and second death
Alma 13	The holy order after the Son of God
Alma 17	Missionary work
Alma 32	Humility, planting the seed of faith
Alma 34	Prayer, atonement, and procrastination
Alma 37	Following the Lord's guidance
Alma 40	Resurrection
Alma 42	Justice and mercy

Chart 54

Chart 55

Key Doctrinal Chapters
Helaman–Moroni

Key Scripture   Helaman 5–Moroni 10

Explanation   Chapters of doctrinal significance in the books of Helaman, 3 Nephi, Ether, and Moroni are listed and briefly summarized in this chart. The account in 3 Nephi 11–27 of Jesus Christ's visitation and instructions to the ancient American people is the crux of the Book of Mormon. Those key chapters testify powerfully of the Savior, expound his gospel, record how he established his church, and fulfill earlier prophecy about Christ.

Key Doctrinal Chapters
Helaman–Moroni

Helaman 5	Righteousness
Helaman 12	The feebleness of mankind
Helaman 14	Prophecies of the signs of Christ's birth
3 Nephi 11	Christ's initial appearance
3 Nephi 12	The new law of Christ
3 Nephi 13	Prayer, single-mindedness
3 Nephi 14	Passing God's judgment
3 Nephi 17	Blessing the sick, children, and parents
3 Nephi 18	The sacrament
3 Nephi 27	The church and gospel of Jesus Christ
Ether 3	Brother of Jared sees premortal Christ
Ether 12	Faith, examples of righteousness
Moroni 7	True goodness; faith, hope, and charity
Moroni 8	Salvation of children
Moroni 10	Testimony, enduring to the end

Chart 55

Chart 56

The Gospel in the Book of Mormon

Key Scriptures   2 Nephi 31; 3 Nephi 11; 27

Explanation   In three major statements about the gospel of Jesus Christ, the Book of Mormon highlights certain principles and ordinances that a person must follow or have completed in order to come fully unto Christ. The gospel of Christ, centered in the atonement, includes belief, repentance, baptism, receiving the Holy Ghost, enduring to the end, and ultimately entering the kingdom of God. The systematic listing of these six elements in 2 Nephi 31, 3 Nephi 11, and 3 Nephi 27 suggests that when the Nephites spoke about the "gospel," they meant particularly these six principles and ordinances.

Source   Noel B. Reynolds, "The Gospel as Taught by Nephite Prophets," in *Reexploring the Book of Mormon,* ed. John W. Welch (Salt Lake City: Deseret Book, 1992), 257–59.

The Gospel
in the Book of Mormon

1. Believe in Christ

2. Repent

3. Be baptized

4. Be cleansed by the Holy Ghost

5. Endure to the end

6. Enter God's kingdom

Found in 2 Nephi 31:2–32:6;

3 Nephi 11:23–39; 27:13–21

Chart 56

Chart 57

Citations of the Word "Covenant"

Key Scripture   3 Nephi 20:26

Explanation   The term *covenant* appears more than 150 times in the Book of Mormon. As this chart illustrates, the covenant relationship with God was important to the Nephites, both those living the law of Moses in the promised new land and those living the gospel of Jesus Christ after the old law was fulfilled. This bar graph displays the number of times that ten Nephite authors, along with the Jaredite prophet Ether, King Benjamin's people, and Christ himself, speak of the "covenant." The number of occurrences is relatively high in two eras, when the promise of the new land to Lehi's posterity and the gospel of Christ are first established in the Americas (see, for example, 2 Nephi 1:5; 3 Nephi 20:26). Incidentally, in those eras there is also a positive correlation between frequent covenant citations and high levels of righteousness.

Source   Victor L. Ludlow, "Covenant Teachings of the Book of Mormon," Book of Mormon Lecture Series (FARMS, 1994).

Citations of the Word "Covenant"
in the Book of Mormon

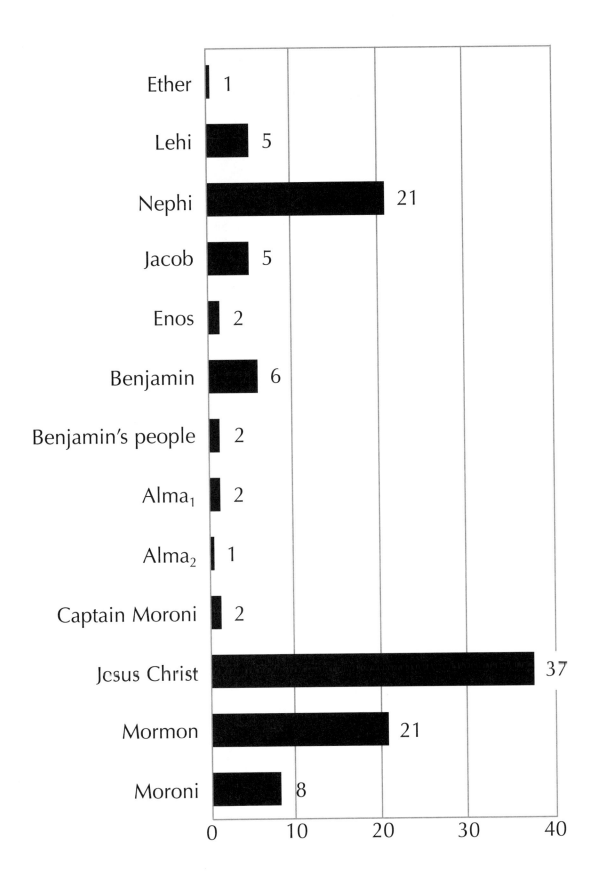

Ether	1
Lehi	5
Nephi	21
Jacob	5
Enos	2
Benjamin	6
Benjamin's people	2
Alma$_1$	2
Alma$_2$	1
Captain Moroni	2
Jesus Christ	37
Mormon	21
Moroni	8

0   10   20   30   40

Chart 57

Chart 58

Book of Mormon
Covenant Language

Key Scriptures Mosiah 5; 18; 3 Nephi 18; Moroni 4–5

Explanation Covenant-making phrases used throughout the Book of Mormon
are similar, regardless of which group of people made the covenants.
This chart compares covenant-language phrases in four particular
settings: after King Benjamin's great speech, with Alma at the Waters
of Mormon, during Christ's administration of the sacrament, and
during Nephite sacrament administration following Christ's visitation. Most of the elements are the same or are similar throughout,
such as the willing commitment to obey God's commandments.
Other elements may vary somewhat. For example, the phrase "God's
people," used commonly in ancient Israel to emphasize collective
salvation, shifts to the phrase "people of [Christ's] church," focusing
more on individual membership and worthiness. Covenant language
shifted slightly after Christ came to the Americas, when intimate
"fold" (shepherd) imagery was replaced by the more institutional
affiliation of covenanters with Christ's larger church.

Book of Mormon Covenant Language

COVENANT PHRASES	Benjamin's covenant with his people	Alma's covenant at Waters of Mormon	Christ's sacrament administration	Nephite sacrament prayers
	Mosiah 5	Mosiah 18	3 Nephi 18	Moroni 4–5
witness to God		18:10	18:7, 10	4:3; 5:2
willing	5:5	18:8–9	18:10	4:3; 5:2
to obey the commandments	5:5, 8	18:10	18:10	4:3
until the end of life	5:8	18:9		
become God's people		18:8		
come into God's fold	5:14	18:8		
become the people of my church			18:5	6:4
called by the name of Christ	5:8		18:11	4:3
remember Christ always	5:12		18:7, 11	4:3; 5:2
have eternal life	5:15	18:9		
have Christ's Spirit		18:10	18:7, 11	4:3; 5:2

Chart 58

Chart 59

Baptism of Alma's People at the Waters of Mormon

Key Scripture   Mosiah 18:7–10

Explanation   Alma, while in hiding at the Waters of Mormon, baptized about two hundred people and formed there the Church of Christ. Before the baptisms, Alma rehearsed to them their preparations and desires to be baptized, their willingness to serve and take upon themselves baptismal covenants, and the blessings promised to them if they remained faithful. This is one of the clearest statements in all of scripture about the covenants made at baptism. The elements of this baptismal speech are listed in this chart.

Baptism of Alma's People at the Waters of Mormon

Mosiah 18:7–10

People's Preparations
They believe Alma's words
They understand repentance and redemption
They have faith on the Lord

People's Willingness
They will bear one another's burdens
They will mourn with those that mourn
They will comfort those in need of comfort
They will stand as witnesses of God

Baptismal Covenants
They covenant to serve God
They covenant to keep God's commandments

Results
They come into the fold of God
They are called God's people

Blessings
They have Christ's Spirit more abundantly
They are redeemed of God
They will be numbered in the first resurrection
They will have eternal life

Chart 59

Chart 60

The Speeches of Alma

Key Scriptures   Alma 5; 7; 12–13; 32–33; 36–42

Explanation   Alma the Younger's first recorded speech (see Mosiah 27:24–31) was the impromptu account of his conversion to the gospel of Jesus Christ. After his conversion, he devoted his life to preaching the gospel to as many people as would listen. These included the righteous, the wicked, the poor, the wealthy, and members of his own family. All of his known speeches or formal statements are cited in this chart, along with the topics and settings of those discourses.

The Speeches of Alma

Reference	Topics	Audience Setting
Mosiah 27:24–31	Alma's conversion	those assembled to pray for Alma
Alma 5	true conversion	backsliding church members in Zarahemla
Alma 7	atonement	righteous people in Gideon
Alma 9	repentance and deliverance	wicked people in Ammonihah
Alma 12–13	the plan and holy order of God	wicked people in Ammonihah
Alma 29	"O that I were an angel"	unknown
Alma 32–33	humility, faith, prayer, atonement	the poor outcasts in Antionum
Alma 36–37	Alma's conversion, following the Lord	his son Helaman
Alma 38	Alma's conversion, wise counsel	his son Shiblon
Alma 39–42	sin, redemption, justice, mercy, resurrection, restoration	his son Corianton

Chart 60

Chart 61

50 Questions of Alma 5
Overview

Key Scripture   Alma 5

Explanation   In one of Alma the Younger's major discourses to the people of Zarahemla, he asks the people fifty rhetorical questions. This chart is an overview of the general issues Alma discusses in Alma 5, such as being personally converted and imagining the judgment day. His fifty searching questions are useful to all people who wish to assess their own personal conversion and standing before God.

50 Questions of Alma 5
Overview

Questions	General Issues
1–5	Remembering God's Acts for His People
6–12	Knowing the Essential Logic of the Gospel
13–17	Being Personally Converted
18–29	Imagining the Judgment Day
30–36	Assessing One's Spiritual Condition
37–38	Identifying with a "Fold"
39–40	Obtaining Spiritual Knowledge
41–50	Refusing to Repent

Chart 61

Chart 62

50 Questions of Alma 5
Questions 1–17

Key Scripture   Alma 5:6–15

Explanation   This chart lists in three groups the first seventeen rhetorical questions Alma asks the people of Zarahemla in Alma 5. First, Alma asks if they have remembered their heritage and God's deliverance of their ancestors. This can have personal application to Latter-day Saints: just as the Nephites were admonished to remember God's deliverance of their ancestors, so should Latter-day Saints remember the sacrifices of the Prophet Joseph Smith and the pioneers—and the Lord's providing them the promised land of Zion. Second, he invites people to ponder the conditions of salvation and the need to believe the prophets of God. Third, he asks penetrating questions about each listener's repentance, change, faith, and hope. Still today, most of these questions invite a clear yes or no answer.

50 Questions of Alma 5
Questions 1–17

Question	Verse

Question   **Verse**

Remembering God's Acts for His People

1. Have you sufficiently retained in remembrance the captivity of your fathers? — 6

2. Have you sufficiently retained in remembrance God's mercy and long-suffering towards your fathers?

3. Have you sufficiently retained in remembrance that he has delivered their souls from hell?

4. Were your fathers destroyed? — 8

5. Were the bands of death broken, and the chains of hell which encircled your fathers about, were they loosed? — 9

Knowing the Essential Logic of the Gospel

6. On what conditions were your fathers saved? — 10

7. On what grounds had they to hope for salvation?

8. What is the cause of your fathers' being loosed from the bands of death, yea, and also the chains of hell?

9. Did not my father Alma believe in the words which were delivered by the mouth of Abinadi? — 11

10. Was Abinadi not a holy prophet?

11. Did Abinadi not speak the words of God?

12. Did my father Alma believe them?

Being Personally Converted

13. Have you spiritually been born of God? — 14

14. Have you received his image in your countenance?

15. Have you experienced this mighty change in your heart?

16. Do you exercise faith in the redemption of him who created you? — 15

17. Do you look forward with an eye of faith?

Chart 62

Chart 63

50 Questions of Alma 5
Questions 18–29

Key Scripture   Alma 5:15–24

Explanation   This chart lists rhetorical questions 18–29 that Alma asks the people of Zarahemla in Alma 5. These dozen questions concern the state of the individual's soul at the final judgment day. Alma wishes to impress upon his audience that there are ultimately only two possible outcomes at the final judgment: eternal joy or eternal remorse. Those who are righteous will have the image of God upon their countenances and will be found spotless and pure; others will be stained and unfit for the presence of God. This dualistic conception, or the doctrine of the Two Ways, is discussed in detail in charts 66–76. The vivid belief that all people will someday stand before God to give an accounting and to be judged is a powerful motivator of moral behavior.

50 Questions of Alma 5
Questions 18–29

Question	Verse

Imagining the Judgment Day

18. Do you view this mortal body raised in immortality, and this corruption raised in incorruption, to stand before God to be judged according to the deeds which have been done in the mortal body? — 15

19. Can you imagine to yourself that you hear the voice of the Lord, saying unto you, in that day: Come unto me you blessed, for behold your works have been works of righteousness upon the face of the earth? — 16

20. Or do you imagine to yourself that you can lie unto the Lord in that day, and say—Lord, my works have been righteous works upon the face of the earth—and that he will save you? — 17

21. Or otherwise, can you imagine yourself brought before the tribunal of God with your soul filled with guilt and remorse, having a remembrance of all your guilt, yea, a perfect remembrance of all your wickedness, yea, a remembrance that you have set at defiance the commandments of God? — 18

22. Can you look up to God at that day with a pure heart and clean hands? — 19

23. Can you look up, having the image of God engraven upon your countenance?

24. Can you think of being saved when you have yielded yourself to become subject to the devil? — 20

25. How will you feel if you shall stand before the bar of God, having your garments stained with blood and all manner of filthiness? — 22

26. What will these things testify against you?

27. Will they not testify that you are a murderer? — 23

28. Will they not also testify that you are guilty of all manner of wickedness?

29. Do you suppose that such an one can have a place to sit down in the kingdom of God, with Abraham, with Isaac, and with Jacob, and also all the holy prophets, whose garments are cleansed and are spotless, pure and white? — 24

Chart 63

Chart 64

50 Questions of Alma 5
Questions 30–40

Key Scripture   Alma 5:26–46

Explanation   In this next series of questions directed to the people of Zarahemla, Alma states that experiencing a change of heart can be temporary and that one must continually strive to be blameless before God. His dualistic view is apparent: those who are blameless are of the fold of God, and all others are of the fold of the devil. In this part of his speech, he guides the spiritual progress of his listeners by directing them in assessing their own spiritual condition, identifying with a community that believes in Jesus Christ, and personally obtaining spiritual knowledge.

50 Questions of Alma 5
Questions 30–40

Question	Verse
Assessing One's Spiritual Condition	

30. If you have experienced a change of heart, and if you have felt to sing the song of redeeming love, can you feel so now? — 26

31. Have you walked, keeping yourself blameless before God? — 27

32. Could you say, if you were called to die at this time, within yourself, that you have been sufficiently humble?

33. Could you say that your garments have been cleansed and made white through the blood of Christ?

34. Are you stripped of pride? — 28

35. Is there one among you who is not stripped of envy? — 29

36. Is there one among you that doth make a mock of his brother, or that heapeth upon him persecutions? — 30

Identifying with a "Fold"

37. If you are not the sheep of the good shepherd, of what fold are you? — 39

38. The devil is your shepherd, and you are of his fold; and now who can deny this?

Obtaining Spiritual Knowledge

39. Do you not suppose that I know of these things myself? — 45

40. How do you suppose that I know of their surety? — 46

Chart 64

Chart 65

50 Questions of Alma 5
Questions 41–50

Key Scripture Alma 5:53–59

Explanation The last ten rhetorical questions that Alma asks the people of Zarahemla are listed in this chart. These questions concern refusing to repent of sins. Alma's phrase "trample the Holy One under your feet" (Alma 5:53) poignantly illustrates that individuals blatantly mock God when they know the source of salvation and yet refuse to repent and partake of that free gift. By ending his speech with these ten questions, Alma places the burden of repentance directly on the shoulders of each person who seeks to live a life pleasing to God.

50 Questions of Alma 5
Questions 41–50

Questions	Verse
Refusing to Repent	

41. Can you withstand these sayings? — 53

42. Can you lay aside these things and trample the Holy One under your feet?

43. Can you be puffed up in the pride of your heart?

44. Will you still persist in the wearing of costly apparel and setting your heart upon the vain things of the world, upon your riches?

45. Will you persist in supposing that you are better than another? — 54

46. Will you persist in the persecution of your brethren, who humble themselves and do walk after the holy order of God, wherewith they have been brought into this church having been sanctified by the Holy Spirit, and they do bring forth works which are meet for repentance?

47. Will you persist in turning your back upon the poor and the needy, and in withholding your substance from them? — 55

48. The names of the righteous shall be written in the book of life, and unto them will I grant an inheritance at my right hand. What have you to say against this? — 58

49. What shepherd is there having many sheep doth not watch over them, that the wolves enter not and devour his flock? — 59

50. If a wolf enter his flock doth the shepherd not drive him out?

Chart 65

Chart 66

The Ways of Life and Death
Overview

Key Scripture   2 Nephi 9

Explanation   Many prophets in the Book of Mormon discuss in great detail the doctrine that men and women can choose to follow one of two courses: the way of life or the way of death. Though each Book of Mormon prophet addresses this doctrine in a unique way, all have in common a dualistic view of reality. This view is similar to ancient Israelite and early Christian worldviews, further supporting the ancient origin of the Book of Mormon. Understanding this dualistic conception of reality in the Book of Mormon is vital to our understanding of salvation and is the framework upon which additional revelation in the Doctrine and Covenants is built. The revelations of the three degrees of glory and the spirit world (see D&C 76; 138), while not dualistic in themselves, can be seen as supplementary to the dualistic Book of Mormon perception. The fact that the Prophet Joseph Smith used little dualism in his own preaching and writing, it has also been argued, is secondary evidence that he was not the author of the Book of Mormon.

Source   Mack C. Stirling, "The Way of Life and the Way of Death in the Book of Mormon," *Journal of Book of Mormon Studies* 6/2 (1997): 152–204.

The Ways of Life and Death
Overview

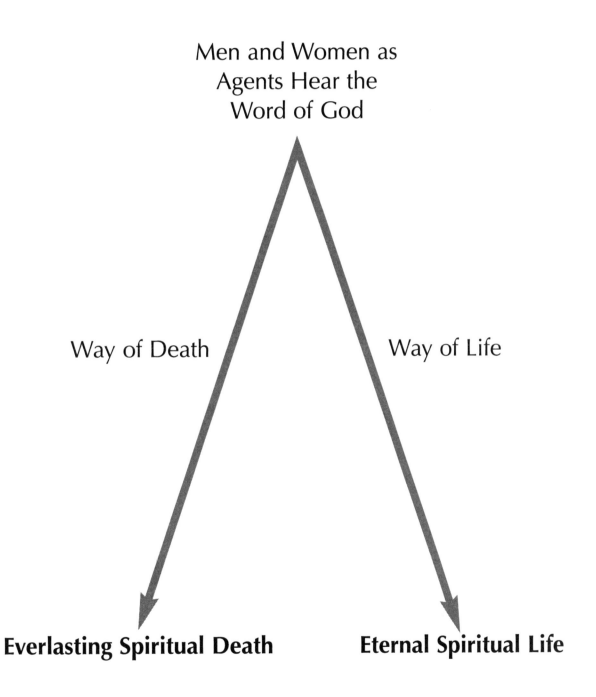

Men and Women as
Agents Hear the
Word of God

Way of Death

Way of Life

Everlasting Spiritual Death

Eternal Spiritual Life

Chart 66

Chart 67

The Ways of Life and Death
The Visionary Perception of Lehi and Nephi

Key Scriptures   1 Nephi 8; 11–15; 2 Nephi 31:17–32:5

Explanation   Lehi and Nephi spoke clearly in terms of the ways of life and death. These well-known, largely metaphorical discussions of the tree of life lay insightful groundwork relevant to nearly every chapter in the Book of Mormon. In the visions of the tree of life, Lehi and Nephi saw a straight and narrow path leading to the tree of life, the only way of life. By contrast, the mists of darkness, fountain of filthy water, forbidden paths, strange roads, and great and spacious building all represent the "broad roads" of the way of death (1 Nephi 12:17). Nephi explains further that, depending on the way he or she chooses, a person belongs to either the church of God or the church of the devil. This view sets the stage for the dualistic discourse apparent elsewhere in the Book of Mormon.

Source   Mack C. Stirling, "The Way of Life and the Way of Death in the Book of Mormon," *Journal of Book of Mormon Studies* 6/2 (1997): 180–86.

The Ways of Life and Death

The Visionary Perception of Lehi and Nephi
(1 Nephi 8; 11–15; 2 Nephi 31:17–32:5)

Men and Women in Dark and Dreary Waste
(1 Nephi 8:7–8)

Large and Spacious Field
(1 Nephi 8:9, 20)

Gate to Way of Death

Being overpowered
by temptation

Having blind eyes
and hard heart

Gate to Way of Life

Faith
Repentance
Baptism
Holy Ghost

Church of the Devil

Church of the Lamb

Broad Path to Death
(1 Nephi 12:17)

Straight and Narrow Path to Life
(1 Nephi 8:19–20)

Consequences

Depths of Hell
(1 Nephi 12:16)

Captivity of Devil
(1 Nephi 14:4)

Cast Out of the
Kingdom of God
(1 Nephi 15:33–36)

Awful Hell Prepared
for Wicked
(1 Nephi 15:26–30)

Blessings

Eternal Life
(2 Nephi 31:20)

Love of God
(1 Nephi 11:21–22; 2 Nephi 31:30)

Being Redeemed by Christ
(1 Nephi 11:10–21)

Kingdom of God
(1 Nephi 15:35)

Chart 67

The Ways of Life and Death
Jacob's Explanation

Key Scripture 2 Nephi 9

Explanation In the blessing he received from his father Lehi, Jacob was told that "there is an opposition in all things" (2 Nephi 2:11). Characteristic of his writing style, Jacob's exposition in 2 Nephi 9 of the ways of life and death is an extensive meditation on the desires of men and women in mortality and how they lead to either spiritual life or death. As this chart shows, Jacob focuses on the inward state of the souls who choose either of these divergent paths. Jacob presents as options only paradise and endless torment as places where a soul may go after final judgment.

Source Mack C. Stirling, "The Way of Life and the Way of Death in the Book of Mormon," *Journal of Book of Mormon Studies* 6/2 (1997): 161–63.

The Ways of Life and Death
Jacob's Explanation (2 Nephi 9)

Men and Women
Choose in Probation

Verses	Wicked Response in Probation
27	transgressing commandments
30, 34–37	despising poor, lying, murdering, committing whoredoms
33, 38	being uncircumcised of heart, dying in sins
39	being carnally minded
40	reviling against the truth
27	wasting days of probation
28	knowing of themselves
30	setting hearts on treasures
28	hearkening not to counsels of God
31–32	neither hearing nor seeing

Righteous Response in Probation	Verses
righteousness	18
enduring crosses and shame of world	18
having faith, repenting, being baptized, enduring	23–24
being spiritually minded	39
loving the truth	40
following the straight and narrow course	41
knocking to approach God	42
letting hearts rejoice in righteousness	49, 52
feasting on that which perisheth not	51
praying continually	52

Spiritual Death
Hell

14	knowledge of guilt and uncleanness
16	filthy still
16, 46	misery and endless torment
46	obtained by the devil
16	death/lake of fire and brimstone

Spiritual Life
Paradise

perfect knowledge of righteousness	14
clothed with purity	14
fulness of joy	18
inherit kingdom of God	18
life eternal	39

Chart 68

Chart 69

The Ways of Life and Death
Benjamin's Explanation

Key Scripture   Mosiah 2–5

Explanation   In Mosiah 2–5, Benjamin explains the ways of life and death to his people and is subsequently met with an overwhelming desire of the people to follow the way of life. Missing from his explanation is information concerning resurrection and the spirit world. Instead, he focuses on the "natural man," emphasizing that one must repent and be spiritually reborn to overcome natural tendencies to do evil. This chart illustrates the characteristics associated with each path—those personal deeds and attributes that land souls either on the left hand of God according to his justice (see Mosiah 2:38–39; 3:26; 5:10) or on the right hand of God according to his mercy (see Mosiah 2:39; 4:2; 5:15).

Source   Mack C. Stirling, "The Way of Life and the Way of Death in the Book of Mormon," *Journal of Book of Mormon Studies* 6/2 (1997): 164–66.

The Ways of Life and Death
Benjamin's Explanation (Mosiah 2–5)

Fall of Adam
Natural Man in Carnal State

Verses	Wicked Response in Probation	Righteous Response in Probation	Verses
2:38	repenting not	having faith, repenting, entering into covenant, which brings remission of sins	3:12; 5:5; 4:2–3
2:32, 37	listing to obey evil spirit	being born again: a mighty change bringing desire to do good	5:2, 7
3:24–25	doing evil works	becoming steadfast and immovable in good works, thereby retaining remission of sins	5:15; 4:11–12, 26
2:36	transgressing contrary to that which has been spoken	being obedient to the end	5:8
5:10	being called by some other name	being called by the name of Christ	5:9
2:38	dying an enemy to God	being sealed to God	5:15

Left Hand of God
Justice

Right Hand of God
Mercy

Verses			Verses
3:26–27	as a lake of fire and brimstone	heaven, eternal life	5:15
2:33	damnation	everlasting salvation	5:15
2:38	shrinking from the presence of God	dwelling with God	2:41
2:38–39	endless torment; suffering wrath of God	never-ending happiness	2:41

Chart 69

Chart 70

The Ways of Life and Death
Abinadi's Explanation

Key Scripture   Mosiah 15–16

Explanation   Abinadi, in Mosiah 15–16, expounds upon the ways of life and death to King Noah and his priests. In this provocative sermon, Abinadi warns Noah that obeying God also means following his prophets, namely, Abinadi. Abinadi preaches that if men and women do not listen to the voice, or mouthpiece, of the Lord, they necessarily follow the way of death. Abinadi also speaks of partial judgment before the resurrection, a concept not found in Alma's, Jacob's, and Benjamin's speeches.

Source   Mack C. Stirling, "The Way of Life and the Way of Death in the Book of Mormon," *Journal of Book of Mormon Studies* 6/2 (1997): 166–68.

The Ways of Life and Death
Abinadi's Explanation (Mosiah 15–16)

Men and Women in Fallen State
Knowledge of God Given; Arm of Mercy Extended

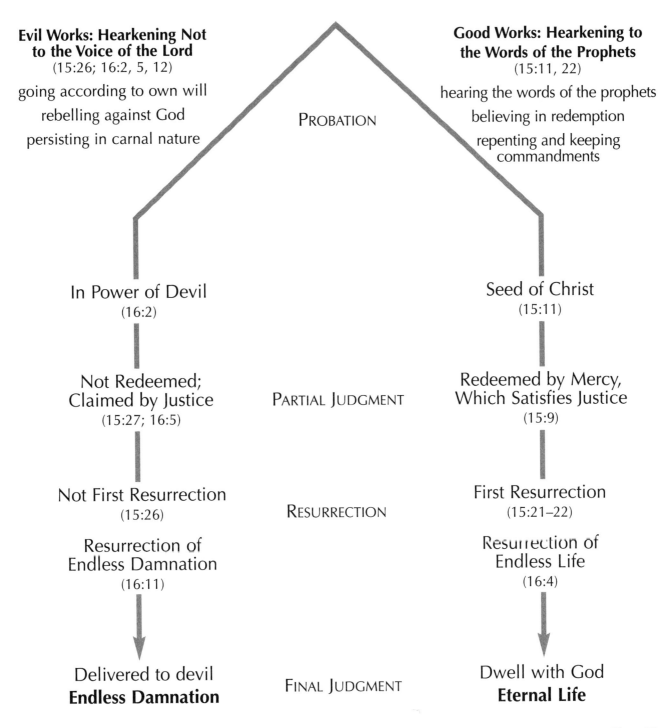

Evil Works: Hearkening Not to the Voice of the Lord
(15:26; 16:2, 5, 12)

going according to own will

rebelling against God

persisting in carnal nature

Good Works: Hearkening to the Words of the Prophets
(15:11, 22)

hearing the words of the prophets

believing in redemption

repenting and keeping commandments

PROBATION

In Power of Devil
(16:2)

Seed of Christ
(15:11)

Not Redeemed;
Claimed by Justice
(15:27; 16:5)

PARTIAL JUDGMENT

Redeemed by Mercy,
Which Satisfies Justice
(15:9)

Not First Resurrection
(15:26)

RESURRECTION

First Resurrection
(15:21–22)

Resurrection of
Endless Damnation
(16:11)

Resurrection of
Endless Life
(16:4)

Delivered to devil
Endless Damnation

FINAL JUDGMENT

Dwell with God
Eternal Life

Chart 70

Chart 71

The Ways of Life and Death
The Voice of the Lord to Alma the Elder

Key Scripture Mosiah 26:20–28

Explanation In Mosiah 26:20–28 the voice of the Lord builds upon Abinadi's discourse, telling Alma the Elder that the ways of life and death can be determined in terms of responding to the Lord's voice. Those who obey the word of the Lord will be found on the right hand of God, while those who do not will dwell in everlasting fire with the devil.

Source Mack C. Stirling, "The Way of Life and the Way of Death," *Journal of Book of Mormon Studies* 6/2 (1997): 168–71.

The Ways of Life and Death
The Voice of the Lord to Alma the Elder
(Mosiah 26:20–28)

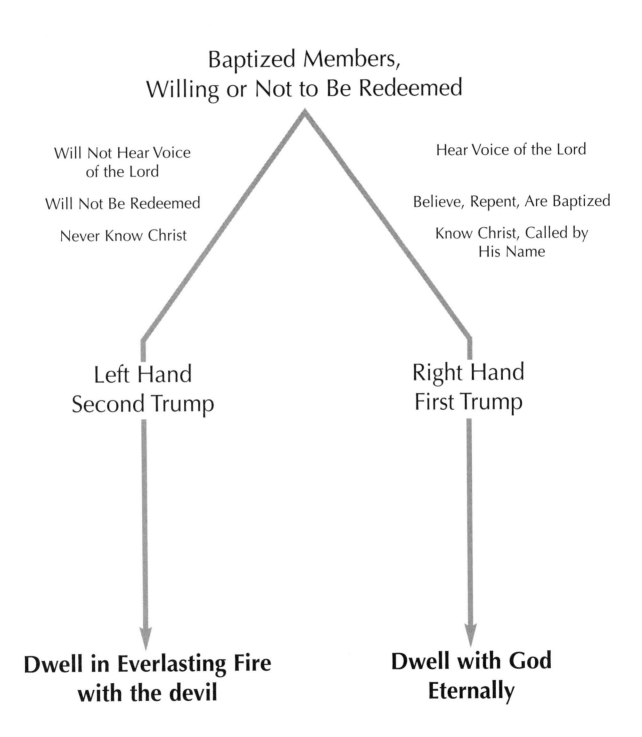

Baptized Members,
Willing or Not to Be Redeemed

Will Not Hear Voice
of the Lord

Will Not Be Redeemed

Never Know Christ

Hear Voice of the Lord

Believe, Repent, Are Baptized

Know Christ, Called by
His Name

Left Hand
Second Trump

Right Hand
First Trump

**Dwell in Everlasting Fire
with the devil**

**Dwell with God
Eternally**

Chart 71

Chart 72

The Ways of Life and Death
Alma the Younger's Explanation in Zarahemla

Key Scripture Alma 5

Explanation Alma the Younger's perception of the gospel was heavily influenced by the teachings of King Benjamin, Abinadi, and his father, Alma. His explanation of the ways of life and death to the people of Zarahemla (see Alma 5) echoes and expounds upon the teachings of his predecessors, emphasizing adherence to the voice of the Good Shepherd as the way to sustain spiritual life. Alma the Younger also states that "whatsoever is good cometh from God, and whatsoever is evil cometh from the devil" (Alma 5:40). Just as humanity's ability to bring forth good works is an element of God's grace, as the foregoing quotation suggests, the very existence of life and the power granted to humanity to proceed in the way of life are also gifts from God.

Source Mack C. Stirling, "The Way of Life and the Way of Death in the Book of Mormon," *Journal of Book of Mormon Studies* 6/2 (1997): 171–73.

The Ways of Life and Death

Alma the Younger's Explanation in Zarahemla
(Alma 5)

Good Shepherd Calls All to
Repent and Partake of Life

Man Hearkens to the
Voice of the Devil
(5:37–39, 41)

Man Hearkens to the Voice
of the Good Shepherd
(5:37–39, 57)

FOLD OF THE DEVIL

FOLD OF THE GOOD SHEPHERD

Is a Child of the Devil (5:41)

awaits everlasting destruction
is in a deep sleep
soul is in darkness
is encircled by chains of hell

Is Born of God (5:14)

is delivered from hell
awakes to God
soul is illuminated
chains of hell are loosed

Commits All Manner of
Wickedness (5:23)

does evil works
is subject to devil
garments are stained

Walks Blameless (5:27, 54)

is sanctified by the Holy Spirit
does good works
has God's image in countenance
garments are washed white

**Is a Child of the
Kingdom of the Devil**

**Sits Down in the
Kingdom of God**

is hewn down and cast out
into the fire

has inheritance at
right hand of God

Chart 72

Chart 73

The Ways of Life and Death
Alma the Younger's Explanation in Ammonihah

Key Scripture   Alma 12:31–37

Explanation   A more detailed illustration of chart 66, this chart illustrates the concise but thorough discourse of Alma the Younger as he explains the ways of life and death to the people of Ammonihah (see Alma 12:31–37). Alma's explanation of the first death can be applied to three different situations: Adam and Eve's transgression in the Garden of Eden, Israel's disobedience to the law of Moses in the wilderness, and personal sin.

Source   Mack C. Stirling, "The Way of Life and the Way of Death in the Book of Mormon," *Journal of Book of Mormon Studies* 6/2 (1997): 158–61.

The Ways of Life and Death
Alma the Younger's Explanation in Ammonihah
(Alma 12:31–37)

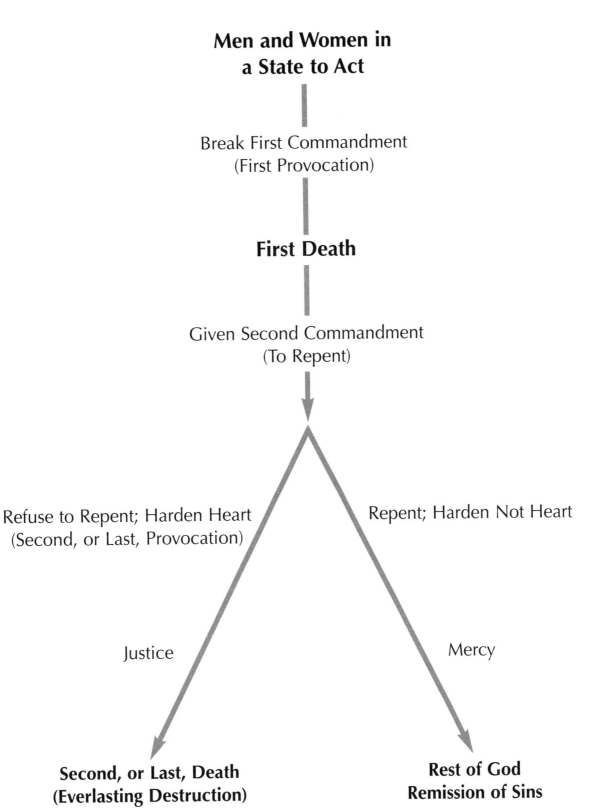

**Men and Women in
a State to Act**

Break First Commandment
(First Provocation)

First Death

Given Second Commandment
(To Repent)

Refuse to Repent; Harden Heart
(Second, or Last, Provocation)

Repent; Harden Not Heart

Justice

Mercy

**Second, or Last, Death
(Everlasting Destruction)**

**Rest of God
Remission of Sins**

Chart 73

Chart 74

The Ways of Life and Death
Alma the Younger's Explanation to Corianton

Key Scripture   Alma 41:3–8

Explanation   Alma the Younger discussed the ways of life and death in both public sermons and private instructions. In Alma 41 he chastises his son Corianton, who had been on a mission to the Zoramites, for boasting and committing sexual sins. In this chapter Alma explains that the doctrine of restoration is inextricably tied with the doctrine of the Two Ways. For example, those who choose evil follow the way of death and will unavoidably be restored to evil, "raised to . . . endless misery to inherit the kingdom of the devil" (Alma 41:4). Like Jacob, Alma focuses on the desires of the people as leading to eternal life or death. And like Benjamin, he sermonizes on casting off the natural man through the mercy of God. Apparently, his private instruction to Corianton was quite convincing, for Corianton was again called to preach and later declared the word of God to the people of the church (see Alma 49:30).

Source   Mack C. Stirling, "The Way of Life and the Way of Death in the Book of Mormon," *Journal of Book of Mormon Studies* 6/2 (1997): 173–76.

The Ways of Life and Death
Alma the Younger's Explanation to Corianton
(Alma 41:3–8)

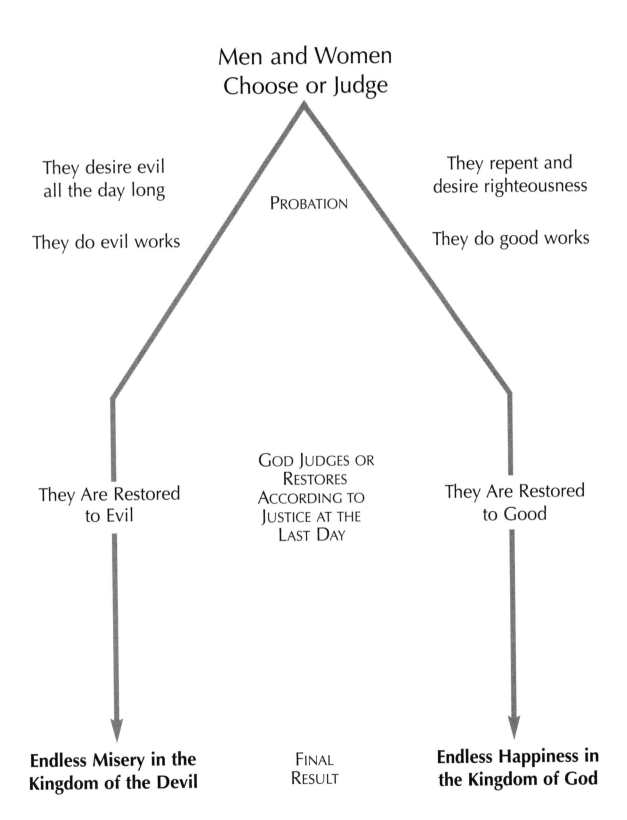

Men and Women
Choose or Judge

PROBATION

They desire evil
all the day long

They do evil works

They repent and
desire righteousness

They do good works

They Are Restored
to Evil

GOD JUDGES OR
RESTORES
ACCORDING TO
JUSTICE AT THE
LAST DAY

They Are Restored
to Good

**Endless Misery in the
Kingdom of the Devil**

FINAL
RESULT

**Endless Happiness in
the Kingdom of God**

Chart 74

Chart 75

The Ways of Life and Death
Mormon's Explanation

Key Scripture   Moroni 7:5–20

Explanation   Moroni included in the Book of Mormon a sermon given by his father, Mormon, which is widely known as including Mormon's discussion on faith, hope, and charity. In this sermon Mormon explains the ways of life and death to introduce the concepts of faith, hope, and charity (see Moroni 7:5–20). He speaks of choosing between good and bitter fountains, which may represent Jesus Christ and the devil as well as us as individuals once we have chosen which fountain to drink from. Choosing which fountain to drink from largely determines what we will ultimately become—a child of Christ or a servant of the devil. For Mormon there is no middle ground.

Source   Mack C. Stirling, "The Way of Life and the Way of Death in the Book of Mormon," *Journal of Book of Mormon Studies* 6/2 (1997): 176–81.

The Ways of Life and Death
Mormon's Explanation (Moroni 7:5–20)

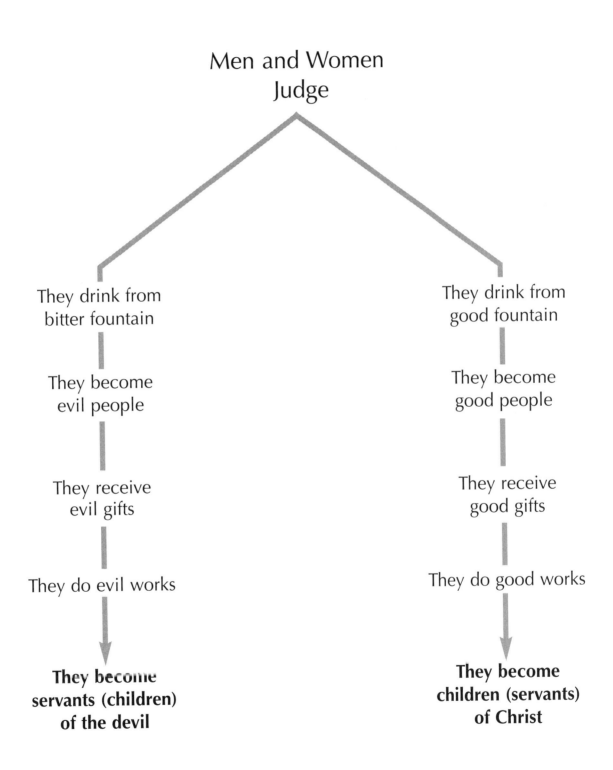

Men and Women
Judge

They drink from
bitter fountain

They become
evil people

They receive
evil gifts

They do evil works

**They become
servants (children)
of the devil**

They drink from
good fountain

They become
good people

They receive
good gifts

They do good works

**They become
children (servants)
of Christ**

Chart 75

Chart 76

The Ways of Life and Death
A Composite View

Key Scriptures   2 Nephi 9; Alma 12; 40; D&C 63:17–18; 76; 88:96–103

Explanation   This chart depicts the ways of life and death as discussed by Jacob and Alma the Younger and supplemented by the Doctrine and Covenants. The views of reality presented by the Book of Mormon and Doctrine and Covenants work hand in hand to provide the most complete representation of the ways of life and death. Adding the three degrees of glory to the framework of the ways of life and death creates a paradigm promoting optimal understanding of reality and the final state of the soul.

Source   Mack C. Stirling, "The Way of Life and the Way of Death in the Book of Mormon," *Journal of Book of Mormon Studies* 6/2 (1997): 199–203.

The Ways of Life and Death
A Composite View
(2 Nephi 9; Alma 12, 40; D&C 63:17–18; 76; 88:96–103)

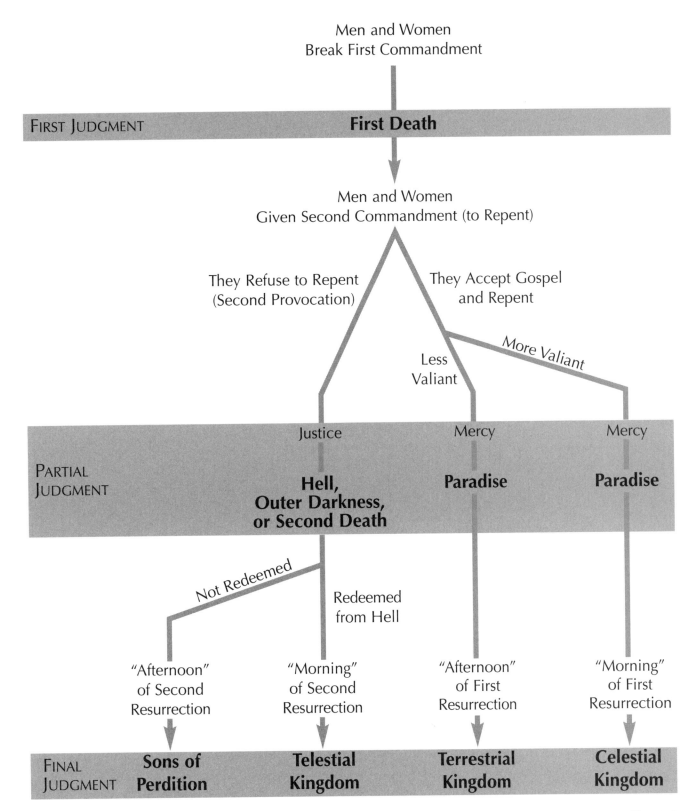

Men and Women
Break First Commandment

FIRST JUDGMENT — **First Death**

Men and Women
Given Second Commandment (to Repent)

They Refuse to Repent
(Second Provocation)

They Accept Gospel
and Repent

Less
Valiant

More Valiant

Justice

Mercy

Mercy

PARTIAL
JUDGMENT

**Hell,
Outer Darkness,
or Second Death**

Paradise

Paradise

Not Redeemed

Redeemed
from Hell

"Afternoon"
of Second
Resurrection

"Morning"
of Second
Resurrection

"Afternoon"
of First
Resurrection

"Morning"
of First
Resurrection

FINAL
JUDGMENT

**Sons of
Perdition**

**Telestial
Kingdom**

**Terrestrial
Kingdom**

**Celestial
Kingdom**

Chart 76

Chart 77

Murmurings of Laman and Lemuel

Key Scripture   1 Nephi 2:11–12

Explanation   Laman and Lemuel murmured incessantly against Lehi, Nephi, and the Lord. One major theme of their complaints was that Nephi, their younger brother, was domineering; another was that the requirements of the Lord, such as living in the wilderness and obtaining the brass plates, were too difficult. This chart catalogs those complaints and others.

Murmurings of Laman and Lemuel

Target of Complaint	Reference	Reason for Complaint
Lehi	1 Nephi 2:11–12	commandment to leave Jerusalem
	1 Nephi 3:5, 28	commandment to return for plates of brass
	1 Nephi 17:20–21, 49	hardship
Nephi	1 Nephi 16:3	Nephi explains Lehi's vision and condemns wickedness
	1 Nephi 16:18, 20	Nephi breaks bow
	1 Nephi 17:17–18	Nephi builds a ship
	2 Nephi 1:26	Nephi rebukes them
	2 Nephi 1:25; 5:3–4	Nephi rules over them
Lord	1 Nephi 3:31	difficulty in obtaining the plates of brass
	1 Nephi 4:4	difficulty in obtaining the plates of brass

Chart 77

Chart 78

Teachings of Korihor

Key Scripture   Alma 30

Explanation   Korihor, an anti-Christ preaching at the time when Alma the Younger was high priest over the land, convinced many Nephites that they should not believe in Jesus Christ or his coming atonement. He taught them instead various philosophies. In Korihor's phrases and arguments, modern readers can find parallels to many schools of thought, such as atheism, nihilism, and relativism, which have long dominated much of secular philosophy. This highly intelligent opponent's tactics were persuasive, but Alma retaliated with pure testimony and the power of God, eliminating Korihor's influence in the land. This chart lists each of the doctrines taught by Korihor in Alma 30 and a modern or standard philosophical counterpart.

Source   Based on the research and assistance of Miriam Horwinski, teaching assistant of John W. Welch, Book of Mormon 121H, Brigham Young University, fall 1997.

The Teachings of Korihor
in Alma 30

Modern Counterpart	Korihorism	Verse
Anti-Christian	"there should be no Christ"	12
Negativism	"bound down under a foolish and vain hope"	13
Agnosticism	"no man can know of anything which is to come"	13
Empiricism	"ye cannot know of things which ye do not see"	15
Psychological explanation	"it is the effect of a frenzied mind"	16
Positivism	"a belief of things which are not so"	16
Sophism	"every man fares in this life according to the management of the creature"	17
Naturalism	"every man prospers according to his genius"	17
Egoism	"every man conquers according to his strength"	17
Relativism	"whatsoever a man does is no crime"	17
Hedonism	"lift up their heads in wickedness"	18
Nihilism	"when a man dies, that is the end thereof"	18
Anti-Religion	"priests usurp power and authority over people"	23
Skepticism	"ye do not know that they are true"	24
Atheism	"a being who never has been seen or known, who never was nor ever will be"	28

Chart 78

Chart 79

The Ways of the Devil

Key Scripture   2 Nephi 28:3–30

Explanation   Embedded in Nephi's prophecy in 2 Nephi 28 are many phrases that describe the conduct of those who follow the devil. These sins, Nephi states, will pervade much of society in the latter days. Today they can be found well disguised as the philosophies and tendencies listed in this chart. Such conditions are symptomatic of society's passive acceptance of "false and vain and foolish doctrines" (2 Nephi 28:9) that can lead people away from God. Knowing how the devil works and being able to see his tactics in operation in the ideologies of the world around us help prevent us from being taken captive by Satan, who leads people "carefully down to hell" (2 Nephi 28:21).

Source   Based on the research and assistance of Miriam Horwinski, teaching assistant of John W. Welch, Book of Mormon 121H, Brigham Young University, fall 1997.

The Ways of the Devil
2 Nephi 28:3–30

Tactic	Quotation	Verse
Misappropriation	"built up, and not unto the Lord"	3
Exclusivism	"I am the Lord's"	3
Disputation	"contend one with another"	4
Sophism	"teach with their learning"	4
Cynicism	"deny the Holy Ghost, which giveth utterance"	4
Secularism	"deny the power of God"	5
Historicism	"the Redeemer hath done his work"	5
Empowerment	"he hath given his power unto men"	5
Skepticism	"believe it not"	6
Naturalism	"he is not a God of miracles"	6
Hedonism	"eat, drink, and be merry"	7
Fatalism	"tomorrow we die"	7
Cavalierism	"it shall be well with us"	7
Appearances	"nevertheless, fear God"	8
Popularism	"many . . . shall say"	8
Rationalizing	"justify in committing a little sin"	8
Criticism	"take the advantage of one because of his words"	8
Entrapment	"dig a pit for thy neighbor"	8
Legalism	"no harm in this"	8
Permissivism	"do all these things"	8
Leniency	"God will beat us with a few stripes"	8

Chart 79

Fadism	"many . . . shall teach after this manner"	9
Sensationalism	"false"	9
Egotism	"vain"	9
Imprudence	"foolish"	9
Arrogance	"puffed up in their hearts"	9
Self-Deception	"hide their counsels from the Lord"	9
Persecutionism	"blood of the saints shall cry"	10
Corruptionism	"they have become corrupted"	11
Oppressionism	"rob the poor"	13
Ostentationism	"because of their fine sanctuaries"	13
Narcissism	"their fine clothing"	13
Supremism	"persecute the meek and the poor in heart"	13
Elitism	"stiff necks and high heads"	13
Immorality	"abominations and whoredoms"	14
Distortionism	"pervert the right way of the Lord"	15
Trivialism	"turn aside the just for a thing of naught"	16
Meanness	"revile against that which is good"	16
Dismissivism	"say that it is of no worth"	16
Tantrumism	"rage in the hearts of the children"	20
Emotionalism	"anger against that which is good"	20
Mollifying Pacifism	"others will he pacify"	21
Materialism	"into carnal security"	21
Toadyism	"others he flattereth"	22
Relativism	"there is no hell"	22
Complacency	"wo be unto him that is at ease in Zion"	24
Secularism	"we need no more of the word of God"	29
Faithless Humanism	"putteth his trust in man"	30

Chart 79

Messages

of the Book of Mormon

Chart 80

Interpretation of Lehi's Vision

Key Scripture 1 Nephi 11–15

Explanation Nephi, after hearing about his father's vision of the tree of life, desired to see the same things his father saw and was granted this request. Upon seeing the tree in vision, he desired to know its interpretation. Nephi then saw the coming of the Son of God and knew that the tree of life represented the love of God. He soon learned the meaning of several other symbols in his father's vision, as this chart illustrates. The angelic ministrant also showed Nephi episodes of world history, including periods of war, colonization, apostasy, and wickedness. Thus in light of 1 Nephi 11–15, the vision of the tree of life can be seen not only as a powerful illustration of God's love shown through the atonement of Jesus Christ, but also as an allegory of the history of the world, as the right-hand column of the chart illustrates.

Source Daniel H. Ludlow, *A Companion to Your Study of the Book of Mormon* (Salt Lake City: Deseret Book, 1976), 101.

Interpretation of Lehi's Vision

Symbol	Interpretation	Examples Given
DARK AND DREARY WASTE 1 Nephi 8:7		
LARGE AND SPACIOUS FIELD 1 Nephi 8:9, 20	The world 1 Nephi 8:20	
TREE OF LIFE 1 Nephi 8:10; 11:25; 15:21–22	Love of God 1 Nephi 11:21–22	The coming of the Son of God 1 Nephi 11:13–22
FRUIT OF THE TREE 1 Nephi 8:11–12		
FOUNTAIN/RIVER OF FILTHY WATER 1 Nephi 8:13; 12:16	Hell and the depths thereof 1 Nephi 12:16; 15:26–36	Wickedness and war 1 Nephi 12:13–15
ROD OF IRON 1 Nephi 8:19	The word of God 1 Nephi 11:25; 15:23–25	The ministry of the Son of God 1 Nephi 11:24–25
MIST OF DARKNESS 1 Nephi 8:23	Temptations of the devil 1 Nephi 12:17	Apostasy, wickedness, war, the great and abominable church, plain and precious things removed from the scriptures 1 Nephi 12:19–23; 13:1–9, 20–29
GREAT AND SPACIOUS BUILDING 1 Nephi 8:26	Pride, wisdom, and vain imaginations of the world 1 Nephi 11:35–36; 12:18	Persecution of the Son of God and those who followed him 1 Nephi 11:26–36

Chart 80

Chart 81

The Allegory of the Olive Tree

Key Scripture   Jacob 5

Explanation   The longest allegory in scripture in Zenos's allegory of the olive tree. In Jacob 5:3, Zenos explains that the tame olive tree represents the house of Israel. From this interpretation, conclusions may be drawn concerning other symbols in the allegory. For example, the young branches taken from the olive tree most likely represent inhabitants of the Americas, the Jews, the lost ten tribes, and a remnant of the house of Israel; and the wild olive tree symbolizes the Gentiles and the nations of the earth. The large numbers on the top half of this chart (1–6) represent the six main stages that Zenos addresses in his allegory: (1) the decaying of the top, (2) the grafting in of the wild tree, (3) the planting of young branches in other parts of the vineyard, (4) the returning of the branches to the main tree, (5) the bitter fruit burned by fire, and (6) the good fruit being gathered and stored. On the bottom half of the chart, these same stages are shown graphically, arranged clockwise around the central figure of the tame tree.

The Allegory of the Olive Tree
Jacob 5

Stage 1 Main top of tame olive tree begins to perish (v. 6) and is burned by fire (v. 9)

Stage 2 Wild olive tree branches are grafted in (v. 10) and bear good fruit (v. 17)

Stage 3 Young branches are grafted in other parts of the vineyard (vv. 8, 13)

Stage 4 Young branches are grafted back into the tame olive tree (v. 52)

Stage 5 Branches that bring forth bitter fruit are cleared (v. 65)

Stage 6 Fruit is good and vineyard is no more corrupt (v. 75)

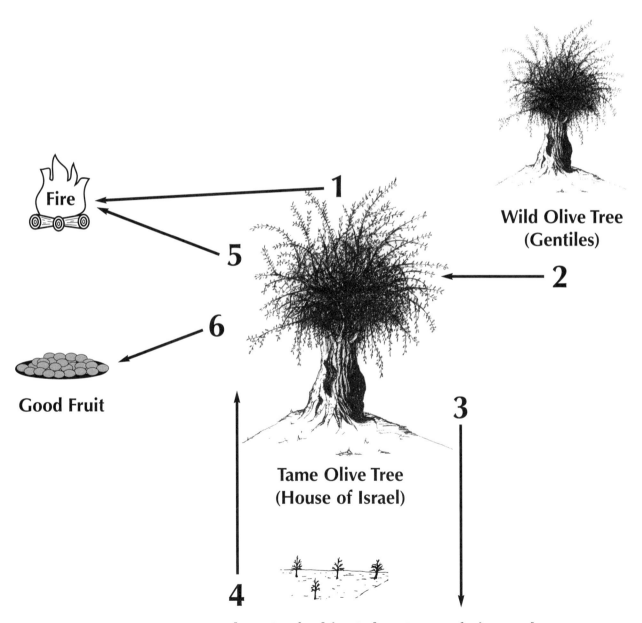

Fire

1

5

**Wild Olive Tree
(Gentiles)**

2

6

Good Fruit

**Tame Olive Tree
(House of Israel)**

3

4

Young Branches Grafted in Other Parts of Vineyard

(New World, Jews, Lost Ten Tribes, Remnant)

Chart 81

Chart 82

Symbolic Elements in Zenos's Allegory

Key Scripture Jacob 5

Explanation Zenos's allegory of the tame and wild olive trees, though complicated, is one of great doctrinal and historical importance, in part
because it represents the past and future history of the house of
Israel. Understanding the elements in this allegory, which are
grouped together and listed on this chart, can lead to added insights
concerning God's dealings with his covenant people. As this data
shows, the allegory is a dynamic interchange between several trees
(or parts of trees) and the master of the vineyard, his servant, and
several laborers. This chart does not interpret these symbols as they
appear in Jacob 5, but it shows that many elements are built into this
extended allegory and thus facilitates in-depth reflection on this text.

Symbolic Elements in Zenos's Allegory

1. The Trees

a tame olive tree
young and tender branches
mother tree
main top
natural branches
root of the main tree
moisture of the root
transplanted branches
a wild olive tree
grafted branches
many other trees
good, tame, natural fruit
bad, wild, bitter fruit
equal fruit

Trees' Doings

growing
waxing old
decaying and perishing
cumbering the ground
overrunning the roots
bringing forth much fruit
becoming corrupt
withering away
growing faster than roots
taking strength
good overcoming evil
thriving exceedingly

2. The Actors

master of the vineyard
servant
a few other servants

Actors' Doings

nourishing
digging about
dunging
pruning/plucking off branches
burning, casting into fire
grafting
planting branches
cutting down trees
grieving
laboring long, caring
sparing
balancing the root and top
preserving
laying up fruit
obeying
rejoicing

3. The Places

a vineyard
nethermost part
poorest spot
poorer than the poorest spot
good spot

Chart 82

Chart 83

Personal Applications of Olive Symbolism

Key Scripture   Jacob 5

Explanation   The tame olive tree in Jacob 5 may represent not only the house of Israel but also each of us personally. Listed in this chart are symbolic elements of the olive tree allegory and possible personal applications of them. While the gathering of the house of Israel is of utmost concern, personal conversion to the gospel of Jesus Christ as a member of the house of Israel may be even more important. Thus Zenos's allegory should be read and applied in terms of individual as well as collective salvation.

Personal Applications of Olive Symbolism

Symbol	Possible Applications
Planted in God's vineyard	Membership in God's church
Olive trees grow slowly	Spiritual growth is slow
Without care olives become wild	We must remain faithful
Each tree needs particular care	Lord knows us individually
Even trees in good soil go wild	Use blessings properly
Branches should balance the roots	Grow patiently and deeply
Olive trees like dry, rocky soil	Adversity can be a blessing
Strong roots will support the stock	Keep spiritual roots strong
Branches should not become lofty	Avoid pride
Pruning is necessary	Repent regularly
Each branch needs light to grow	Keep Light of Christ in all
Prunings must not cumber the ground	Completely remove evil
Grafting will preserve the stock	Draw strength from others
Dunging is necessary	Study, ponder, and pray
Olive oil is very valuable	The worth of souls is great
Pressure is needed to extract oil	Attaining purity takes work
"What could I have done more?"	God does all he can for us
"It grieveth me to lose this tree"	God loves his children
"Spare it a little longer"	The Lord is patient with us

Chart 83

Chart 84

Five Keys to Understanding Isaiah

Key Scripture   2 Nephi 25

Explanation   To his faithful followers in the Americas, the Lord gave a commandment to "search these things diligently; for great are the words of Isaiah" (3 Nephi 23:1). That commandment implies that understanding the gospel of Jesus Christ and the words of Isaiah go hand in hand. Unfortunately, many find the writings of Isaiah hard to understand. Nephi may have been aware of this difficulty, for he addresses his latter-day audience specifically in 2 Nephi 25, giving us five keys to help facilitate comprehension of Isaiah's words. These keys include being filled with the spirit of prophecy, living righteously in the last days, and understanding the geography and rhetorical tradition of the Jews.

Source   Donald W. Parry, "Nephi's Keys to Understanding Isaiah (2 Nephi 25:1–8)," in *Isaiah in the Book of Mormon,* ed. Donald W. Parry and John W. Welch (Provo, Utah: FARMS, 1998), 47–65.

Five Keys to Understanding Isaiah
Given in 2 Nephi 25

1   Understand the "manner of prophesying among the Jews"   25:1

2   Do not do "works of darkness" or "doings of abominations"   25:2

3   Be filled with the spirit of prophecy   25:4

4   Be familiar with regions around Jerusalem   25:6

5   Live during the days that the prophecies of Isaiah are fulfilled   25:7

Chart 84

Chart 85

King Benjamin's Coronation of Mosiah

Key Scriptures   Mosiah 1–5; 1 Kings 1:34, 39; 2 Kings 11:12, 14, 17; 23:3; 2 Chronicles 6:13

Explanation   The coronation of Mosiah by King Benjamin was a grand ceremonial event that parallels the installation of kings in ancient Israel and other Near Eastern countries of antiquity, suggesting that the Nephites continued to practice Old World traditions in the Americas. Coronations were important ritual acts in the ancient Near East, including, among other things, anointing the new king, installing him in office with insignia, and presenting him to the people—elements that Benjamin's ceremony also contained. Old Testament parallels to Mosiah's coronation can be found in 1 Kings 1:34, 39; 2 Kings 11:12, 14, 17; 23:3; and 2 Chronicles 6:13.

Source   Stephen D. Ricks, "Kingship, Coronation, and Covenant in Mosiah 1–6," in *King Benjamin's Speech: "That Ye May Learn Wisdom,"* ed. John W. Welch and Stephen D. Ricks (Provo, Utah: FARMS, 1998), 233–75.

King Benjamin's Coronation of Mosiah

Israelite Pattern	Book of Mormon Parallel or Adaptation
The Sanctuary Was the Site of the Coronation	All the people gathered at the temple at Zarahemla, the site chosen for Benjamin's address to the people and for the consecration of his son Mosiah as king (Mosiah 1:18)
	Mosiah was then presented to the people in the public gathering at the temple (Mosiah 2:30)
The King Stood on a Royal Dais, Platform	Benjamin constructed a tower from which he spoke to the people gathered (situated in tents) at the temple (Mosiah 2:7)
Installing in Office with Insignia	Benjamin gave Mosiah the official records of the people (the plates of brass and the plates of Nephi), the sword of Laban, and the miraculous Liahona (Mosiah 1:15–16)
	King Mosiah was known to possess "two stones" (Mosiah 28:13)
Anointing	Benjamin consecrated his son Mosiah to be a ruler and a king over his people (Mosiah 6:3)
Presentation of the New King	Mosiah is presented to the people as their king (Mosiah 2:30)
	The people respond by accepting the king's declarations (Mosiah 4:2; 5:2–4)
Receiving a Throne Name	A royal name was given to the rulers over the Nephites (Jacob 1:10–11)
	Benjamin revealed to all his people a new name at this coronation (Mosiah 3:8)
Divine Adoption of the King	By covenant, all the people became God's sons and daughters on his right hand (Mosiah 5:6–12)

Chart 85

Chart 86

Three Steps in Benjamin's Logic on Service

Key Scripture   Mosiah 2–5

Explanation   King Benjamin, in his great discourse to the people in the land of Zarahemla, answers the question "Why should we serve?" In his speech recorded in Mosiah 2–5, he provides a logical yet somewhat surprising explanation for service. Benjamin is well-known for his famous dictum on service in Mosiah 2:17. Actually, he mentions service two other times as he develops this topic more fully. This chart considers these three statements. They deal with service to God, our debt to God, and knowing God. On one level, a certain logic is embedded within each of these individual statements. On another level, the relationship between them is also logical and interdependent. If we serve men, then we only (merely) serve God. This does not win us great credit, for when we serve God, he blesses us and we are continually in his debt. Thus we have no reason to boast. Why, then, should we serve? If we are humble in our service, we will know God. Knowing the Master whom we serve is the great blessing that profits us more than anything else. This, to Benjamin, is the ultimate reason for service.

Source   John W. Welch, "Benjamin's Speech: A Masterful Oration," in *King Benjamin's Speech: "That Ye May Learn Wisdom,"* ed. John W. Welch and Stephen D. Ricks (Provo, Utah: FARMS, 1998), 77–82.

Three Steps in Benjamin's Logic on Service

1 **All service is merely service to God.**

Therefore, serving fellow beings produces no reason to boast, unless serving God produces some reason to boast.

"When ye are in the service of your fellow beings ye are only in the service of your God" (Mosiah 2:17)

2 **But no matter how much we serve God, we remain unprofitable servants.**

Therefore, we have no reason to boast.

"If ye should serve him with all your whole souls yet would ye be unprofitable servants" (Mosiah 2:21)

3 **We do not serve God to get ahead with God or man, but to know the voice by which we are called.**

Therefore, service to God is valuable, but not in ways people always think.

"For how knoweth a man the master whom he has not served?" (Mosiah 5:13)

Chart 86

Chart 87

Overview of Benjamin's Speech

Key Scripture Mosiah 2–5

Explanation This chart is an outline of the chiastic nature of King Benjamin's speech to the people at the temple of Zarahemla. In it are seven major sections separated by interruptions or intervening ceremonial acts. The overall structure of the text follows an A–B–C–D–C'–B'–A' pattern: the atonement of Jesus Christ is the crux, or center, of the speech (section D), the angel's and Benjamin's testimonies of the atonement are found on either side of it (sections C and C'), the behavior of the people is addressed in sections B and B', and sections A and A' address God and his relationship with the people. Further chiasms can be found on the sentence level, indicating that this speech was highly structured for the occasion. The evidence of chiasmus in the Book of Mormon attests to its artistry and antiquity. For a more detailed explanation of chiasmus, refer to chart 124.

Source John W. Welch, "Parallelism and Chiasmus in Benjamin's Speech," in *King Benjamin's Speech: "That Ye May Learn Wisdom,"* ed. John W. Welch and Stephen D. Ricks (Provo, Utah: FARMS, 1998), 325–28.

Overview of Benjamin's Speech

Supporting Elements in Mosiah 1–6

Preparations (1:1–2:8)
Successor named and new name to be given; people gathered but not yet numbered; tower constructed

First Interruption (2:29–30)
Coronation proclamation

Second Interruption (2:41–3:1)
Remember, remember, the Lord has spoken; Benjamin calls again for attention

Third Interruption (3:27–4:4)
Thus has the Lord commanded, amen; the people fall to the ground and confess; atoning blood is applied; joy and remission; Benjamin begins to speak again

Fourth Interruption (4:30–5:6)
Remember, and perish not; covenant response of the people; Benjamin accepts their covenant

Final Acts (6:1–3)
Names recorded of all who accepted the name; Mosiah consecrated; priests appointed; people dismissed

Words of Speech in Mosiah 2–5

A. All are indebted to God (2:9–28)
God is the heavenly king; God has physically created and sustains all people; people should serve and thank God; the hope of exaltation after death

B. Consequences of obedience or disobedience (2:31–41)
Obedience brings victory and prosperity (compare Leviticus 26); prohibition of contention; rebellion and disobedience bring pain and anguish; all are eternally indebted to Heavenly Father

C. The angel's testimony of Christ's deeds (3:2–10)
The Lord Omnipotent will come down in power and goodness; the sacred name of God; the suffering and death of Jesus Christ

D. Sanctification by the atonement of Christ (3:11–27)
The only possibility of reconciliation; putting off the natural man and becoming a saint; people will be judged according to their works

C'. Benjamin's testimony of God's goodness (4:4–12)
God is good, patient, long-suffering; believe in God; God is all-powerful, loving, and glorious; call upon the name of the Lord daily

B'. Righteous behavior of the redeemed (4:13–30)
Living in peace and social order (compare Leviticus 25); prohibition of contention; because God imparts, all must give to those in need; avoid guilt and sin

A'. The sons and daughters of God (5:6–15)
God has spiritually begotten you this day; the only head to make you free from debt; excommunication upon breach of obligations; covenant people know God by serving him; the hope of exaltation after death

Chart 87

Chart 88

Benjamin's Themes
Related to the Israelite New Year

Key Scripture Mosiah 2–5

Explanation Ancient Israelites celebrated several holy days, many elements of which have become the modern Jewish celebrations of Rosh ha-Shanah (New Year), Yom Kippur (Day of Atonement), and Sukkot (Feast of Tabernacles). These three particular celebrations took place during the early autumn season, specifically during the seventh month of the year. Because the Nephites and Mulekites originally came from Jerusalem, it is likely that they continued some of these festival traditions in the Americas. As this chart shows, King Benjamin's speech in Mosiah 2–5 contains themes especially pertinent to the Israelite New Year, suggesting that this speech was delivered near that time of the year. Benjamin's proclamation of his son Mosiah as king at this time is especially fitting, considering that part of the ancient Israelite New Year celebration included proclaiming or sustaining the king or high priest as an authority figure. Each element on this chart is found both in Israelite tradition and in Benjamin's speech. The similarities between Benjamin's speech and ancient Israelite celebrations are circumstantial evidence attesting to the historical backgrounds and divine origins of the Book of Mormon.

Source Terrence L. Szink and John W. Welch, "King Benjamin's Speech in the Context of Ancient Israelite Festivals," in *King Benjamin's Speech: "That Ye May Learn Wisdom,"* ed. John W. Welch and Stephen D. Ricks (Provo, Utah: FARMS, 1998), 160–74, 200.

Benjamin's Themes
Related to the Israelite New Year

admonitions
the attributes of God
being sealed to God
covenant making
creation
divine judgment
forsaking sin
God's involvement in history
guilt before God
judgment
kingship of God
law
the long-suffering of God
the Lord Omnipotent
man's nature and nothingness
preaching and prophecy
rebirth and resurrection
remembrance
reverence and fear of God
sacrifice
testimony against the people
warnings against sin
wisdom

Chart 88

Chart 89

Benjamin's Themes
Related to the Day of Atonement

Key Scripture   Mosiah 2–5

Explanation   The Day of Atonement is one of the most sacred holidays in Jewish culture. In preexilic Israel it included ritual atonement in the temple and a series of holy assemblies. Because Benjamin's speech in Mosiah 2–5 and its surrounding context emphasizes several topics particularly significant to this day of religious celebration, it is possible that Benjamin gave the speech on or near the Day of Atonement. In fact, he refers to the atonement overtly seven times—a number that represented spiritual perfection and that was used in connection with rituals performed on the Day of Atonement and during other times of purification mentioned in the book of Leviticus. This holy day was also a time of forgiveness for the people of Israel who confessed their sins and repented; similarly, the people of Benjamin were spiritually reborn after they confessed and repented of their sins. Each element in this chart, listed alphabetically, is found both in Israelite texts and in Benjamin's speech.

Source   Terrence L. Szink and John W. Welch, "King Benjamin's Speech in the Context of Ancient Israelite Festivals," in *King Benjamin's Speech: "That Ye May Learn Wisdom,"* ed. John W. Welch and Stephen D. Ricks (Provo, Utah: FARMS, 1998), 174–83, 201.

Benjamin's Themes
Related to the Day of Atonement

atonement

balancing order and diligence

being made free from sin

belief in the Messiah

belief in God

blessings

blood

blotting out names of transgressors

the commandments of God

confession and repentance

conversion

eternal rewards and punishments

faith

the fall of Adam

the fallen state of humanity

foundation of the world

giving to the poor

the goodness of God

humility

ignorant sin

indebtedness to God

inscribing names of the righteous

joy and blessings

knowing the divine name

left hand

the means of salvation

the name of God

preparations

pride

purification

rebellion against God

repentance

right hand

sacrifice and purifications

scapegoat, driving ass out

service to God and fellowman

submission

suffering and works of the Messiah

unintentional sin

Chart 89

Chart 90

Benjamin's Themes
Related to the Feast of Tabernacles

Key Scripture   Mosiah 2–5

Explanation   Sukkot, or the Feast of Tabernacles, as it is currently celebrated represents the events associated with the exodus from Egypt, although it was probably originally an agricultural celebration. Although it is not possible to know exactly which parts of this celebration were observed in Jerusalem during Lehi's lifetime, there are several significant parallels between the fully developed celebration of Sukkot and King Benjamin's speech and the events associated with it. These elements, shared by both Israelite and Nephite observances, include a pilgrimage to the temple, sitting in tents, reading the law, coronating a king, and renewing the covenant.

Source   Terrence L. Szink and John W. Welch, "King Benjamin's Speech in the Context of Ancient Israelite Festivals," in *King Benjamin's Speech: "That Ye May Learn Wisdom,"* ed. John W. Welch and Stephen D. Ricks (Provo, Utah: FARMS, 1998), 183–90, 201.

Benjamin's Themes
Related to the Feast of Tabernacles

becoming sons and daughters of God
booths/tents
coronation
covenant
deliverance
earthly king
the effect of knowing God
family
giving thanks and praise
heavenly king
joy in the commandments
keeping the commandments
kingship
knowing God by serving God
law and order
one's accountability after being warned
praise
pilgrimage
remembrance
rejoicing and thanksgiving
sacrifice
temple assembly
thanksgiving and praise

Chart 90

Chart 91

Benjamin's Themes
Related to Sabbatical and Jubilee Years

Key Scripture   Mosiah 2–5

Explanation   In addition to scheduling his speech during the season of the fall festival complex, King Benjamin may have also timed it to be given at the end of a sabbatical year, which came once every seven years. During this year, the land was not to be tilled, the yield was given to the poor, and debtors and slaves (or servants) were released from their obligations. Similarly, at the end of his speech Benjamin commands his people to "till the land," which would make sense if the people had not been working in the fields during the sabbatical year and were preparing to resume agricultural activity. Benjamin also tells the people to settle their debts with their neighbors. These parallels are quite striking.

But this is not all. Textual evidence indicates that this may also have been a jubilee year, which occurred every seventh sabbatical year and offered a new economic beginning for the poor in the land and spiritual renewal for all. Parts of the jubilee text, found in Leviticus 25, and parts of Mosiah 2 and 4 essentially mirror each other. Topics such as settling debts, succoring the poor, depending on God, and prospering in the land, listed on this chart, are all present in both texts. Benjamin's speech was one of monumental importance to the Nephites who still lived under the law of Moses. No wonder Mormon chose to include this speech in its entirety.

Source   Terrence L. Szink and John W. Welch, "King Benjamin's Speech in the Context of Ancient Israelite Festivals," in *King Benjamin's Speech: "That Ye May Learn Wisdom,"* ed. John W. Welch and Stephen D. Ricks (Provo, Utah: FARMS, 1998), 190–99, 202.

Benjamin's Themes
Related to Sabbatical and Jubilee Years

blessings

debt recognition

forgiveness

freedom

land

love

peaceful living

prosperity

purification and renewal

reading of the law

rendering to each his due

returning things borrowed

riches and generosity

service and servants

slaves released

Chart 91

Comparative Studies

of the Book of Mormon

Chart 92

A Comparison of Lehi's Dream and Nephi's Vision

Key Scripture   1 Nephi 8; 11–14

Explanation   Though Nephi and Lehi both experienced the vision of the tree of life, they explained it and possibly perceived it somewhat differently. They saw the same vision, for Nephi "saw the things which [his] father saw, and the angel of the Lord did make them known unto [him]" (1 Nephi 14:29). But Lehi's vision is recorded as being completely allegorical, while Nephi's vision of the tree of life expanded further into a view of the future of the world and Nephi's posterity, including specific historical occurrences like the birth of Jesus Christ and the latter-day restoration of the gospel to Lehi's seed. On this chart the elements in these visions are compared and contrasted. Viewing these two texts together may yield new insights concerning both of these visions of the tree of life.

A Comparison of Lehi's Dream and Nephi's Vision

Reference	Lehi's Dream: 1 Nephi 8	Nephi's Vision: 1 Nephi 11–14	Reference
8:4	Dark and dreary wilderness	High mountain	11:1
8:5	Man dressed in white robe	Spirit speaks	11:2, 11
8:6	Man leads the way	Spirit's introductory questions	11:2
8:7–8	Man leaves (implied)	Spirit departs	11:12
8:7–8	Dark and dreary waste	Jerusalem	11:13
8:8	Prayer for mercy		
8:9	Large and spacious field		11:7, 13–18, 20–25
8:10	Tree	Tree	
8:10	Fruit desirable to make happy	Love of God most desirable	11:22
8:11	Fruit sweet and white above all	Virgin most beautiful and fair	11:15
8:12	Soul filled with joy	Carried away in the spirit	11:19
8:12	Desire to share with family		
8:14	Head of river near the tree	Fountain of living waters	11:25
8:15	Call with loud voice	Christ, John, apostles preach	11:24–31
8:15–16	Come partake of fruit		
8:17–18	Laman, Lemuel do not partake	People reject Christ	11:32–33
8:19	Rod of iron	Rod of iron	11:25
8:20	Straight and narrow path	The apostles preach	11:34
8:20	Large and spacious field	Large and spacious building	11:35
8:21	Numberless concourses coming	Multitudes like sand	12:1
8:23	Mist of darkness	Mists of darkness	12:17
8:23	Lose their way and are lost	Broad roads and are lost	12:17
8:24	Others come to tree and partake	Four generations	12:10–12
8:26	River is a divider	Great gulf divideth them	12:18
8:26	Great and spacious building	Large and spacious building	12:18
8:27	Fine dress, mocking	Pride and vain imaginations	12:18
8:28	They fell away	The good are overpowered	12:19
8:29	[Break in Nephi's recitation]	War between seed	12:20–23
8:30	Other multitudes partake	Gentile nations	13:3
8:31	Great and spacious building	Great and abominable church	13:4–9
		Restoration of Lehi's seed through a great and marvelous work	13:10–14:7
8:32	Many drowned in the depths	Whore upon the waters	14:11
8:32	Many are lost in strange roads	Wars and chaos	14:16

Chart 92

Chart 93

Three Biblical Archetypes Compared to Nephi's Construction of the Ship

Key Scriptures   1 Nephi 17–18; Genesis 1–2; 6–9; Exodus 24; 31; 39–40; Joshua 18

Explanation   Unlike modern writers, who value originality and consider writing to be intellectual property, writers of antiquity valued repetition. For example, ancient Hebrew writers consistently repeated and alluded to previous narratives, and the Nephites did the same. This chart highlights one specific instance of this. As is shown here, Nephi's account of the construction of his ship closely parallels three other narratives about beginnings: the creation, the flood, and the construction of the biblical tabernacle. This suggests that Nephi purposefully included allusions to these biblical texts when recounting his own story of creation, a practice consistent with ancient Hebraic writing.

Source   Alan Goff, "Boats, Beginnings, and Repetitions," *Journal of Book of Mormon Studies* 1/1 (1992): 67–84.

Three Biblical Archetypes
Compared to Nephi's Construction of the Ship

	Creation	Deluge	Tabernacle	Nephi's Ship
Work Declared Good	"God saw everything that he had made, and, behold, it was very good" (Gen. 1:31).	God establishes a covenant (Gen. 9:11–17).	"Moses did look upon all the work, and, behold, they had done it as the Lord had commanded, even so had they done it" (Ex. 39:43).	"After I had finished the ship, according to the word of the Lord, my brethren beheld that it was good" (1 Ne. 18:4).
Completion Formula	"Thus the heavens and the earth were finished, and all the host of them" (Gen. 2:1).	"Thus did Noah; according to all that God commanded him, so did he" (Gen. 6:22; cf. 7:5).	"The children of Israel did according to all that the Lord commanded Moses, so did they" (Ex. 39:32; cf. 39:43; 40:33).	"I had finished the ship, according to the word of the Lord" (1 Ne. 18:4).
Blessing Pronounced	"God blessed the seventh day, and sanctified it" (Gen. 2:3).	"God blessed Noah and his sons" (Gen. 9:1).	"Moses blessed them" (Ex. 39:43).	"We were blessed in abundance" (1 Ne. 18:24).
Multiply and Fill the Earth	"God said unto them, Be fruitful, and multiply, and replenish the earth" (Gen 1:2).	"Bring forth with thee every living thing . . . that they may breed abundantly in the earth, and be fruitful, and multiply upon the earth" (Gen. 8:17; cf. 9:1).	"The whole congregation of Israel assembled together at Shiloh, and set up the tabernacle of the congregation there. And the land was subdued before them" (Josh. 18:1).	"We did begin to till the earth, and we began to plant seeds" (1 Ne. 18:24).
Curious Workmanship	The variety of species is emphasized (Gen. 1:11–12, 20–22, 24–25).	Divine pattern for building the ark specified (Gen. 6:14–16).	"I have filled [Bezaleel] with the spirit of God, in wisdom, . . . and in all manner of workmanship, to devise cunning works . . . in gold, and in silver, and in brass" (Ex. 31:3–4).	"We did work the timbers of curious workmanship. And the Lord did show me from time to time after what manner I should work the timbers of the ship" (1 Ne. 18:1; cf. 18:2).
Mountain Theophany			"The Lord said unto Moses, Come up to me into the mount, and be there. . . . And Moses rose up, and . . . went up into the mount of God" (Ex. 24:12–13).	"The voice of the Lord came unto me, saying: Arise, and get thee into the mountain. And it came to pass that I arose and went up into the mountain, and cried unto the Lord" (1 Ne. 17:7; cf. 17:8).

Chart 93

Chart 94

1 Nephi and the Exodus

Key Scripture 1 Nephi 4:2

Explanation Lehi's group saw themselves as reenacting the exodus of the Israelites from Egypt. Just as God had called Moses and Joshua to lead the children of Israel out of oppressive conditions, across a sea and the river Jordan, and into the promised land, so he called Lehi to lead his group out of Jerusalem, across the ocean, and to a new land of promise. Nephi thought of Moses when he exhorted his brothers to be "strong like unto Moses," who had delivered his people out of captivity (1 Nephi 4:2). As a typology, that first exodus, mainly in the Old Testament book of Exodus, became a pattern whose motifs may be found throughout Nephi's story of this second exodus. By extension, many of these themes can also be found in accounts of other Book of Mormon groups who were likewise delivered from captivity and fled into the wilderness. It is a pattern that still holds today in the personal conversion of individuals who flee evil and seek the Lord.

Sources Terrence L. Szink, "Nephi and the Exodus," in *Rediscovering the Book of Mormon,* ed. John L. Sorenson and Melvin J. Thorne (Salt Lake City: Deseret Book and FARMS, 1991), 38–51; S. Kent Brown, "The Exodus: Seeing It as a Test, a Testimony, and a Type," *Ensign,* February 1990, 54–57; S. Kent Brown, "The Exodus Pattern in the Book of Mormon," *BYU Studies* 30/3 (1990): 111–26; "Nephi and the Exodus," *Ensign,* April 1987, 64–65; and Mark J. Johnson, "The Exodus of Lehi Revisited," in *Pressing Forward with the Book of Mormon,* ed. John W. Welch and Melvin J. Thorne (Provo, Utah: FARMS, 1999), 54–58.

1 Nephi and the Exodus

1 Nephi	Exodus	Motifs Common to Both Accounts
1:6	3:2	fire present at calling of Lehi and Moses
1:6; 16:16	13:21	Lord's guidance
1:20	1:11–16	oppressive conditions
2:2	3:7–18	Lord's command to depart
2:6–7	3:18; 15:22; 20:25	sacrifice to the Lord after three days' journey
2:11–12; 5:2; 16:20	15:24; 16:2–3	murmuring against the Lord
2:15; 3:9; 10:16	18:7; 33:8	dwelling in tents
2:20	3:17	promise of a new land of inheritance
4:12	17:8–13	victory over enemies
7:6–7	14:12	rebellious desire to return
9:1–4	17:14	a record of the journey
11:1–14:27	19:19–31:18	instruction from God on a high mountain
15:6–16:5	19:3–25	prophet who teaches with divine instruction
16:10	7:9–21; 8:16; 14:16	miraculous objects (liahona, rod)
16:34	Josh. 24:32	a burial
17:3–5	16:11–18	Lord's provision of ready-to-eat food
17:4	16:35; Deut. 8:2	prolonged wandering in the wilderness
17:6	16:3; 17:1	afflictions in the wilderness
17:26; 18:8–23	14:21–22, 29; 15:19	crossing a sea
17:52	34:30	a transfiguration
17:55	14:31; 20:12	acknowledgment of the Lord's power
18:7	18:3–4	two sons born in the wilderness
18:8	14:21	Lord's providential wind
18:9	32:18–19	wicked revelry
18:20	32:10	death warnings from the Lord
18:23–25	Josh. 11:23	inheritance of a promised land
19:11	20:18	thunderings and lightnings at God's presence

Chart 94

Chart 95

Three Trees in the Book of Mormon

Key Scriptures Jacob 5; 1 Nephi 8; Alma 5; 32

Explanation The tree is the primary symbol in three significant sections in the Book of Mormon, showing the development of Nephite theology: Zenos's allegory in Jacob 5, Lehi's dream in 1 Nephi 8, and Alma's discourses on righteousness in Alma 5 and 32. This chart compares the three symbolic trees and the differences in their messages concerning the house of Israel.

In Zenos's allegory, the tame olive tree symbolizes the house of Israel as a whole. Groups or individuals are branches or leaves on this tree. Collectively speaking, the Lord does all he can to save his vineyard and will redeem the house of Israel after grafting, or gathering, the branches of Israel together in the last days.

When Lehi was physically separated from the house of Israel, and knowing that salvation was not to be found in Jerusalem in his day, the focus of his view of salvation shifted. Instead of focusing on collective salvation, he invited individual men and women to come to a new tree and partake of the fruit of the tree of life, or Christ's atonement, which leads to individual salvation.

In Alma's pluralistic society, salvation was portrayed even more as a matter of individual choice. Alma's allegorical tree symbolizes the personal righteousness that grows inside each individual through planting the seed of Christ's atonement and God's love in one's heart.

Three Trees in the Book of Mormon

Zenos's Olive Tree

The House of Israel
Collective Salvation

Lehi's Tree of Life

The Love of God
Blessedness

Alma's Tree of Righteousness

Personal Righteousness
and Testimony

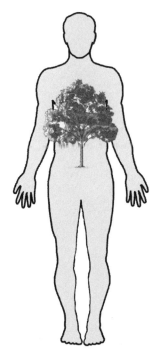

Chart 95

Chart 96

Isaiah Passages
Listed by Book of Mormon Reference

Key Scripture   3 Nephi 23:1

Explanation   Prophets in the Book of Mormon, including the Lord himself, repeatedly declared the importance of reading Isaiah's prophecies. They emphasized this point by quoting extensively from Isaiah in their own sermons and writings. This chart lists Book of Mormon passages that quote or paraphrase the words of Isaiah, which held great meaning for the Nephites and also apply to us today. The main Nephite prophets who quoted Isaiah were Nephi, Jacob, and Abinadi. Next to the Book of Mormon references in this chart are corresponding references in the book of Isaiah.

Source   Royal Skousen, "Textual Variants in the Isaiah Quotations in the Book of Mormon," in *Isaiah in the Book of Mormon,* ed. Donald W. Parry and John W. Welch (Provo, Utah: FARMS, 1998), 369–71.

Isaiah Passages
in the Book of Mormon
Listed by Book of Mormon Reference

Direct Quotations

1 Nephi 20:1–21:26	Isaiah 48:1–49:26
2 Nephi 6:6–7	Isaiah 49:22–23
2 Nephi 6:16–8:25	Isaiah 49:24–52:2
2 Nephi 9:50	Isaiah 55:1
2 Nephi 12:1–24:32	Isaiah 2:1–14:32
2 Nephi 26:18	Isaiah 29:5
2 Nephi 27:2–5	Isaiah 29:6–10
2 Nephi 27:25–35	Isaiah 29:13–24
2 Nephi 30:9	Isaiah 11:4
2 Nephi 30:11–15	Isaiah 11:5–9
Mosiah 12:21–24	Isaiah 52:7–10
Mosiah 14:1–12	Isaiah 53:1–12
Mosiah 15:6	Isaiah 53:7
Mosiah 15:29–31	Isaiah 52:8–10
3 Nephi 16:18–20	Isaiah 52:8–10
3 Nephi 20:32	Isaiah 52:8
3 Nephi 20:34–35	Isaiah 52:9–10
3 Nephi 20:36–38	Isaiah 52:1–3
3 Nephi 20:39–40	Isaiah 52:6–7
3 Nephi 20:41–45	Isaiah 52:11–15
3 Nephi 21:8	Isaiah 52:15
3 Nephi 22:1–17	Isaiah 54:1–17

Paraphrases

1 Nephi 10:7	Isaiah 40:3
1 Nephi 13:37	Isaiah 52:7
1 Nephi 14:7	Isaiah 29:14
1 Nephi 17:36	Isaiah 45:18
1 Nephi 22:6	Isaiah 49:22–23
1 Nephi 22:8	Isaiah 29:14
1 Nephi 22:8	Isaiah 49:22–23
1 Nephi 22:10	Isaiah 52:10
1 Nephi 22:11	Isaiah 52:10
2 Nephi 6:15	Isaiah 29:6
2 Nephi 9:51	Isaiah 55:2
2 Nephi 25:17	Isaiah 11:11
2 Nephi 25:17	Isaiah 29:14
2 Nephi 26:15–16	Isaiah 29:3–4
2 Nephi 26:17	Isaiah 29:11
2 Nephi 26:25	Isaiah 55:1
2 Nephi 27:6–9	Isaiah 29:4
2 Nephi 27:15–19	Isaiah 29:11–12
2 Nephi 28:9	Isaiah 29:13
2 Nephi 28:9	Isaiah 29:15
2 Nephi 28:14	Isaiah 29:13
2 Nephi 28:16	Isaiah 29:21
2 Nephi 28:30	Isaiah 28:10
2 Nephi 28:30	Isaiah 28:13
2 Nephi 29:1	Isaiah 11:11
2 Nephi 29:1	Isaiah 29:14
2 Nephi 29:2	Isaiah 5:26
2 Nephi 29:2	Isaiah 49:22
2 Nephi 29:3	Isaiah 5:26
Mosiah 15:10	Isaiah 53:10
Mosiah 15:14	Isaiah 52:7
Mosiah 15:15–18	Isaiah 52:7
Helaman 12:16	Isaiah 51:10
Helaman 12:16	Isaiah 44:27
3 Nephi 21:29	Isaiah 52:12
Moroni 10:31	Isaiah 52:1–2
Moroni 10:31	Isaiah 54:2

Chart 96

Chart 97

Isaiah Passages
Listed by Isaiah Reference

Key Scriptures   3 Nephi 23:1; Mormon 8:23

Explanation   This chart organizes important Isaiah references in the Book of Mormon according to their order of appearance in the book of Isaiah. In 3 Nephi 23:1, Jesus Christ emphasizes the importance of studying Iaiah's writings: "A commandment I give unto you that ye search these things diligently; for great are the words of Isaiah." The direct quotations listed in this chart come from three parts of Isaiah, namely, chapters 2–14, 29, and 48–55:1.

Source   Royal Skousen, "Textual Variants in the Isaiah Quotations in the Book of Mormon," in *Isaiah in the Book of Mormon,* ed. Donald W. Parry and John W. Welch (Provo, Utah: FARMS, 1998), 369–71.

Isaiah Passages
in the Book of Mormon
Listed by Isaiah Reference

Direct Quotations

Isaiah 2:1–14:32	2 Nephi 12:1–24:32
Isaiah 11:4	2 Nephi 30:9
Isaiah 11:5–9	2 Nephi 30:11–15
Isaiah 29:5	2 Nephi 26:18
Isaiah 29:6–10	2 Nephi 27:2–5
Isaiah 29:13–24	2 Nephi 27:25–35
Isaiah 48:1–49:26	1 Nephi 20:1–21:26
Isaiah 49:22–23	2 Nephi 6:6–7
Isaiah 49:24–52:2	2 Nephi 6:16–8:25
Isaiah 52:1–3	3 Nephi 20:36–38
Isaiah 52:6–7	3 Nephi 20:39–40
Isaiah 52:7–10	Mosiah 12:21–24
Isaiah 52:8	3 Nephi 20:32
Isaiah 52:8–10	Mosiah 15:29–31
Isaiah 52:8–10	3 Nephi 16:18–20
Isaiah 52:9–10	3 Nephi 20:34–35
Isaiah 52:11–15	3 Nephi 20:41–45
Isaiah 52:15	3 Nephi 21:8
Isaiah 53:1–12	Mosiah 14:1–12
Isaiah 53:7	Mosiah 15:6
Isaiah 54:1–17	3 Nephi 22:1–17
Isaiah 55:1	2 Nephi 9:50

Paraphrases

Isaiah 5:26	2 Nephi 29:2
Isaiah 5:26	2 Nephi 29:3
Isaiah 11:11	2 Nephi 25:17
Isaiah 11:11	2 Nephi 29:1
Isaiah 28:10	2 Nephi 28:30
Isaiah 28:13	2 Nephi 28:30
Isaiah 29:3–4	2 Nephi 26:15–16
Isaiah 29:4	2 Nephi 27:6–9
Isaiah 29:6	2 Nephi 6:15
Isaiah 29:11	2 Nephi 26:17
Isaiah 29:11–12	2 Nephi 27:15–19
Isaiah 29:13	2 Nephi 28:9
Isaiah 29:13	2 Nephi 28:14
Isaiah 29:14	1 Nephi 14:7
Isaiah 29:14	1 Nephi 22:8
Isaiah 29:14	2 Nephi 25:17
Isaiah 29:14	2 Nephi 29:1
Isaiah 29:15	2 Nephi 28:9
Isaiah 29:21	2 Nephi 28:16
Isaiah 40:3	1 Nephi 10:7
Isaiah 44:27	Helaman 12:16
Isaiah 45:18	1 Nephi 17:36
Isaiah 49:22	2 Nephi 29:2
Isaiah 49:22–23	1 Nephi 22:6
Isaiah 49:22–23	1 Nephi 22:8
Isaiah 51:10	Helaman 12:16
Isaiah 52:1–2	Moroni 10:31
Isaiah 52:7	1 Nephi 13:37
Isaiah 52:7	Mosiah 15:14
Isaiah 52:7	Mosiah 15:15–18
Isaiah 52:10	1 Nephi 22:10
Isaiah 52:10	1 Nephi 22:11
Isaiah 52:12	3 Nephi 21:29
Isaiah 53:10	Mosiah 15:10
Isaiah 54:2	Moroni 10:31
Isaiah 55:1	2 Nephi 26:25
Isaiah 55:2	2 Nephi 9:51

Chart 97

Chart 98

Outlines of Passages Quoting Isaiah

Key Scripture   2 Nephi 12–24

Explanation   When Nephite prophets quoted Isaiah, they used a quoting formula of sorts, usually consisting of an introduction, a quotation, an explanation of the quotation, and a conclusion. This chart outlines the structures of four major scriptural passages in which Book of Mormon prophets quote Isaiah at length. Though each passage varies slightly from the four-part quoting formula, the pattern is definite, helping readers to follow the thoughts of Isaiah and to make good use of the explanations provided by Nephi, Jacob, and Abinadi.

Source   John Gee, "'Choose the Things That Please Me': On the Selection of the Isaiah Sections in the Book of Mormon," in *Isaiah in the Book of Mormon,* ed. Donald W. Parry and John W. Welch (Provo, Utah: FARMS, 1998), 75–83.

Outlines of Passages Quoting Isaiah

NEPHI ADDRESSES HIS BRETHREN

Introduction
1 Nephi 19:22–24

Quotation of Isaiah 48:1–49:26
1 Nephi 20:1–21:26

Explanation
1 Nephi 22:1–31

THE WORDS **JACOB** SPOKE TO THE PEOPLE OF NEPHI

Introduction
2 Nephi 6:1–5

Quotation of Isaiah 49:22–23
2 Nephi 6:6–7

Explanation
2 Nephi 6:8–15

Quotation of Isaiah 49:24–52:2
2 Nephi 6:16–8:25

Discourse Conclusion
2 Nephi 9:1–54

NEPHI WRITES MORE OF THE WORDS OF **ISAIAH**

Introduction
2 Nephi 11:1–8

Quotation of Isaiah 2:1–14:32
2 Nephi 12:1–24:32

Explanation
2 Nephi 25:1–27:2

Quotation of Isaiah 29:7–11
2 Nephi 27:3–6

Explanation
2 Nephi 27:7–16

Quotation of Isaiah 29:11–12
2 Nephi 27:17–19

Explanation
2 Nephi 27:20–24

Quotation of Isaiah 29:13–24
2 Nephi 27:25–35

Discourse Conclusion
2 Nephi 28:1–30:10

Quotation of Isaiah 11:5–9
2 Nephi 30:11–15

The End
2 Nephi 30:16–18

ABINADI'S DISCOURSE

Question on Isaiah 52:7–10
Mosiah 12:20–24

Question & Answer
Mosiah 12:25–32

Quotation of Exodus 20:2–4
Mosiah 12:34–36

Explanation of Exodus 20:2–17
Mosiah 13:25–35

Quotation of Isaiah 53:1–12
Mosiah 14:1–12

Explanation of Isaiah 53:1–12
Mosiah 15:1–28

Quotation of Isaiah 52:8–10
Mosiah 15:29–31

Conclusion
Mosiah 16:1–15

Chart 98

Chart 99

Four Stages of the Nephite Prophetic View

Key Scripture   1 Nephi 11–14

Explanation   Understanding Isaiah's writings in the Book of Mormon is difficult for many students of the scriptures. But becoming familiar with the way the Nephite prophets viewed the future can help reveal the profound insights of Isaiah. Nephi's writings in 1 Nephi 11–14 establish four basic elements that represent to some extent Nephite prophecy in general. These four elements, or stages of history, concern the coming of Jesus Christ, his rejection and the scattering of the Jews, the day of the Gentiles, and the restoration of Israel and ultimate victory of good over evil. When Nephi or Jacob quotes a section from Isaiah, it is because Isaiah is speaking about one of these stages. For example, as this chart shows, Nephi quotes Isaiah 48 and 49 in articulating stages 2 and 3 in 1 Nephi 20–21. Viewing the quoted Isaiah passages in this context helps readers of the Book of Mormon to understand better the meaning and importance of Isaiah's writings.

Source   John W. Welch, "Getting through Isaiah with the Help of the Nephite Prophetic View," in *Isaiah in the Book of Mormon*, ed. Donald W. Parry and John W. Welch (Provo, Utah: FARMS, 1998), 19–26.

Four Stages of the Nephite Prophetic View
in 1 Nephi 11–14 and 1 Nephi 19–22

1 Christ's coming   1 Nephi 11   1 Nephi 19

2 His rejection by the   1 Nephi 12   1 Nephi 20
Jews and their scattering   (Isaiah 48)

3 The day of the Gentiles   1 Nephi 13   1 Nephi 21
                                                        (Isaiah 49)

4 The restoration of   1 Nephi 14   1 Nephi 22
Israel and the ultimate
victory of good over
evil

Chart 99

Chart 100

Treaty-Covenant Pattern in the Old Testament and Benjamin's Speech

Key Scripture   Mosiah 1–6

Explanation   King Benjamin's speech in Mosiah 2–5 had the desired effect: the people of Nephi were willing to make covenants with the Lord to keep his commandments (see Mosiah 5:5–6). In his discourse, Benjamin used the same pattern of covenant making that Moses and Joshua employed for the children of Israel, most likely during the Feast of Tabernacles. This chart highlights some of the similarities between Benjamin's pattern and Old Testament covenant-making conventions. It is also interesting to note that Hittite treaties composed in the fourteenth and thirteenth centuries B.C. also exhibit the same six characteristics listed on this chart: the preamble, antecedent history, terms of the covenant, formal witness, blessings and curses, and recital of the covenant and deposit of the text. (In the chart the designations *a* and *b* in the scriptural references refer to the first half of a verse and to the second half, respectively.)

Source   Stephen D. Ricks, "Kingship, Coronation, and Covenant in Mosiah 1–6," in *King Benjamin's Speech: "That Ye May Learn Wisdom,"* ed. John W. Welch and Stephen D. Ricks (Provo, Utah: FARMS, 1998), 256–60.

Treaty-Covenant Pattern
in the Old Testament and Benjamin's Speech

Elements	Exodus 19:3b–8	Exodus 20–24	Deuteronomy	Joshua 24	Mosiah 1–6
Preamble	19:3b	20:1	1:1–5	24:1–2a	1:1–2:9a
Antecedent History	19:4	20:2	1:6–3:29	24:2b–13, 16b–18a	2:9b–21, 23–30
Terms of the Covenant	19:5–6	20:3–23:19	4–26	24:14, 18b, 23	2:22, 24b, 31–41; 4:6–30
Formal Witness	19:8	24:3	31:19	24:16a, 19a, 21–23	5:2–8
Blessings and Curses	19:5	23:20–33	27:9–28:68	24:19b–20	3:24–27; 5:9–15
Recital of the Covenant/ Deposit of the Text	19:7	24:4–8	27:1–8; 31:9, 24–26	24:25–27	2:8, 9a; 6:1–3, 6

Chart 100

Chart 101

Benjamin's and Mosiah's Covenant Ceremonies Compared with Old Testament Rituals

Key Scriptures Mosiah 1–6; Exodus 19:3–8; 20–24; Joshua 24; Deuteronomy 1–31

Explanation In Mosiah 1–6 and 25, Benjamin and Mosiah each direct a ceremony of spiritual renewal among the Nephite population. These ceremonies are similar to many other formal covenant-making ceremonies found in the Old Testament, beginning with the ceremony at Sinai (see Exodus 24) and including the ceremonies at Shechem (see Joshua 24) and Mizpeh (see 1 Samuel 10). In each of these, the king or religious leader of the people directs the ceremony, for ancient Hebrew kings were seen as mediators between God and the people. Other similar elements include gathering an assembly of the people by royal decree to make covenants, publicly reading the law or basis of the covenant, establishing or expounding upon a legal document, writing the speech down, and participating in cultic acts (ranging from building an altar to being baptized) to physically demonstrate acceptance of the covenant made. These similarities are further evidence of the Book of Mormon's Old Testament roots and strongly suggest that the Nephites conscientiously followed established laws and customs brought with them from Jerusalem.

Sources Todd R. Kerr, "Ancient Aspects of Nephite Kingship in the Book of Mormon," *Journal of Book of Mormon Studies* 1/1 (1992): 110–111. See Stephen D. Ricks, "Treaty/Covenant Patterns in King Benjamin's Address," *BYU Studies* 24 (spring 1984): 151–62.

Benjamin's and Mosiah's Covenant Ceremonies
Compared with Old Testament Rituals

Elements	Exodus 24	Joshua 24	1 Samuel 10	Mosiah 1–6	Mosiah 25
Leader	Moses	Joshua	Samuel	Benjamin	Mosiah
Assembly	read in the audience of the people (v. 7)	gathered all the tribes of Israel to Shechem (v. 1)	called people together unto the Lord at Mizpeh (v. 17)	the people gathered themselves throughout all the land (2:1)	caused that all the people should be gathered together (v. 1)
Legal Document	book of the covenant (v. 7)	set them a statute and an ordinance (v. 25)	manner of the kingdom (v. 25)	my, my father's, my son's, and God's commandments (2:31)	
Public Reading	read in the hearing of the people	said unto the people (v. 22)	told the people the manner of the kingdom (v. 25)	opened his mouth and began to speak (4:4; cf. 2:9)	read and caused to be read (v. 5)
Writing	wrote all the words of the Lord (v. 4)	wrote the words in the book of the law of God (v. 26)	wrote it in a book (v. 25)	words which he spake should be written (2:8)	
Cultic Act	built an altar (v. 4)	took a stone and set it under an oak by the sanctuary of the Lord (v. 26)	laid it up before the Lord (v. 25)	sacrifices and ordinances according to law of Moses (2:3); names recorded (6:1)	baptism (v. 17)

Chart 101

Elements Found in Great Farewell Addresses

Key Scripture Mosiah 1–6

Explanation In ancient classical and biblical farewell addresses, certain themes appear consistently. William S. Kurz has identified twenty elements commonly found in the final farewell addresses of famous men shortly before their deaths. Moses' farewell speech contains sixteen of these elements, while the farewell speeches of the apostle Paul and Socrates include fourteen and eleven elements, respectively. Sixteen, and possibly nineteen, of these elements can be found in the carefully preserved text of Benjamin's farewell address, making it perhaps the best example of this speech genre on record. This chart lists Kurz's twenty elements and shows where the elements can be found in Benjamin's farewell speech.

Sources John W. Welch and Daryl R. Hague, "Benjamin's Speech: A Classic Ancient Farewell Address," in *Reexploring the Book of Mormon,* ed. John W. Welch (Salt Lake City: Deseret Book and FARMS, 1992), 120–22; see also John W. Welch and Daryl R. Hague, "Benjamin's Sermon as a Traditional Ancient Farewell Address," in *King Benjamin's Speech: "That Ye May Learn Wisdom,"* ed. John W. Welch and Stephen D. Ricks (Provo, Utah: FARMS, 1998), 105; and William S. Kurz, "Luke 22:14–38 and Greco-Roman and Biblical Farewell Addresses," *Journal of Biblical Literature* 104 (1985): 251–68.

Elements Found in Great Farewell Addresses

Biblical and Classical Speech Elements	Benjamin's Speech (Mosiah 1–5)
1. The speaker summons his successors	1:9–10; 2:1, 9
2. He cites his own mission as an example	2:12–14, 18
3. He states that he fulfilled his duty	2:15, 27–31
4. He refers to his impending death	1:9; 2:26, 28
5. He exhorts his audience	2:9, 40–41; 5:12
6. He issues warnings and final injunctions	2:31–39; 3:12, 25; 4:14–30; 5:10–11
7. He blesses his audience	Possibly "blessed" in 2:41
8. Farewell gestures	Possibly in 2:28
9. He names tasks for his successors	1:15, 16; 2:31; 6:3
10. He theologically reviews history	2:34–35; 3:13–15
11. The speaker reveals future events	3:1, 5–10
12. Promises are given	2:22, 31; 4:12; 5:9
13. He appoints/refers to successor	1:15–16; 2:31; 6:3
14. Rest bewail the loss of the leader	Not found
15. Future degeneration addressed	3:23–27; 4:14–15
16. Sacrifices and covenant renewal	2:3; 5:1–7
17. Care is given for those left	4:14–26; 6:3
18. Consolation to inner circle	5:15
19. Didactic speech	3:16–21
20. *Ars moriendi*	Possibly in 2:28

Chart 102

Chart 103

Alma's Quotation of Lehi

Key Scriptures   1 Nephi 1:8; Alma 36:22

Explanation   Book of Mormon prophets, in addition to quoting scripture from the brass plates, quoted other Nephite prophets who had gone before them. For example, Alma 36:22 quotes Lehi's words found in 1 Nephi 1:8. Because Alma was the keeper of the small plates, he would have had access to Lehi's words. Alma's verbatim quoting of these twenty-one words has interesting implications. These two passages are separated from each other by several hundred pages of text. Because Joseph Smith dictated the Book of Mormon without notes, he would, if he recognized the quotation at all, not likely have been able to remember the original version word for word except by divine inspiration.

Source   John W. Welch, "Textual Consistency," in *Reexploring the Book of Mormon*, ed. John W. Welch (Salt Lake City: Deseret Book and FARMS, 1992), 21–22.

Alma's Quotation of Lehi

1 Nephi 1:8

And being thus over-
come with the Spirit,
he was carried away in
a vision, even that he
saw the heavens open,
and he thought he
*saw God sitting upon
his throne, surrounded
with numberless
concourses of angels,
in the attitude of
singing and praising
their God.*

Alma 36:22

Yea, methought I saw,
even as our father Lehi
*saw, God sitting upon
his throne, surrounded
with numberless
concourses of angels,
in the attitude of
singing and praising
their God;*
yea, and my soul did
long to be there.

Chart 103

Chart 104

Helaman's Quotation of Benjamin

Key Scriptures Mosiah 3:18; Helaman 5:9

Explanation Like Alma, Helaman was familiar with the prophecies of his ancestors. As this chart demonstrates, Helaman quoted and paraphrased Benjamin, whose words he considered highly important, when he encouraged his sons to remember that salvation comes only through the atonement of Jesus Christ.

Source John W. Welch, "Textual Consistency," in *Reexploring the Book of Mormon,* ed. John W. Welch (Salt Lake City: Deseret Book and FARMS, 1992), 23.

Helaman's Quotation of Benjamin

Mosiah 3:18

But men drink damnation to their own souls except they humble themselves and become as little children, and believe that salvation was, and is, and is to come, in and *through the atoning blood of Christ,* the Lord Omnipotent.

Helaman 5:9

O remember, remember, my sons, the words which king Benjamin spake unto his people; yea, remember that there is no other way nor means whereby man can be saved, only *through the atoning blood of Jesus Christ,* who shall come; yea, remember that he cometh to redeem the world.

Chart 104

Chart 105

Samuel's Quotation of Benjamin

Key Scriptures   Mosiah 3:8; Helaman 14:12

Explanation   Though Samuel did not explicitly state that he was quoting Benjamin, his words in Helaman 14:12 are a precise repetition of Benjamin's key words in Mosiah 3:8. Samuel could have known of the teachings of Benjamin through the ministry of Helaman's sons Lehi and Nephi to the Lamanites. Because Helaman stressed that his sons should remember the words of Benjamin (see Helaman 5:9), it is likely that Lehi and Nephi used exact quotes of Benjamin in their proselytizing. In Mosiah 3:8, Benjamin revealed to his people, in connection with their covenant with God, the name and titles of their Lord God Omnipotent. This took place at Zarahemla. A century later, Samuel the Lamanite stood on the walls of that same city and called the people to repentance. His use of Benjamin's covenantal language probably struck them especially powerfully.

Source   John W. Welch, "Textual Consistency," in *Reexploring the Book of Mormon,* ed. John W. Welch (Salt Lake City: Deseret Book and FARMS, 1992), 22.

Samuel's Quotation of Benjamin

Mosiah 3:8

And he shall be called *Jesus Christ, the Son of God, the Father of heaven and earth, the Creator of all things from the beginning;* and his mother shall be called Mary.

Helaman 14:12

And also that ye might know of the coming of *Jesus Christ, the Son of God, the Father of heaven and of earth, the Creator of all things from the beginning;* and that ye might know of the signs of his coming, to the intent that ye might believe on his name.

Chart 105

Chart 106

Three Accounts of Alma's Conversion

Key Scriptures Mosiah 27; Alma 36; 38

Explanation Alma's conversion is documented in three places in the Book of Mormon. This chart compares the rhetorical situation of each of these accounts and shows how the context of the situation may have in part determined the way Alma expressed his conversion story each time he told it. For example, Alma's initial account of his conversion (see Mosiah 27:7–37) is spontaneous and detailed, perhaps because it had just occurred and was still very vivid in his mind. In this account, he uses direct, antithetical parallelism to emphasize that the atonement had miraculously changed him from one former state into a new person.

Alma's account to his son Helaman (see Alma 36) is the longest and most elaborate. This is perhaps because Alma gave this account in a blessing to his first son. To emphasize his pivotal acceptance of Jesus Christ as the Savior—the turning point in his life—Alma expresses his conversion story in the form of an extended chiasm.

Alma's narrative account in Alma 38, given to his second son, Shiblon, is much shorter. Alma focuses on the mercy of Christ in this account and counsels Shiblon not to "boast" in his wisdom or strength. Though each account differs from the others, all were appropriate for the contexts in which they were given.

Three Accounts of Alma's Conversion

	Mosiah 27:7–37	Alma 36:1–30	Alma 38:4–8
When	about 100 B.C. immediately after conversion	about 73 B.C. 27 years after conversion	about 73 B.C. 27 years after conversion
Told by	Alma and Mosiah	Alma	Alma
Audience	multitude of people	Helaman	Shiblon
Tone	spontaneous	deliberate	brief
Technique	antithetical parallelism	chiasmus	narrative
Feelings	snatched, redeemed	relief, exquisite joy	peace to my soul
Sphere	public	personal, spiritual	personal, moral
Length	long	medium long	short
Angel's Words	long quote (vv. 13–16)	short quote (v. 9)	no quote
Causal Forces	prayers of God's people	Alma's cry for mercy	God's mercy
Called on	not mentioned	Jesus, thou Son of God	the Lord Jesus Christ
Unique Parts	Alma's evil deeds detailed (vv. 8–10, 30) affirmation of God's power (v. 18) angel departed (v. 17) Alma carried before a multitude (vv. 19, 21) God's declaration of judgment on all (vv. 25–27) the redeemed become God's sons and daughters (v. 25) Alma persecuted as he preaches (v. 32)	Alma heard no more (v. 11); sons of Mosiah hear more	angel face to face (v. 7) God sent angel in mercy (v. 7)

Chart 106

Shared Words in the Three Accounts of Alma's Conversion

Key Scriptures   Mosiah 27; Alma 36; 38

Explanation   The three accounts of Alma's conversion recorded in the Book of Mormon contain many shared or similar phrases, leading us to believe that Alma had repeated his story often and in a distinctive manner. The use of shared words in these three accounts is circumstantial evidence of the authenticity of the Book of Mormon, since, in spite of the different settings of these accounts and the textual layers of compilation, abridgment, and translation, Alma's unique, underlying personal voice can still be heard and identified.

Shared Words in the Three Accounts of Alma's Conversion

Mosiah 27:7–37	Alma 36:1–30	Alma 38:4–8
destroy the church	destroy the church	work of destruction
angel of the Lord	his holy angel	his angel
voice of thunder	voice of thunder	voice of thunder
fell to the earth	fell to the earth	
arise and stand	arose and stood	
remember captivity	remember captivity and bondage	thou wast in bonds
	Lord delivered them	Lord delivered thee
	trust in God	trust in God
	trials, troubles, afflictions	trials, troubles, afflictions
	lifted up at last day	lifted up at last day
	know not of myself	know not of myself
born of the spirit	born of God	born of God
be cast off	be destroyed	
not open his mouth	not open my mouth	
not move hands	not move limbs	
fast two days, nights	out three days, nights	out three days, nights
	heart cried for mercy	
limbs received strength	limbs received strength	
everlasting burning	everlasting chains	
gall of bitterness	gall of bitterness	most bitter pain
marvelous light	marvelous light	
pained no more	pains no more	
many to the knowledge	many born of God	

Chart 107

Chart 108

Women in the Book of Mormon

Key Scriptures   1 Nephi 16:7; Jacob 2:31–35

Explanation   Although women do not receive prominent attention in all parts of the Book of Mormon, they are referred to more often than most readers realize. Six are mentioned by name (Eve, Sarah, Mary, Sariah, Isabel, Abish); others are known by title (such as Ishmael's daughters, King Lamoni's wife, or Morianton's maidservant). Many more women are recognized collectively, primarily in their roles as wives, mothers, and daughters, but also as sisters, maids, and widows. Women are also mentioned frequently as members of numerous groups, multitudes, cities, or general populations. Only two women (Isabel and the daughter of Jared) are seen explicitly in negative roles; most others (notably the twenty-four Lamanite daughters and the mothers of Helaman's stripling warriors) are seen as strong, righteous individuals. The totals on this chart do not include pronoun references or metaphorical allusions to women.

Sources   Allison Welch, student of John W. Welch, Book of Mormon 121H, Brigham Young University, fall 1997; and Donna Lee Bowen and Camille S. Williams, "Women in the Book of Mormon," in Daniel H. Ludlow, ed., *Encyclopedia of Mormonism*, 5 vols. (1992), 4:1577–80.

Women in the Book of Mormon

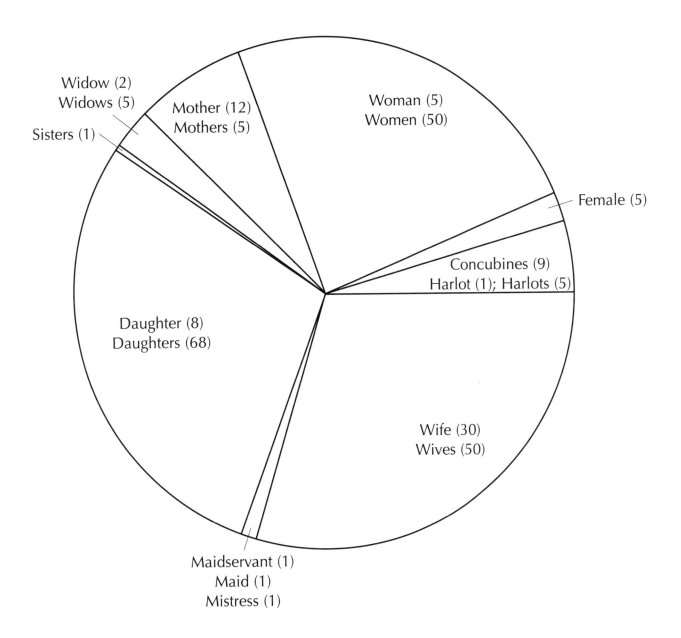

Widow (2)
Widows (5)

Sisters (1)

Mother (12)
Mothers (5)

Woman (5)
Women (50)

Female (5)

Concubines (9)
Harlot (1); Harlots (5)

Daughter (8)
Daughters (68)

Wife (30)
Wives (50)

Maidservant (1)
Maid (1)
Mistress (1)

Specific Women Mentioned in the Book of Mormon

Title	Number	Specific Women Mentioned
Known by name	6	Eve, Sarah, Mary, Sariah, Isabel, Abish
Known as wives or queens	12	Lehi's, Ishmael's, Nephi's, Lamoni's, Lamoni's father's, Amalickiah's, Coriantum's, Akish's, Zoram's, Laman's, Lemuel's, Sam's
Known as daughters	at least 44	Ishmael's (5 or more), Laman's (2 or more), Lemuel's (2 or more), Lehi's (2 or more), Lamoni's (2 or more), Jared's, Coriantumr's (2 or more), Cohor's (2 or more), Corihor's (2 or more), 24 Lamanite daughters

Chart 108

Chart 109

Missionary Work

Key Scripture   Alma 17–23

Explanation   The importance of missionary work is a prominent theme in the Book of Mormon. This chart lists and compares the work of many of the ancient American missionaries, the people they preached to, the degree of success they had, and the scriptural references pertaining to their missionary labors. Reactions to the gospel message varied, despite the quality of missionaries in the field.

Source   Maryanne Butler, student of John W. Welch, Book of Mormon 121H, Brigham Young University, fall 1997.

Missionary Work

Missionaries	People Taught	Reaction of the People	References
ABINADI	King Noah and priests	Alma$_1$ converted	Mosiah 11–17
ALMA$_1$	people of Noah	204 converted	Mosiah 18
AMMON$_1$	people of Limhi	converted/renewed	Mosiah 21
ALMA$_2$	people of Zarahemla people of Gideon people of Melek people of Ammonihah	3,500 converted repented many converted rejected message	Alma 4–6 Alma 7 Alma 8:3–6 Alma 8:6–13
ALMA$_2$ AND AMULEK	people of Ammonihah	Zeezrom and others converted; many rejected message and were destroyed	Alma 8:14–14:29;15:12; 16:2–3
	land of Sidom	many converted	Alma 15
	land of Zarahemla	many converted, strengthened	Alma 16
	Zoramites in Antionum	the poor and many others converted	Alma 31–34; 35:6–7; 14

Chart 109

SONS OF MOSIAH	land of Zarahemla	many converted	Mosiah 27:32–36, 37:9
	land of Ishmael	many converted (including King Lamoni)	Alma 17–20; 21:23; 23:9
	city of Jerusalem	rejected message	Alma 21
	land of Middoni	imprisoned missionaries; later many converted	Alma 21; 23
	King Lamoni's father and others (land of Nephi)	converted	Alma 22
	people of Shilom, Shemlon, Lemuel, Shimnilom	many converted	Alma 23:4–5, 12–13
Zoramites in Antionum	the poor and many others converted	Alma 31:6–7; 35:6–7, 14	
CORIANTON	Zoramites in Antionum	rejected message	Alma 31:7; 39
HELAMAN	Lamanites at war with Gadianton band	many converted	Helaman 3
NEPHI AND LEHI	apostates	many converted	Helaman 5
LAMANITES	wicked Zarahemla	many converted	Helaman 6
SAMUEL	wicked Zarahemla	some converted	Helman 13–15
JESUS CHRIST	great multitude	all converted	3 Nephi 11–28
MORMON	Nephites	few converted	Mormon 3

Chart 109

Money

in the Book of Mormon

Chart 110

King Mosiah's Monetary System

Key Scripture Alma 11:1–19

Explanation King Mosiah's system of weights and measures established equiva-
lencies between amounts of silver, gold, and grains. This chart
compares the precious metals with their grain equivalents, as
described in Alma 11. These measurements for the most part
increase exponentially, much like the ancient Egyptian system of
measurement (see chart 113). In King Mosiah's system, the limnah
or onti, worth "the value of . . . all" measurements (Alma 11:10),
was worth the sum of the gold senine, seon, and shum or the silver
senum, amnor, and ezrom.

Source Robert F. Smith, "Weights and Measures in the Time of Mosiah II"
(FARMS, 1983).

King Mosiah's Monetary System
Alma 11:1–19

Silver Measure	Gold Equivalent	Grain Equivalent	Math Ratio
leah		$1/8$ measure	1, or 2^0
shiblum		$1/4$ measure	2, or 2^1
shiblon		$1/2$ measure	4, or 2^2
senum	senine	1 measure	8, or 2^3
	antion	$1 1/2$ measures	12
amnor	seon	2 measures	16, or 2^4
ezrom	shum	4 measures	32, or 2^5
onti	limnah	7 measures	

Chart 110

Chart 111

The Utility of the Gold Antion

Key Scripture Alma 11:19

Explanation Under King Mosiah's monetary system, the gold antion was worth one and a half measures of silver or other commodities (see Alma 11:15, 19). It functioned as a useful commercial unit since it allowed more measures of grain or other items to be purchased with fewer units of precious metal, as this chart shows. Using as few monetary units as possible in the marketplace was most likely an advantage.

Source John W. Welch, "Weighing and Measuring in the Worlds of the Book of Mormon," *Journal of Book of Mormon Studies* 8/2 (1999).

The Utility of the Gold Antion

Computing Half Measures	With the Gold Antion Value = 1.5		Without the Gold Antion*	With the Silver Shiblon Value = .5	
1.5	1 weight		impossible	2 weights	1 + .5
2.5	2 weights	1 + 1.5	impossible	2 weights	2 + .5
3.5	2 weights	2 + 1.5	impossible	3 weights	2 + 1 + .5
4.5	3 weights	1 + 2 + 1.5	impossible	3 weights	2 + 2 + .5
5.5	2 weights	4 + 1.5	impossible	3 weights	4 + 1 + .5
6.5	3 weights	4 + 1 + 1.5	impossible	3 weights	4 + 2 + .5

*If payment was to be in gold only

Chart 111

Chart 112

The Utility of the Onti and Limnah

Key Scripture Alma 11: 1–19

Explanation While the Nephite system of weights and measures was not based on a decimal system, as are all modern currencies, it was more efficient, for example, than the system of coinage used today in the United States. As this chart shows, under Mosiah's system (see Alma 11:1–19) the onti and limnah were worth seven times a senum of silver or senine of gold. This enabled consumers in Nephite society to use fewer weights to weigh out or purchase more measures of grain than if they had been using the decimal system.

The Utility of the Onti and Limnah

Measures	Nephite Currency Number of Weights Required Using Senum/Senine, Amnor/Seon, Ezrom/Shum, Onti/Limnah		American Currency Number of Coins Required Using Pennies, Nickels, Dimes	
1	1		1	
2	1		2	1+1
3	2	2 +1	3	1+1+1
4	1		4	1+1+1+1
5	2	4 +1	1	
6	2	4 + 2	2	5+1
7	1		3	5+1+1
8	2	7 + 1	4	5+1+1+1
9	2	7 + 2	5	5+1+1+1+1
10	3	7 + 2 + 1	1	
11	2	7 + 4	2	10+1
12	3	7 + 4 + 1	3	10+1+1
13	3	7 + 4 + 2	4	10+1+1+1
14	2	7 + 7	5	10+1+1+1+1
15	3	7 + 7 + 1	2	10+5
16	3	7 + 7 + 2	3	10+5+1
17	4	7 + 7 + 2 + 1	4	10+5+1+1
18	3	7 + 7 + 4	5	10+5+1+1+1
19	4	7 + 7 + 4 + 1	6	10+5+1+1+1+1
20	4	7 + 7 + 4 + 2	2	10+10
Average	2.4		3.05	

Chart 112

Chart 113

Egyptian Hieroglyphs for Grain Measurement

Key Scripture Alma 11:1–19

Explanation Egyptian hieroglyphs offer a parallel to King Mosiah's monetary system. The grain measure in ancient Egypt was represented by the eye of Horus. Each part of the eye represented a fraction of the grain measure. There were six parts. The smallest measure was 1/64, represented by the tear duct; the next was 2/64, represented by the eyelash; and so on. The sum of all the parts equaled 63/64, which was considered the full measure. Mosiah's weights and measures were similarly exponential, with the largest equaling "the value of . . . all" (Alma 11:10) of the main lesser amounts. Although the Nephite system is not exactly the same as the Egyptian, the similarities corroborate the report that the Nephite kings studied "the language of the Egyptians" (Mosiah 1:4) and drew on their Old World backgrounds well after their arrival in the New World.

Sources Alan H. Gardiner, *Egyptian Grammar* (London: Oxford University Press, 1957), 197–99; and Richard J. Gillings, *Mathematics in the Time of the Pharoahs* (New York: Dover, 1986), 210.

Egyptian Hieroglyphs
for Grain Measurement

Measure	Hieroglyph	Fraction
Full Measure		$\dfrac{63^{*}}{64}$
Half Measure		$\dfrac{32}{64}$
Quarter Measure		$\dfrac{16}{64}$
Eighth Measure		$\dfrac{8}{64}$
Sixteenth Measure		$\dfrac{4}{64}$
Thirty-Second Measure		$\dfrac{2}{64}$
Sixty-Fourth Measure		$\dfrac{1}{64}$

*Compare Alma 11:10: "the value of them all"

Chart 113

Law

in the Book of Mormon

Charts 114–27

Chart 114

Legal Traditions
Related to Biblical Law

Key Scripture 2 Nephi 25:25

Explanation This chart can be seen as a genealogy of law. As part of the brass plates brought to the Americas by Lehi and his family, the Torah (the five books of Moses containing the Mosaic law) governed Lehi's seed until Jesus Christ fulfilled the law and established his higher law. The Jewish Mishnah and Talmud, as well as the Dead Sea Scrolls of the Essenes, were also based on the law of Moses. Originally, some critics faulted the Book of Mormon because it did not depict the Nephites as following the law of Moses in a way that perfectly cohered with the law of Moses as interpreted under rabbinical Judaism. The Dead Sea Scrolls, however, indicate that the Essenes also interpreted the law of Moses differently than the Pharisees did, showing that the law of Moses was interpreted in more than one way in antiquity and that the independent Nephite tradition could have adhered to the law of Moses while not following all of the laws in the same manner as did the Jews.

Legal Traditions Related to Biblical Law

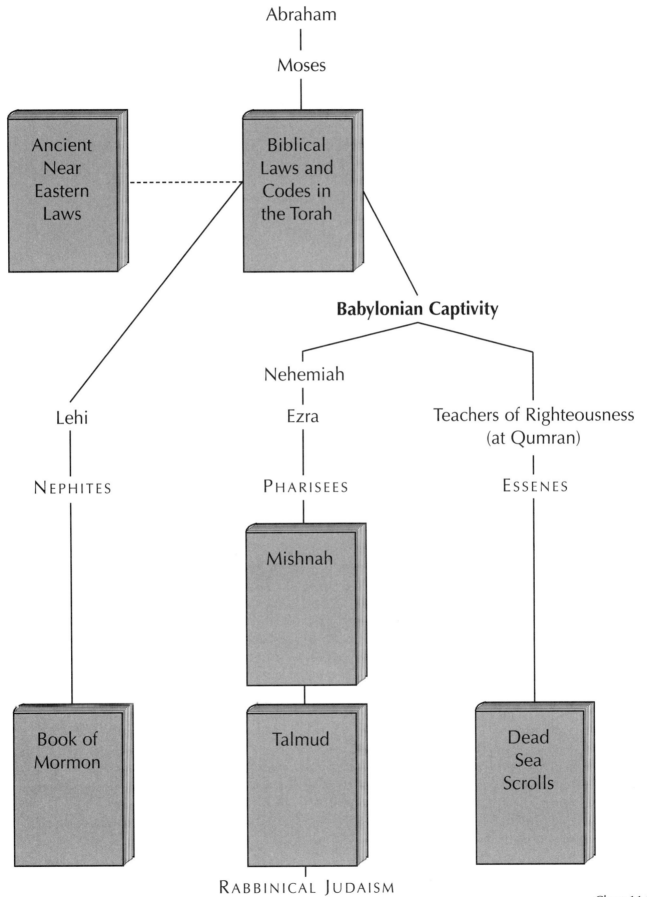

Abraham

Moses

Ancient Near Eastern Laws

Biblical Laws and Codes in the Torah

Babylonian Captivity

Lehi

Nehemiah

Teachers of Righteousness (at Qumran)

NEPHITES

Ezra

PHARISEES

ESSENES

Mishnah

Book of Mormon

Talmud

Dead Sea Scrolls

RABBINICAL JUDAISM

Chart 114

Chart 115

When Is It Better for One Man to Perish Than an Entire Nation?

Key Scriptures 1 Nephi 4; 2 Samuel 20; 2 Kings 24

Explanation The Spirit told Nephi that the Lord had delivered Laban into Nephi's hands and that it was better for Laban to die than for an entire nation to perish because of unbelief (see 1 Nephi 4:11–13). Though this case is extremely rare, ancient Israelite law authorized the slaying of a particular man at least two other times. This chart compares Nephi's situation with two similar incidents found in the Bible: the beheading of the rebel Sheba and the execution of King Jehoiakim. Five conditions were present in each of these instances: The (1) recognized leader of Israel pronounced judgment upon a (2) specifically named person (3) guilty of some form of rebellion or disobedience that (4) would result in the destruction of at least part of Israel (5) unless the innocent people turned the traitor over for execution. Under these special circumstances, the law sanctioned the death of one instead of requiring innocent people to perish or be destroyed.

Source John W. Welch and Heidi Harkness Parker, "Better That One Man Perish," FARMS Update, *Insights* (June 1998): 2.

When Is It Better for One Man to Perish Than an Entire Nation?

Five Conditions	Sheba 2 Samuel 20 ca. 100 B.C.	Jehoiakim 2 Kings 24 ca. 598 B.C.	Laban 1 Nephi 4 ca. 597 B.C.
1 Judgment issued by the recognized leader of Israel	David (king of Israel)	Nebuchadnezzar (king of Judah)	Jehovah (king of all)
2 Person already guilty of offense against the leader	rebellion	treason	disobedience
3 Person specifically identified for death	Sheba named	Jehoiakim named	Laban delivered
4 Those surrendering person are innocent	city of Abel innocent	the council innocent	Nephi innocent
5 People face inevitable destruction if they refuse to surrender person	city of Abel attacked by Joab	Jerusalem threatened	nation would perish
Result	Sheba beheaded	Jehoiakim taken to Babylon and presumably executed	Laban beheaded

Chart 115

Chart 116

Did Lehi Organize His Posterity into Seven Tribes?

Key Scriptures   Jacob 1:13; 4 Nephi 1:36–38; Mormon 1:8; Genesis 49

Explanation   Before his death, Lehi gave blessings and counsel to his posterity (see 2 Nephi 4:1–11). At this time, he may have organized them into seven tribes: Nephites, Jacobites, Josephites, Zoramites, Lamanites, Lemuelites, and Ishmaelites (see Jacob 1:13; 4 Nephi 1:38; Mormon 1:8). While Nephite and Lamanite governments came and went, the tribal structure of their society endured, suggesting that Lehi's children considered his organization of tribes binding and constitutional. The patriarch "father Lehi," as he is called by Enos, Benjamin, Alma, Helaman, Nephi, and Mormon, parallels Jacob/Israel in many respects, for both organized a people of God in a new land of promise by dividing their children into groups.

Sources   John L. Sorenson, John A. Tvedtnes, and John W. Welch, "Seven Tribes: An Aspect of Lehi's Legacy," in *Reexploring the Book of Mormon*, ed. John W. Welch (Salt Lake City: Deseret Book and FARMS, 1992), 93–95; see John W. Welch, "Lehi's Last Will and Testament: A Legal Approach," in *Second Nephi: The Doctrinal Structure*, ed. Monte S. Nyman and Charles D. Tate Jr. (Provo, Utah: BYU Religious Studies Center, 1989), 68–70.

Did Lehi Organize His Posterity into Seven Tribes?

1. Nephites*

2. Jacobites

3. Josephites

4. Zoramites

5. Lamanites

6. Lemuelites

7. Ishmaelites

*Sam's lineage was numbered by Lehi with Nephi's

Chart 116

Chart 117

Ancient Sealed, Doubled Documents

Key Scriptures 2 Nephi 27:7–15; Jeremiah 32:10–14

Explanation In formal Israelite legal documents, there were two parts, as documented by Jeremiah: one part that was sealed, and one part that was open (see Jeremiah 32:10–14). Seals were placed on the closed portion, and witnesses signed the end of the document, attesting to its authenticity. Finally, the sealed doubled documents were placed in containers and preserved. The pictures at the bottom of this chart show the process by which ancient manuscripts containing one closed part and one open part were folded and sealed.

The Book of Mormon, as 2 Nephi 27:7–15 indicates, followed this ancient process of sealing and authenticating a text. The plates of Nephi had two parts: one open and one closed. Seals kept the closed part secure, and as promised anciently, witnesses were provided who signed the Book of Mormon after it was translated. Interestingly enough, the testimonies of the Three and Eight Witnesses were originally placed at the back of the Book of Mormon, at the end of the document, just as ancient Hebrew law would have required. The plates were preserved in a stone container until the Lord directed Joseph Smith to translate them.

Source John W. Welch, "Doubled, Sealed, Witnessed Documents: From the Ancient World to the Book of Mormon," in *Mormons, Scripture, and the Ancient World: Studies in Honor of John L. Sorenson,* ed. Davis Bitton (Provo, Utah: FARMS, 1998), 393–94, 402.

Ancient Sealed, Doubled Documents

	Jeremiah 32:10–14	2 Nephi 27:7–15
	Jeremiah took the deed (scroll)	Nephi describes the plates (book)
part sealed	"that which was sealed according to the law and custom" (v. 11) part "which is sealed" (v. 14)	"the things which are sealed" (v. 8) "the words which are sealed" (v. 10)
part open	"and that which was open" (v. 11) part "which is open" (v. 14)	"he shall deliver the words" (v. 9) "these words which are not sealed" (v. 15)
seals	"and sealed it" (v. 10)	"the book shall be sealed" (v. 7)
witnesses	"and took the witnesses" (v. 10)	"three witnesses" (v. 12); "many witnesses" (v. 14)
preserved	"put them in an earthen vessel that they may continue many days" (v. 14)	"kept in the book until the own due time of the Lord" (v. 10)

Chart 117

Chart 118

Sealed or Sealed-Up Documents

Key Scriptures   2 Nephi 27; Ether 3–5

Explanation   Nephi, the brother of Jared, and Moroni all commented on sealed or sealed-up portions of the Book of Mormon, the brother of Jared's vision, and Moroni's abridgment of the brother of Jared's writings. *Sealed (hatom),* as used in Jeremiah 32, has various meanings. *Hatom* means literally that a seal has been placed on a document, but it also implies that the document may be "unavailable" or "complete." Similarly, in their discussions of the sealed portion of the Book of Mormon, Book of Mormon prophets generally used the term *sealed* to express that a document was literally closed with a seal and *sealed up* to indicate that a document was unavailable. Knowing these definitions can help readers follow the accounts in 2 Nephi 27 and Ether 3–5.

Source   John W. Welch, "Doubled, Sealed, Witnessed Documents: From the Ancient World to the Book of Mormon," in *Mormons, Scripture, and the Ancient World: Studies in Honor of John L. Sorenson,* ed. Davis Bitton (Provo, Utah: FARMS, 1998), 432–33.

Sealed or Sealed-Up Documents

	2 Nephi 27 Nephi's conception of the Nephite record	**Ether 3–4** Instructions to the brother of Jared concerning his record	**Ether 4–5** Moroni's comments on his abridgment of the writings of the brother of Jared
Will the document be in a sealed format?	Yes. The book itself will be "sealed"	No. The record will be "sealed up"	Not indicated
Will the document be in two distinct parts?	Yes, words that are "not sealed" and words that are "sealed"	No	Yes
Will the document be supported by witnesses?	Yes, three and a few others	Not indicated	Yes, three, joined by the Godhead
When will the document come forth?	"The own due time of the Lord"	Part when Jesus comes in the flesh, part in due time	When the Gentiles repent and become clean and have faith
What does the document contain?	"A revelation from God, from the beginning of the world to the ending"	Vision of the pre-mortal Christ and "all the inhabitants of the earth"	Things the brother of Jared saw
Is there a curse associated with rejecting the record?	Yes	Not indicated	Yes
Is the document to be sealed or sealed up again?	Yes, after the text has been read	Not expected	Yes, so it would not be destroyed
Was anything else sealed up with the record?	No	Two stones	The interpreters

Chart 118

Chart 119

How Do You Say "Law" in Hebrew?

Key Scriptures   2 Nephi 5:10; Mosiah 6:6; Alma 8:17; 30:3; 58:40; Helaman 3:20; 15:5; 1 Kings 2:3

Explanation   The Hebrew language uses at least six different words that are translated into English as the word *law*. *Torah* refers to the law, especially the law of Moses, while *mishpat* signifies judgment or standards based on the law. *Huqqah* and *hoq* are similar in meaning, suggesting not only formal ordinances but also general codes of behavior. *Mitzvah* denotes divine commandments in general, and *edut*, while a more ambiguous term, often signifies a written law. For example, King David counseled Solomon to keep God's "statutes *[huqqot]*, and his commandments *[mitzvot]*, and his judgments *[mishpatim]*, and his testimonies *[edot]*, as it is written in the law *[torah]* of Moses" (1 Kings 2:3). Similarly, Nephi states that his people observed "the judgments, and the statutes, and the commandments of the Lord in all things, according to the law of Moses" (2 Nephi 5:10). The striking similarities between these texts reveal that the Hebrew-speaking Nephites and the ancient Israelites conceived law in much the same way.

Source   John W. Welch, "Statutes, Judgments, Ordinances, and Commandments," in *Reexploring the Book of Mormon*, ed. John W. Welch (Salt Lake City: Deseret Book and FARMS, 1992), 62–65.

How Do You Say "Law" in Hebrew?

Hebrew	Usual translation	Meanings and contexts
torah	law, law of Moses	teachings, instructions
mishpat	judgment	pronouncement of a verdict, standards of behavior
huqqah	statute, ordinance	custom, manner, decree, portion, order, prescription, limit
hoq	statute, ordinance	the masculine form of *huqqah*, used in place of *huqqah* (note: *statute* and *ordinance* do not appear together in the Book of Mormon)
mitzvah	commandment	frequently signifies divine commandments, *bar mitzvah* = "son of the commandment"
edut	testimony, witness	often a monument, stele, or book of the law

Chart 119

Chart 120

Jacob's Ten Woes
and the Ten Commandments

Key Scripture   2 Nephi 9

Explanation   In 2 Nephi 9, Jacob pronounces a "wo" or curse upon the people of Nephi who do not keep the commandments. This chart shows that the specific sins he denounces are similar to several of the sins committed when the Ten Commandments are broken. The two lists are not identical, but it is evident that they are related at several levels. Both give ten warnings, woes, commands, or prohibitions. The fourth commandment (addressing the Sabbath day) and the eighth commandment (prohibiting stealing) are not on Jacob's list, possibly because they were not a problem for Jacob's isolated audience to keep. (Note that each item in the chart is numbered according to its order in the scriptural passage it appears in.)

Source   John W. Welch, "Jacob's Ten Commandments," in *Reexploring the Book of Mormon,* ed. John W. Welch (Salt Lake City: Deseret Book and FARMS, 1992), 69–72.

Jacob's Ten Woes and the Ten Commandments

2 Nephi 9:27, 30–38	Compare Exodus 20:3–17
1. Wo unto them who knowingly transgress God's commandments	1. Thou shalt have no other gods before me
2. Wo unto the rich who despise the poor and make their treasure their god	10. Thou shalt not covet
3. Wo unto the deaf who will not hear	5. Honor (hear) thy father and thy mother
4. Wo unto the blind who will not see	
5. Wo unto the uncircumcised of heart	3. Thou shalt not take the name of the Lord thy God in vain
6. Wo unto the liar	9. Thou shalt not bear false witness
7. Wo unto the murderer who deliberately kills	6. Thou shalt not kill
8. Wo unto them who commit whoredoms	7. Thou shalt not commit adultery
9. Wo unto those who worship idols	2. Thou shalt not make unto thee any graven image
10. Wo unto all those who die and remain in their sins	

Chart 120

Chart 121

Legal Cases and Procedures in the Book of Mormon

Key Scripture Mosiah 29:25–29

Explanation The main purpose of the Book of Mormon is, of course, religious; but its pages also report more than a dozen important lawsuits or legal procedures. This chart helps a person to appreciate the number and variety of legal procedures reported in the Book of Mormon. These accounts provide significant information about aspects of the Nephite legal system, such as accusations, arrests, imprisonments, executions, judges, witnesses, and rules of law. Most of these legal cases arose during the reign of the judges, when the role of the judicial system had been greatly expanded. That period in Nephite history saw great internal turmoil. Those problems teach how important it is for a free and open society to honor, obey, and sustain the law in order to survive, let alone thrive.

Legal Cases and Procedures
in the Book of Mormon

The Case of Sherem against Jacob	Jacob 7
The Arrest of Ammon	Mosiah 7:6–16
The Trial of Abinadi	Mosiah 12–17
The Trial of Nehor	Alma 1:1–15
The Trial of Alma and Amulek	Alma 14
The Imprisonment of Aaron and Brethren	Alma 21:12–14
The Trial of Korihor	Alma 30
The Political Imprisonment of King-Men	Alma 51:19
The Trial of Pachus's Men and the King-Men	Alma 62:9–10
The Case of Paanchi	Helaman 1:1–10
The Imprisonment of Nephi and Lehi	Helaman 5:21–22
Gadianton Trials of Their Defectors	Helaman 6:24
The Trial of Seantum	Helaman 9
The Execution of Zemnarihah	3 Nephi 4:28–33
The Trial of Captured Robbers	3 Nephi 5:4–5
Corrupt Execution of Inspired Prophets	3 Nephi 6:20–24
Complaint against the Corrupt Judges	3 Nephi 6:25–30

Chart 121

Chart 122

Three Diverse Opponents
of the Nephites

Key Scriptures   Jacob 7; Alma 1; 30

Explanation   The trials of three major opponents of Nephite leadership—Sherem, Nehor, and Korihor—are documented in the Book of Mormon (see Jacob 7; Alma 1; 30). The situations and outcomes of those trials are compared in this chart. Although each of these men had his own style and persuasive tactics and each case is historically unique and distinctive, they were similar in their attempt to lead people down various "broad roads"—away from Christ and to spiritual death.

Three Diverse Opponents of the Nephites

	Sherem	Nehor	Korihor
Date	ca. 500 B.C.	91 B.C.	ca. 74 B.C.
Location	Land/city of Nephi	Land/city of Zarahemla	Zarahemla/Jershon/Gideon/Antionum
Labeled anti-Christ	No	No	Yes
Theology	Theist, traditionalist	Theist, universalist	Atheist
Politics	Reactionary, royalist	Populist	Radical
View on priest	Should keep law	Should be paid	Oppress the poor
Religion	Pro law of Moses	Law irrelevant	Opposed law of Moses
Impact of preaching	Led away hearts	Many believed, gave money	Led away hearts; sin and whoredoms
Nature of legal action or offense	Blasphemy, false prophecy, falsely accused Jacob of leading people into apostasy	Killed Gideon; convicted of enforcing priest-craft with the sword	Reviled against priests and God, committed blasphemy
Arrested	No	Yes	Yes
Status	Plaintiff	Defendant	Defendant with counterclaims
Court	Divine justice	One judge	Several judges
Accepted scriptures	Yes	Unclear	No
Warned	Indirectly	No	Yes
Requested sign	Yes	No	Yes
Sign-giver hesitancy	Yes, tempting God	Not applicable	No, better one perish
Divine sign	Smitten to the earth but could still speak	None	Struck dumb but could still write and walk
Judicial verdict	No	Yes	No
Confession	Sincere, complete	Involuntary	Incomplete
Penalty	Divine justice	Capital punishment	Ostracism, trampled
Death	Nonhuman causes	Human, legal	Human, extralegal
Publicity	Public confession	Ignominious death	Result heralded
Precedent established	Legitimized Christiani-zation of the law of Moses	Gave original juris-diction to chief judge under the new reign of judges	Held that speech acts were still punishable under the law of Mosiah

Chart 122

Chart 123

Legal Charges Brought against Abinadi

Key Scriptures Mosiah 12–17; Alma 13:20; Exodus 20:16; 22:28; Leviticus 24:16; Deuteronomy 18:18–22

Explanation Though the charges proved unfounded, Abinadi was accused by Noah's priests of violating Mosaic law. This chart lists (1) the four charges brought against Abinadi, (2) the Mosaic laws on which each accusation rested, and (3) the false evidence that Noah's priests used to accuse him. The priests of Noah knew the law of Moses thoroughly enough to twist it and use it against Abinadi when he prophesied against Noah and of Jesus Christ. Although the first three charges all failed, they were at least nominally grounded in the law. Abinadi was finally put to death for having "reviled the king" (Mosiah 17:12), which is prohibited in Exodus 22:28. Ultimately, however, these tactics worked to the priests' own undoing. As Alma later counseled the city of Ammonihah: "Behold, the scriptures are laid before you; if ye will wrest [twist] them it shall be to your own destruction" (Alma 13:20).

Legal Charges Brought against Abinadi

Charge	Evidence	Mosaic Law in Question
1. Lying (Mosiah 12:14)	Abinadi said the people had hardened their hearts and had committed evil abominations (Mosiah 12:1)	"Thou shalt not bear false witness" (Exodus 20:16)
2. False prophecy (Mosiah 12:14)	"He pretendeth the Lord hath spoken it" (Mosiah 12:12)	"The prophet [who] shall presume to speak a word in my name, which I have not commanded . . . , shall die" (Deuteronomy 18:20)
3. Blasphemy (Mosiah 17:7–8)	Abinadi said God himself would come down (Mosiah 7:26–28; 15:1–8)	"He that blasphemeth the name of the Lord, he shall surely be put to death" (Leviticus 24:16)
4. Reviling against the king (Mosiah 17:12)	Abinadi said Noah's life would be as a garment in a hot furnace (Mosiah 12:3, 10–12)	"Thou shalt not revile the gods, nor curse the ruler of thy people" (Exodus 22:28)

Chart 123

Chart 124

Did Abinadi Prophesy against King Noah on Pentecost?

Key Scripture   Mosiah 11–17

Explanation   Abinadi may very well have prophesied to King Noah and his priests on or near the day of Pentecost, as textual clues in Mosiah 11–17 suggest. Pentecost in ancient Israel was a three-day festival in May celebrating the new wheat and bounty of spring. It was also a time for carefully listening to and celebrating the law of Moses, since God gave the law to Moses on Sinai at approximately this time in the year. Abinadi's cursing of grain and sending destruction upon crops are a reversal of the themes celebrated at Pentecost. Ironically, at the same time when the priests should have been venerating the Law, Abinadi rehearsed to them the Ten Commandments and chastised them for not keeping it. These and other clues listed in this chart are further evidence attesting to the Book of Mormon's roots in ancient Israel.

Source   John W. Welch, Gordon C. Thomasson, and Robert F. Smith, "Abinadi and Pentecost," in *Reexploring the Book of Mormon*, ed. John W. Welch (Salt Lake City: Deseret Book and FARMS, 1992), 135–38.

Did Abinadi Prophesy against King Noah on Pentecost?

Israelite Pentecost	Abinadi
celebrating first grain harvest	cursed grain (Mosiah 12:6)
rejoicing in bounty	sent hail, winds, insects (Mosiah 12:6)
fifty days after Passover	specific day unknown
remembering deliverance from bondage in Egypt	prophesied that the people would be brought into bondage (Mosiah 11:21)
celebrating the giving of the Ten Commandments to Moses (Exodus 20)	recited the Ten Commandments given to Moses (Mosiah 13:12–24)
Moses' face shone (Exodus 34)	Abinadi's face shone (Mosiah 13:5)
Sinai became a furnace (Exodus 19)	prophesied that Noah's life would be like a garment in a furnace (Mosiah 12:3)
three-day festival (Exodus 19:11)	cast into prison three days (Mosiah 17:6)
stern admonitions	stern admonitions
use of Psalm 50	use of ideas in Psalm 50
"Our God shall come" (Psalm 50:3)	"God . . . shall come down (Mosiah 15:1)
"What hast thou to do to declare my statutes?" (Psalm 50:16)	"What teach ye this people?" (Mosiah 12:27)
"[Thou] hast been partaker with adulterers" (Psalm 50:18)	"Why do ye commit whoredoms?" (Mosiah 12:29)

Chart 124

Chart 125

Benjamin and the Law of the King

Key Scripture   Mosiah 1–5

Explanation   Deuteronomy 17:15–20 presents the requirements to be king under the law of Moses. According to this "paragraph of the king," a righteous king must read and keep the law and fear the Lord, and he should not be lifted up above his brethren or seek for riches. King Benjamin addressed each of these themes in his great speech, explaining how he had been faithful to his people and the Lord in keeping these commandments. These parallels are especially strong in Mosiah 2:12–14, which suggests that Benjamin had read and followed the scriptures on the brass plates, of which Deuteronomy was a part. This shows that Benjamin's concept of kingship was completely at home in ancient Israel and in accordance with God's regulations.

Source   John W. Welch, "Benjamin, the Man: His Place in Nephite History," in *King Benjamin's Speech: "That Ye May Learn Wisdom,"* ed. John W. Welch and Stephen D. Ricks (Provo, Utah: FARMS, 1998), 34.

Benjamin and the Law of the King

	Deut.	Mosiah
The Lord shall choose him	17:15	1:10; 2:30
He shall be one of thy brethren	17:15	2:11
He shall not return the people to Egypt	17:16	3:14
He shall not multiply to himself silver and gold	17:17	2:12
He shall have a copy of the Law	17:18	1:3
He shall read the Law all his days	17:19	1:7
He shall fear the Lord	17:19	2:37–40
He shall keep all the Law	17:19	1:5; 5:5
His heart shall not be lifted up above his brethren	17:20	2:26
He shall turn not aside to the right hand or left	17:20	5:8–10
His days shall be prolonged in the kingdom	17:20	2:31

Chart 125

Chart 126

The Law of Apostate Cities

Key Scripture   Alma 9–16

Explanation   In Deuteronomy 13:12–18 the Lord commands the Israelites to destroy the truly apostate cities in the land. They were to decide whether a city was wicked according to certain conditions set forth in the Law. As this chart illustrates, these conditions are similar to the conditions of Ammonihah before the Lamanites destroyed it. After this city was annihilated, it remained uninhabited for many years but was eventually built up again. The law of Moses deemed that the ruins of a wicked city should never be built up; but this prohibition apparently could be revoked or could expire after a period of time, as evidenced in the Old Testament by the authorized rebuilding of several cities. Ammonihah similarly remained uninhabited for just over seven years, a ritual cleansing period, and was then built up again. This and other evidences support the assertions that Alma, as bearer of the brass plates, knew that Ammonihah was an apostate city according to the law of Moses, and that Alma reported the destruction of that city in such a way as to show that all the legal requirements and procedures regarding the destruction of an apostate city had been satisfied.

Source   John W. Welch, "The Destruction of Ammonihah and the Law of Apostate Cities," in *Reexploring the Book of Mormon,* ed. John W. Welch (Salt Lake City: Deseret Book and FARMS, 1992), 176–79.

The Law of Apostate Cities

Deuteronomy 13:12–18	Ammonihah (Alma 9–16)
certain men gone out from among you	Nehorites
withdrawn the inhabitants of their city	withdrew from Nephites
serve other gods	turned from God
children of Belial	Satan had great hold
inquire and search diligently	Alma visits personally
smite all inhabitants with the sword	everyone killed
destroy utterly	everything destroyed
a heap forever	bodies heaped up
abomination	desolation of Nehors

Chart 126

Chart 127

A Comparison of Nephite Law Lists

Key Scriptures   2 Nephi 26:32; Mosiah 2:13; Alma 1:32; 16:18; 23:3; 30:10; Helaman 3:14; 4:12; 6:23; 7:21; Ether 8:16; Exodus 20–23.

Explanation   The law of Moses, written on the brass plates, was rigorously followed by the Nephites, whose prophets often referred directly or indirectly to it in recitations of various lists of crimes. More than ten such law lists are shown on this chart. Each of these law lists is unique. But when they are all merged into a single composite list, it becomes clear that they collectively proscribe the list of crimes found in Exodus 20–23 and some additional ones, such as power mongering and confining people to dungeons. Such striking parallels and clusters show the relatedness of the five books of Moses to the most frequently condemned crimes in the Book of Mormon.

A Comparison of Nephite Law Lists

Crimes Prohibited	2 Ne. 26:32	Mosiah 2:13	Alma 1:32	Alma 16:18	Alma 23:3	Alma 30:10	Hel. 3:14	Hel. 4:12	Hel. 6:23	Hel. 7:21	Ether 8:16	Ex. 20–23
Abominations							X					X
Adultery		X		X	X	X		X				X
Babblings			X									X
Confinement in dungeons		X										
Contentions	X							X				X
Costly apparel			X									X
Deceivings				X								X
Denying prophecy								X				X
Deserting								X				X
Envy	X		X	X								X
False witness										X		X
Idleness			X									X
Idolatry			X									X
Lasciviousness				X								X
Lying	X		X	X				X			X	X
Malice	X			X								X
Mocking the sacred								X			X	
Murder	X	X	X	X	X	X	X	X	X	X	X	X
Taking name of God in vain	X											X
Oppressing poor								X				X
Persecuting			X									X
Plunder		X		X	X		X	X	X	X	X	X
Power mongering											X	
Pride			X					X				X
Revilings				X								X
Robbing		X	X	X		X	X					X
Seeking riches		X						X		X		X
Slavery		X										X
Smiting weak								X				X
Sorceries			X									X
Stealing	X	X	X	X	X	X		X	X	X		X
Strife			X	X								X
Whoredoms	X		X			X		X			X	X
Wickedness		X	X		X	X		X	X	X	X	X
Withholding food								X				
Withholding clothing								X				

Chart 127

Word Studies

of the Book of Mormon

Charts 128–35

Chart 128

Chiasmus in Leviticus 24:13–23

Key Scripture Leviticus 24:13–23

Explanation Chiasmus is a style of writing known in antiquity and used by many ancient and some modern writers. It consists of arranging a series of words or ideas in one order, and then repeating it in reverse order. In the hands of a skillful writer, this literary form can serve several purposes. The repeating of key words in the two halves underlines the importance of the concepts they present. Furthermore, the main idea of the passage is emphasized by its placement at the turning point where the second half begins. Thus chiasms, in general, place their most important elements in the center. Chiasmus can be found in biblical texts, as Leviticus 24:13–23 demonstrates. It is one of the clearest examples of chiasmus in the Bible. In this case "breach for breach, eye for eye, tooth for tooth" is the central formulation. Other words important to the structure of the chiasm are italicized.

Source John W. Welch, "Chiasmus in Biblical Law: An Approach to the Structure of Legal Texts in the Hebrew Bible," in *Jewish Law Association Studies IV*, ed. Bernard Jackson (Atlanta: Scholars, 1990), 5–22.

Chiasmus in Leviticus 24:13–23

And the Lord spake unto Moses, saying,

Bring forth him that hath *cursed without the camp;* and let all that heard him . . . *stone him.*

And thou shalt speak unto the children of Israel, saying,

Whosoever curseth his God shall bear his sin. . . . the *stranger,* as [well as] he that is *born in the land.* . . .

And he that *killeth any man* shall surely be put to death.

And he that *killeth a beast* shall make it good; beast for beast.

And if a man cause a *blemish* in his neighbour; as he hath done, so shall it be done to him;

Breach for breach,
eye for eye,
tooth for tooth:

as he hath caused a *blemish* in a man, so shall it be done to him again.

And he that *killeth a beast,* he shall restore it:

and he that *killeth a man,* he shall be put to death.

Ye shall have one manner of law, as well for the *stranger,* as for *one of your own country.* . . .

And Moses spake to the children of Israel,

that they should bring forth him that had *cursed out of the camp,* and *stone him* with stones.

And the children of Israel did as the Lord commanded Moses.

Chart 128

Chart 129

Chiasmus in Matthew 13:13–18

Key Scripture   Matthew 13:13–18

Explanation   The Savior used chiasmus on occasion. In this chart Jesus Christ is quoting Isaiah (Esaias), embedding Isaiah's chiastic structure in his own larger discourse, which is also a chiasm. The Savior here begins and ends with a reference to parables and includes as the center of his chiasm the prophecy of Isaiah that many will close their eyes and refuse to see that Jesus is the Christ.

Source   John W. Welch, "Chiasmus in the Book of Mormon," *BYU Studies* 10 (autumn 1969): 69–84.

Chiasmus in Matthew 13:13–18

Therefore speak I to them in *parables:*

 because they seeing *see* not; and hearing they *hear* not, neither do they understand.

  And in them is fulfilled the *prophecy* of Esaias, which saith,

   By hearing ye shall *hear,* and shall not understand;

   and seeing ye shall *see,* and shall not perceive:

    For this people's *heart* is waxed gross,

     and their *ears* are dull of *hearing,*

      and their *eyes*

       they have *closed;*

       lest at any time they should *see*

      with their *eyes,*

     and *hear* with their *ears,*

    and should understand with their *heart,* and should be converted, and I should heal them.

   But blessed are your eyes, for they *see:*

  and your ears, for they *hear.*

 For verily I say unto you, That many *prophets* and righteous men have desired to *see* those things which ye see, and have not seen them; and to *hear* those things which ye hear, and have not heard them.

Hear ye therefore the *parable* of the sower.

Chart 129

Chart 130

Chiasmus in Mosiah 3:18–19

Key Scripture Mosiah 3:18–19

Explanation King Benjamin's complex ceremonial speech in Mosiah 2–5 contains several excellent examples of chiasmus. The overall structure of the speech is chiastic and houses smaller chiasms within it. (For a more detailed representation of the speech of Benjamin as a whole, see chart 84.) This chart shows only one of the chiasms found in Benjamin's speech. Notably, the main chiasms in Benjamin's speech concern the doctrine of Jesus Christ—the doctrine Benjamin wants to emphasize. This particular chiasm, which comes at the midpoint of the entire speech, concerns the crucial process of being spiritually reborn through the atonement of Christ.

Source John W. Welch, "Chiasmus in the Book of Mormon," *BYU Studies* 10 (autumn 1969): 69–84; and John W. Welch, "Parallelism and Chiasmus in King Benjamin's Speech," in *King Benjamin's Speech: "That Ye May Learn Wisdom,"* ed. John W. Welch and Stephen D. Ricks (Provo, Utah: FARMS, 1998), 347–54.

Chiasmus in Mosiah 3:18–19

except they *humble* themselves

    and become as little *children,* and believe that

        salvation was, and is, and is to come, in and through the *atoning blood of Christ, the Lord Omnipotent.*

           For the *natural man*

               is an enemy to *God,*

                  and *has been* from the fall of Adam,

                  and *will be,* forever and ever,

               unless he yields to the enticings of the *Holy Spirit,*

           and putteth off the *natural man*

        and becometh a saint through the *atonement of Christ the Lord,*

    and becometh as a *child,*

submissive, meek, *humble,* patient, full of love, willing to submit to all things

Chart 130

Chart 131

Chiasmus in Mosiah 5:10–12

Key Scripture   Mosiah 5:10–12

Explanation   King Benjamin uses chiasmus several times in his great speech in Mosiah 2–5. In Mosiah 5:10–12 he emphasizes the central importance of taking upon oneself the name of Christ. In this concluding section of his speech, the people enter into a covenant with God and are called the children of Christ. They receive the name of Christ, which will never be blotted out, except by transgression. Transgression therefore receives the focus as the center of this chiasm, which stands at the center of this final section of the entire speech. Benjamin's skillful use of this literary form shows that he carefully and deliberately prepared his masterful oration.

Source   John W. Welch, "Chiasmus in the Book of Mormon," *BYU Studies* 10 (autumn 1969): 69–84; and John W. Welch, "Parallelism and Chiasmus in King Benjamin's Speech," in *King Benjamin's Speech: "That Ye May Learn Wisdom,"* ed. John W. Welch and Stephen D. Ricks (Provo, Utah: FARMS, 1998), 369–73.

Chiasmus in Mosiah 5:10–12

And now it shall come to pass, that whosoever shall not take upon him the *name of Christ*

   must be *called* by some other name;

      therefore, he findeth himself on the *left hand of God.*

         And I would that ye should *remember* also, that this is the name that I said I should give unto you

            that never should be *blotted out,*

               except it be through *transgression;*

               therefore, take heed that ye do not *transgress,*

            that the name be not *blotted out* of your hearts.

         I say unto you, I would that ye should *remember* to retain the name written always in your hearts,

      that ye are not found on the *left hand of God,*

   but that ye hear and know the voice by which ye shall be *called,* and also,

the *name* by which he shall call you.

Chart 131

Chart 132

Chiasmus in Alma 36

Key Scripture   Alma 36

Explanation   In his blessing to his son Helaman, Alma uses chiasmus in recounting his conversion to the gospel of Jesus Christ. This chart illustrates the deep structure of Alma 36. Jesus Christ is the crux of the chiasm, just as he is the center of the gospel and the only means whereby salvation can be attained. The turning point in Alma's conversion was not the appearance of the angel or the fear of eternal banishment, but calling on the name of Jesus Christ, the Son of God. Fittingly, Alma makes this spiritual turning point the literary focal point of this entire chapter, one of the finest examples of chiastic composition anywhere in world literature.

Source   John W. Welch, "A Masterpiece: Alma 36," in *Rediscovering the Book of Mormon*, ed. John L. Sorenson and Melvin J. Thorne (Salt Lake City: Deseret Book and FARMS, 1991), 114–31.

Chiasmus in Alma 36

My son give ear to my *words* (v. 1)
  Keep the commandments and ye shall *prosper in the land* (v. 1)
   Do *as I* have done (v. 2)
    Remember the captivity of our fathers (v. 2)
     They were in *bondage* (v. 2)
      He surely did *deliver* them (v. 2)
       Trust in God (v. 3)
        Supported in *trials, troubles, and afflictions* (v. 3)
        Lifted up at the *last day* (v. 3)
         I know this not of myself but *of God* (v. 4)
          Born of God (v. 5)
           I sought to destroy the church (v. 6–9)
            My *limbs* were paralyzed (v. 10)
             Fear of being in the *presence of God* (vv. 14–15)
              Pains of a damned soul (v. 16)
               Harrowed up by the memory of sins (v. 17)
                I remembered *Jesus Christ, a son of God* (v. 17)
                I cried, *Jesus Christ, son of God* (v. 18)
               Harrowed by the memory of sins no more (v. 19)
              Joy as exceeding as was the *pain* (v. 20)
             Long to be in the *presence of God* (v. 22)
            My *limbs* received strength again (v. 23)
           I labored to bring souls to repentance (v. 24)
          Born of God (v. 26)
         Therefore *my knowledge* is *of God* (v. 26)
        Supported under *trials, troubles, and afflictions* (v. 26)
       Trust in him (v. 27)
      He will *deliver* me (v. 27)
     And *raise me up at the last day* (v. 28)
    As God brought our fathers out of *bondage* and captivity (vv. 28–29)
   Retain a *remembrance of their captivity* (v. 29)
  Know *as I* do know (v. 30)
Keep the commandments and ye shall *prosper in the land* (v. 30)
This according to his *word* (v. 30)

Chart 132

Chart 133

Chiasmus in Helaman 6:7–13

Key Scripture   Helaman 6:7–13

Explanation   Yet another example of chiasmus, in this case a report of the events in a particular Nephite year, is found in Helaman 6:7–13. Because the report is a fine literary unit, the account was most likely originally written as a single entry in the Nephite annals that Mormon copied verbatim into his record from the large plates of Nephi. The sixty-fourth year of the reign of the judges was an unusual year, one in which the Nephites and Lamanites cooperatively enjoyed economic prosperity, peace, and free trade—an unprecedented occurrence. The chiastic form of the report for this year underscores its importance. In the chart, notice that *Zedekiah* and *Lord* are paired together at the center of the chiasm. The *-yah* at the end of *Zedekiah* represents the Hebrew word for "Lord"; thus the chiasm was probably even more evident in its original language than it is today in English.

Source   John W. Welch, "Chiasmus in Helaman 6:7–13," in *Reexploring the Book of Mormon,* ed. John W. Welch (Salt Lake City: Deseret Book, 1992), 230–32.

Chiasmus in Helaman 6:7–13

And behold, there was *peace* in all the land,

[Freedom of travel and trade in *both lands* is discussed]

And it came to pass that they became exceedingly *rich*, both the Lamanites and the Nephites;

and they did have an exceeding *plenty* of *gold, and of silver*, and of all manner of *precious metals, both* in the *land* south and in the *land* north.

Now the land *south*

was called *Lehi*, and

the land *north*

was called *Mulek*,

which was after the son of *Zedekiah;**

for the *Lord*

did bring *Mulek*

into the land *north*,

and *Lehi* into

the land *south*.

And behold, there was *all manner* of *gold* in *both* these *lands*, and of *silver*, and of *precious ore of every kind;*

and there were also curious workmen, who did work all kinds of ore and did refine it; and thus they did become *rich*.

[Economic prosperity in *both lands* is discussed]

And thus the sixty and fourth year did pass away in *peace*.

*The Hebrew word for *Lord* constitutes the theophoric suffix *-yah*, which is at the end of the name Zedekiah.

Chart 133

Chart 134

"It Came to Pass"
Occurrences in the Book of Mormon

Key Scripture   1 Nephi 1:4

Explanation   This chart compares the frequency of the phrase "it came to pass" and its closely related formulations in books of the Book of Mormon. The number of times the phrase is used (expressed as a total and as a percentage) and the rate of occurrence (expressed as one occurrence every so many words) are listed for each individual book, varying considerably. Some readers wonder why these words occur so often in the Book of Mormon compared with the Bible. Actually, the Hebrew word *wayehi* is translated in the King James Version of the Bible as "it came to pass," but it is also translated as "it happened, came, had come, became, arose, was, now," and so forth. Therefore, what was an extremely common phrase in the Bible appears to be less so because it was translated into various phrases instead of a single one. Apparently, Joseph Smith was quite consistent in translating it with the phrase "it came to pass" every time. Incidentally, in much the same way, some books in the Bible have a high frequency of "it came to pass," while others do not.

Source   Robert F. Smith, "'It Came to Pass' in the Bible and the Book of Mormon" (FARMS, 1984).

"It Came to Pass"
Occurrences in the Book of Mormon

	Instances of "it came to pass" in the 1830 edition	Percentage of total "it came to pass" phrases	Average rate of occurrence (instances/words)
1 Nephi	208	14.1	108.9
2 Nephi	52	3.5	525.4
Jacob	48	3.3	174.7
Enos	6	0.4	164.8
Jarom	4	0.3	164.8
Omni	13	0.9	97.8
Words of Mormon	6	0.4	137.3
Mosiah	168	11.4	170.3
Alma	433	29.3	178.6
Helaman	135	9.2	138.2
3 Nephi	154	10.4	173.4
4 Nephi	20	1.4	89.5
Mormon	63	4.3	137.6
Ether	166	11.3	89.4
Moroni	0	0	0

Chart 134

Chart 135

Wordprints and the Book of Mormon

Key Scripture   Helaman 3:13

Explanation   Modern computers have given birth to a new science of analyzing word patterns in documents whose authorship is disputed. By wordprint analysis, it is now possible with a high degree of certainty to tell which suspected authors did not write a given work. Wordprinting is based on the somewhat surprising fact that every author that has been studied thus far subconsciously uses sixty-five identifiable patterns, involving words such as *and, the, of,* and *that,* at rates that, from a statistical standpoint, differ significantly from those of other authors. The higher the number of "rejections" or differences, the less likely it is that the tested samples were written by the same person.

This chart shows the results of tests that were run by John L. Hilton, comparing writings of Nephi and Alma with the words of Joseph Smith, Oliver Cowdery, and Solomon Spaulding. In every set comparing the Book of Mormon texts against these three writers, at least seven (and often many more) rejections were measured. These results yield strong statistical evidence that the wordprints of Joseph Smith, Oliver Cowdery, and Solomon Spaulding are not measurable in the Book of Mormon.

Source   John L. Hilton, "Wordprints and the Book of Mormon," in *Reexploring the Book of Mormon,* ed. John W. Welch (Salt Lake City: Deseret Book and FARMS, 1992), 221–26.

Wordprints and the Book of Mormon

	Tests	Number of Rejections														
		0	1	2	3	4	5	6	7	8	9	10	11	12	13	14	15
Nephi vs. Nephi	3			x		x	x										
Alma vs. Alma	3		x	x	x												
Smith vs. Smith	3	x		xx													
Cowdery vs. Cowdery	1		x														
Spaulding vs. Spaulding	1			x													
Nephi vs. Alma	9			x			xx	xx	x	x	x	x					
Smith vs. Nephi	6					x				xx		x	x	x			
Smith vs. Alma	6				xx	x	x		xx								
Cowdery vs. Nephi	6							x	x				xx		x	x	
Cowdery vs. Alma	6								xx xx	x	x						
Spaulding vs. Nephi	5												x	x	x		x	x
Spaulding vs. Alma	6							x x x		xx				x			

Clearly different author

Chart 135

War

in the Book of Mormon

Chart 136

Wars in the Book of Mormon

Key Scripture Alma 43–62

Explanation There are several major wars or periods of warfare documented in the Book of Mormon. The approximate dates and locations of these wars, along with accompanying scriptural references, are listed in this chart. Having names and dates for these wars can help readers keep all of this confusing action straight. Although the Book of Mormon is a complex record, it is still very clear and purposeful.

Source John W. Welch, "Why Study Wars in the Book of Mormon?" in *Warfare in the Book of Mormon,* ed. Stephen D. Ricks and William J. Hamblin (Salt Lake City: Deseret Book and FARMS, 1990), 6–15.

Wars in the Book of Mormon

Date	War	Location	Reference
500–100 B.C.	Early tribal wars	Land of Nephi	Jacob 1:10, 14; Enos–Omni
160–150 B.C.	Wars of King Laman's sons	City of Nephi and the land of Zarahemla	Omni 1:24; W of M 1:13–14; Mosiah 9–10
87 B.C.	War of Amlici	Zarahemla, hill Amnihu, and river Sidon	Alma 2–3
81 B.C.	Destruction of Ammonihah	Ammonihah, west of Zarahemla	Alma 16:1–11; 24:1–25:14
77 B.C.	War of the Ammonite secession	Zarahemla, the land of Jershon	Alma 28
74 B.C.	Zoramite war	Between Antionum and Jershon	Alma 43–44
72 B.C.	First Amalickiahite war	Ammonihah, Noah, the east coast near narrow neck of land	Alma 46:1–50:11
67–61 B.C.	Second Amalickiahite war (seven years' war)	Throughout land of Zarahemla	Alma 51–62
52 B.C.	Rebellion of Paanchi	City of Zarahemla	Hel. 1:1–13
51 B.C.	War of Tubaloth	Cities of Zarahemla and Bountiful	Hel. 1:14–34
38, 35–30 B.C.	War of Moronihah	Land of Zarahemla	Hel. 4
26–19 B.C.	War of Gadianton and Kishkumen	The entire land, but centered in the land of Zarahemla	Hel. 6:15–11:20
A.D. 13–22	War of Giddianhi and Zemnarihah	From Zarahemla to Bountiful	3 Ne. 2:11–4:28
A.D. 30	Rebellion of Jacob	Land of Zarahemla	3 Ne. 6:14–7:14
A.D. 322, 327–28	Final Nephite wars, phase I	Land of Zarahemla and northward	Morm. 1:6–2:9
A.D. 346–350	Final Nephite wars, phase II	Lands of Zarahemla, Jashon, and Shem	Morm. 2:16–3:1
A.D. 361–85	Final Nephite wars, phase III	The narrow neck of land and all the land northward	Morm. 3:4–6:15

Chart 136

Chart 137

Data on Wars
Involving the Nephites

Key Scripture Alma 43–62

Explanation This three-page chart is a more detailed representation of the fifteen Nephite wars listed in chart 134. It tracks each major war's approximate dates and locations, as well as its causes and results. Though the wars are very different from each other, they share some interesting patterns. For example, several of the wars were caused when one group of people tried to separate from the main group. Apparently, the Nephites were restricted in their travel, and defection from the land was considered an act of treason and a cause for armed intervention. Another pattern is that opponents to the government chose to strike right after a new leader had taken office or when the government or the church was weakened by dissension. Amalickiah's wars, for instance, were initiated when dissenters banded together and desired a king, shortly after Alma left and Helaman was newly in office (see Alma 45:23–46:7). Studying the amazingly consistent complexity and sensible realism of these war accounts brings to light the real-life issues and dynamics behind the Nephite history told in the Book of Mormon.

Source John W. Welch, "Why Study Wars in the Book of Mormon?" in *Warfare in the Book of Mormon,* ed. Stephen D. Ricks and William J. Hamblin (Salt Lake City: Deseret Book and FARMS, 1990), 6–15.

Data on Wars Involving the Nephites

	War	Dates	Location	Causes	References	Results
1.	Early tribal wars	6th–2nd century B.C.	Land of Nephi	A popular and fraternal hatred; resentment; desire to destroy the Nephites	Jacob 1:10, 14; Enos–Omni	Nephites did not thrive and later left land of Nephi
2.	Wars of King Laman's sons	160–150 B.C.	City of Nephi, land of Zarahemla	Lamanite fear of growing Nephite strength; Lamanite belief that Nephi had wronged his elder brothers	Mosiah 9–10; Omni 1:24; W of M 1:13–14	Established land of Zarahemla as Nephite territory and land of Nephi as Lamanite territory
3.	War of Amlici	87 B.C./ 5th year of reign of judges (R.J.)	Zarahemla, hill Amnihu, river Sidon	Political unrest caused by changing the government from a kingship to a judgeship	Alma 2–3	Uneasy peace in Zarahemla with Alma as chief judge
4.	Destruction of Ammonihah	81 B.C./ 11 R.J.	Ammonihah	Lamanites seeking revenge on the Nehorites for causing a civil war	Alma 16:1–11; 24:1–25:14	Virtual elimination of Nehorites as a political force
5.	War of the Ammonite secession	77 B.C./ 15 R.J.	Zarahemla, land of Jershon	Lamanites attack in retaliation for the Ammonite secession	Alma 28	Ammonites established in land of Jershon
6.	Zoramite war	74 B.C./ 18 R.J.	Between Antionum and Jershon	Lamanites attack in retaliation for the Zoramite secession	Alma 43–44	Important use of innovative armor; a Zoramite oath never to attack again

Chart 137

War	Dates	Location	Causes	References	Results
7. First Amalickiahite war	72 B.C./ 20 R.J.	Ammonihah, Noah, east seacoast near the narrow neck of land	Political unrest caused by Amalickiah, who dissented from Nephites with political ambitions	Alma 46:1– 50:11	Amalickiah defeated, but he swore to return and to kill Captain Moroni
8. Second Amalickiahite war (seven years' war)	67–61 B.C./ 25–31 R.J.	Throughout land of Zarahemla	Return of Amalickiah, coinciding with the armed revolt of the king-men and his brother Ammoron's assumption of the Lamanite kingship	Alma 51–62	A very costly Nephite victory
9. Rebellion of Paanchi	52 B.C./ 40 R.J.	City of Zarahemla	Dispute over Pahoran, son of Pahoran, becoming chief judge	Hel. 1:1–13	Paanchi executed; Pahoran assassinated
10. War of Tubaloth	51 B.C./ 41 R.J.	Cities of Zarahemla and Bountiful	After the turmoil of Paanchi's rebellion, Coriantumr tried to capture the throne of Zarahemla	Hel. 1:14–34	The rise of Gadianton robbers
11. War of Moronihah	38, 35–30 B.C./54, 57–62 R.J.	Land of Zarahemla	Continuing dissension in the church	Hel. 4	Half of Nephite lands occupied by dissenters; Nephi resigns judgment seat

Chart 137

War	Dates	Location	Causes	References	Results
12. War of Gadianton and Kishkumen	26–19 B.C./ 66–73 R.J.	Entire land, but centered in the land of Zarahemla	Assassinations of chief judges Cezoram and his son; Gadianton robbers attain power	Hel. 6:15– 11:20	The famine declared by Nephi ended the war as Gadianton's band dissolved
13. War of Giddianhi and Zemnarihah	A.D. 13–22	From Zarahemla to Bountiful	Gadianton robbers come out of the hills to obtain food and to regain control of the government	3 Ne. 2:11– 4:28	Unification of the victorious Lamanites and Nephites against the threat of the robbers
14. Rebellion of Jacob	A.D. 30	Land of Zarahemla	Lachoneus tried to expose corrupt judges, who in retaliation tried to make Jacob king	3 Ne. 6:14– 7:14	Collapse of reign of judges; degeneration into tribal society
15. Final Nephite wars, phase I	A.D. 322, 327–28	Land of Zarahemla and northward	Overpopulation; infestation of robbers	Morm. 1:6– 2:9	Nephites driven back to the narrow neck of land
Final Nephite wars, phase II	A.D. 346–350	Lands of Zarahemla, Jashon, and Shem	Continual Lamanite aggressions	Morm. 2:16– 3:1	Nephites enter ten-year peace with Lamanites
Final Nephite wars, phase III	A.D. 361–385	Narrow neck of land and all the land northward	Lamanite greed; gross wickedness on both sides	Morm. 3:4– 6:15	Eventual annihilation of Nephite people

Chart 137

Chart 138

The Two Final Battles

Key Scriptures   Mormon 6; Ether 15

Explanation   This chart compares the final battles of both the Jaredite and Nephite civilizations, which took place near the same hill (see Ether 15:11). Moroni, the only known Nephite survivor of the battle at Cumorah, was the narrator of the account in the book of Ether that involves the final Jaredite battle at Ramah. He must have been deeply impressed by the parallels between the two wars of annihilation. In both cases, nations of great promise were wiped away. Because of their wickedness, the Spirit of God "ceased to strive" with both peoples (Mormon 5:16; Ether 15:19). In this chart the dates, places, numbers of soldiers, outcomes, and other statistics of these battles are contrasted. Despite the consequent collapse of these civilizations, a remnant of Lehi's seed was preserved, fulfilling the promises made by the Lord to Lehi, Nephi, Enos, and other righteous Nephites.

The Two Final Battles

	Jaredites	**Nephites**
when	ca. 300 B.C.	385 A.D.
where	hill Ramah	hill Cumorah (hill Ramah)
who	Coriantumr and Shiz	Nephites and Lamanites
how many	2 million or more	at least 220,000 Nephites
who gathered	men, wives, children	men, wives, children
outcome	both sides destroyed	Nephites destroyed
Spirit	ceased to strive with	ceased to strive with
prophet	Ether	Mormon
account	Ether 13–15	Mormon 6–7
record	24 gold plates	plates of Mormon
survivor	Coriantumr	Moroni

Chart 138

Chart 139

Ancient Steel Weapons

Key Scripture   1 Nephi 4:9

Explanation   This chart compares a dagger of Hittite origin found in King Tut-ankhamen's tomb with Nephi's description of Laban's sword. The high-quality Middle Eastern sword found in the tomb compares with the description in 1 Nephi surprisingly well. Although not related to each other, these two swords both come from the ancient Near East before Lehi's departure from Jerusalem. Laban's sword, which lasted for thousands of years while the Nephite record keepers safeguarded it and used it ceremonially and in wars from generation to generation (see Words of Mormon 1:13), was reproduced "many" times by the Nephites as they prepared to defend themselves from the Lamanites (see 2 Nephi 5:14).

Source   William J. Hamblin and A. Brent Merrill, "Swords in the Book of Mormon," in *Warfare in the Book of Mormon*, ed. Stephen D. Ricks and William J. Hamblin (Salt Lake City: Deseret Book and FARMS, 1990), 334–35.

Ancient Steel Weapons

Nephi's Description of the Sword of Laban

"And I beheld his sword, and I drew it forth from the sheath thereof; and the hilt thereof was of pure gold, and the workmanship thereof was exceedingly fine, and I saw that the blade thereof was of the most precious steel."
—*1 Nephi 4:9*

Dagger from King Tutankhamen's Tomb

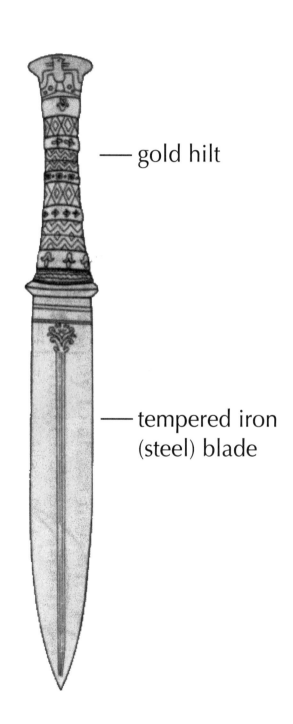

— gold hilt

— tempered iron (steel) blade

Chart 139

Chart 140

Comparison of European and Mayan Armor

Key Scripture Alma 43

Explanation European and Mayan warriors used similarly named pieces of armor, such as head gear, breastplates, body gear, and gauntlets, but the styles and materials they used were very different. The Book of Mormon mentions breastplates, shields, armor, head-plates, arm-shields, animal skins, thick clothing, and bucklers as types of armor. What were they like? Mayan soldiers used thick protective jackets made of double-thick quilted cotton that were often worn under animal skins. Nephite breastplates were probably also similar to Mayan breastplates, which were made of materials such as wood, bone, shells, jade, stones, and pieces of metal. The term *head-plates* in the Book of Mormon is unusual, but Mayan records may again help to clarify: Mayan headplates, or carved jade plaques, were worn attached to leather or cloth headbands. Hats that were protected with plates of stone, wood, or metal could also be considered head-plates. Mayan shields were usually made of reeds, cloth, or wood. Armor terminology in the Book of Mormon interestingly reflects differences between Old World and New World armor. The Book of Mormon uses biblical terms when ancient Near Eastern and Mesoamerican armors are similar but different terminology when Mesoamerican armor (e.g., *head-plate*) differs significantly from Old World armor (e.g., *helmet*), thus indicating the precision of the Book of Mormon accounts.

Source William J. Hamblin, "Armor in the Book of Mormon," in *Warfare in the Book of Mormon,* ed. Stephen D. Ricks and William J. Hamblin (Salt Lake City: Deseret Book and FARMS, 1990), 401, 413.

Comparison of European and Mayan Armor

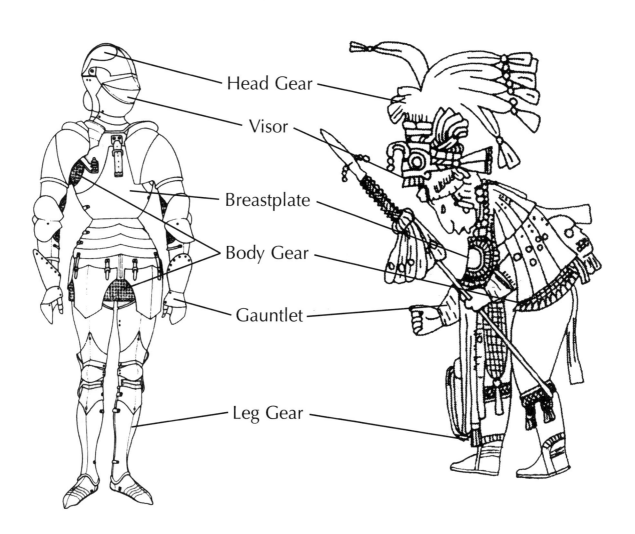

Head Gear

Visor

Breastplate

Body Gear

Gauntlet

Leg Gear

Chart 140

Chart 141

Number of Months Involving Nephite Military Actions

Key Scripture Alma 43–62

Explanation John L. Sorenson, an archaeologist who has devoted his life to the study of ancient Mesoamerica and how it corresponds to the history of the Nephite, Lamanite, and Jaredite peoples in the Book of Mormon, concludes that "Nephite wars were typically carried out early in the dry season as permitted by the agricultural maintenance pattern and when weather conditions were most suited for military campaigns. . . . The Nephite seasonality pattern for warfare agrees remarkably well with what we know from Mesoamerica about seasons for fighting and for cultivation and harvest." As this chart illustrates, November and February were the months in which the most warfare was conducted. Other months were reserved for cultivation and harvesting of crops, taxing, celebrating according to the law of Moses, and so forth.

Source John L. Sorenson, "Seasonality of Warfare in the Book of Mormon and in Mesoamerica," in *Warfare in the Book of Mormon,* ed. Stephen D. Ricks and William J. Hamblin (Salt Lake City: Deseret Book and FARMS, 1990), 455–57.

Number of Months Involving Nephite Military Actions

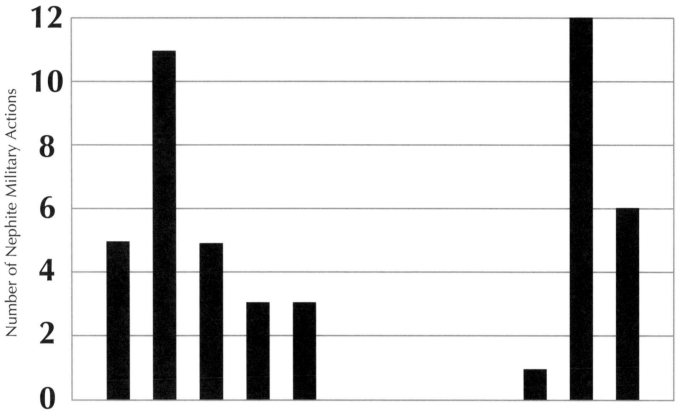

Nephite Calendar	Probable Julian Equivalent
First Month	25 February–26 March
Second Month	27 March–25 April
Third Month	26 April–25 May
Fourth Month	26 May–24 June
Fifth Month	25 June–24 July
Sixth Month	25 July–23 August
Seventh Month	24 August–22 September
Eighth Month	23 September–22 October
Ninth Month	23 October–21 November
Tenth Month	22 November–21 December
Eleventh Month	27 December–25 January
Twelfth Month	26 January–24 February

Five extra days would then complete the year

Chart 141

Chart 142

References to Nephite Fortifications Recorded in the Book of Mormon

Key Scripture   2 Nephi 26:2

Explanation   As is shown by this graph, the Book of Mormon records that more known fortifications were built between 75 B.C. and A.D. 15 than at any other time in Nephite history. The building of these fortifications can be divided into four Nephite periods and one Lamanite period: (1) the Nephites in the land of Nephi from the sixth century B.C. to the third century B.C., (2) Zeniff's rebuilding of the wall of Nephi in the second century B.C., (3) extensive work by Captain Moroni and his successors from approximately 75 B.C. until at least A.D. 15, (4) the Lamanites' effort in the first century B.C., and (5) the Nephites in the final wars before their destruction (late fourth century A.D.). In the first period, the Nephites "began to fortify [the] cities" that they claimed as an "inheritance" (Jarom 1:7), in addition to the city of Nephi (see Jacob 7:25). In the second period, the walls of the city of Nephi must have been prominent, for they are mentioned four times (see Mosiah 7:10; 9:8; 21:19; 22:6). The innovative construction of fortifications at several sites is described in considerable detail during the third period (see Alma 49:2–22; 50:1–11; 53:3–7). More than ten fortified cities are mentioned specifically in this major period, and at least five sites in the final period.

Source   John L. Sorenson, "Fortifications in the Book of Mormon Account Compared with Mesoamerican Fortifications," in *Warfare in the Book of Mormon,* ed. Stephen D. Ricks and William J. Hamblin (Salt Lake City: Deseret Book and FARMS, 1990), 438–43.

References to Nephite Fortifications
Recorded in the Book of Mormon

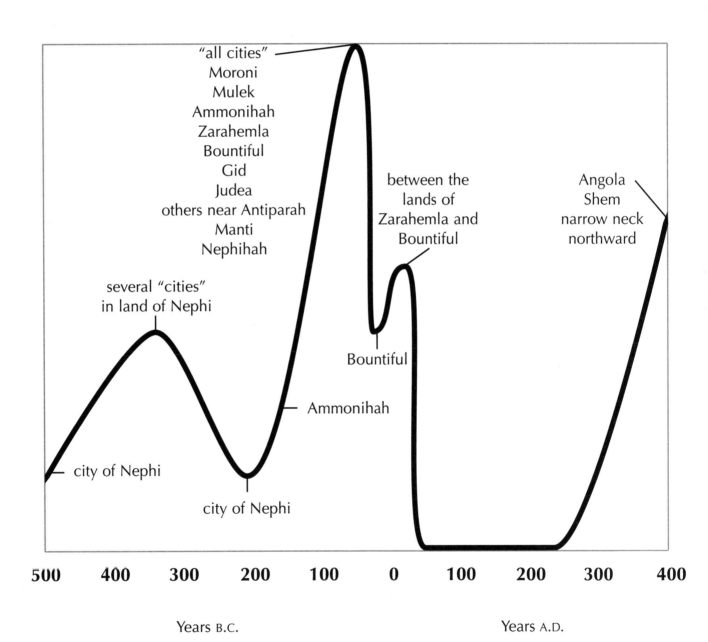

Chart 142

Chart 143

Mesoamerican Fortified and Defensive Sites by Period

Explanation Archaeologists have now identified numerous fortified sites in Meso-america. In the early periods, these fortifications consisted of earthen barriers, stone walls with gates, wooden palisades, isolated guard posts, elevated defensive sites, and moats or ditches. The peoples in that land were once thought to be strictly peaceful, but that idea has been proven wrong. Although the numbers in this chart are tentative (dependent as they are on the accidents of archaeological discovery), it is interesting to note that the number of known fortified sites sharply increases in the period when the Nephites also experienced their years of greatest military conflict.

Source John L. Sorenson, "Fortifications in the Book of Mormon Account Compared with Mesoamerican Fortifications," in *Warfare in the Book of Mormon*, ed. Stephen D. Ricks and William J. Hamblin (Salt Lake City: Deseret Book and FARMS, 1990), 429, 437.

Mesoamerican Fortified and Defensive Sites by Period

Period	Definite	Possible
Early Pre-Classic (pre-1000 B.C.)	0	1
Early Middle Pre-Classic (1000–600 B.C.)	0	2
Late Middle Pre-Classic (600–400 B.C.)	5	1
Late Pre-Classic (400–50 B.C.)	30	2
Proto-Classic (50 B.C.–A.D. 200)	26	8
Early Classic (A.D. 200–400)	14	8
Middle Classic (A.D. 400–650)	11	13
Late Classic (A.D. 650–850)	27	11
Epi-Classic (A.D. 850–1000)	12	10
Post-Classic (A.D. 1000–Conquest)	177	16

Chart 143

Cycles

in the Book of Mormon

Chart 144

Nephite Cycle of Righteousness
Mormon's Warning for Us Today

Key Scripture   Alma 37:13

Explanation   Nowhere is the cycle of righteousness more apparent in the Book of Mormon than during the reign of the judges. The judges governed from 91 B.C. until A.D. 31, when the chief judge was murdered and the government overthrown. During the reign of the judges, the Nephites constantly fluctuated in their level of righteousness. Other factors, such as degrees of peace, political unity, and prosperity no doubt affected their commitment to the gospel; however, the righteousness of the people affected the other factors in a more direct way. This overview of the Nephite cycle of righteousness can be used to identify general trends in the complex examples presented by the following graphs in this section. Beginning at the top of the chart, the scriptures in each cycle can be followed around the circle clockwise until the final destruction recorded in Mormon 4–6, after which no repentance occurred.

Nephite Cycle of Righteousness
Mormon's Warning for Us Today

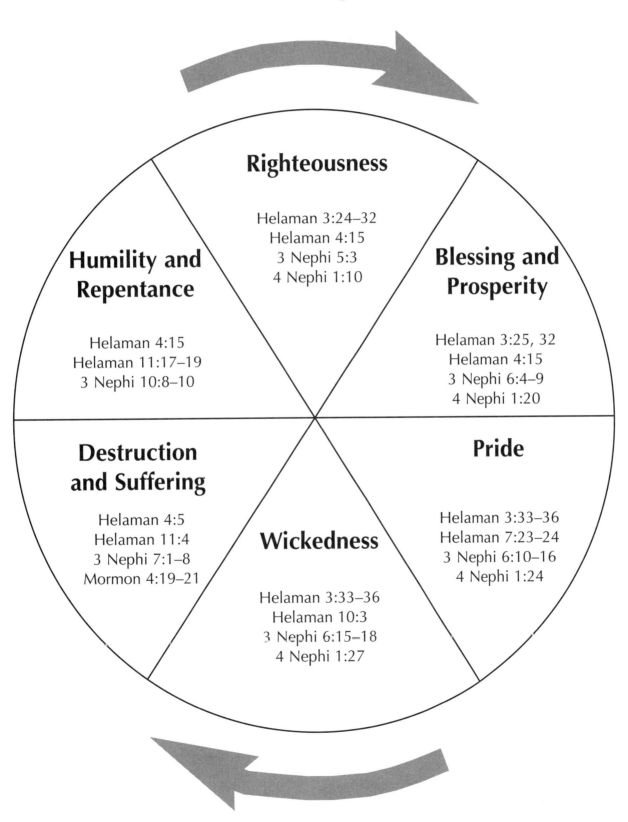

Righteousness

Helaman 3:24–32
Helaman 4:15
3 Nephi 5:3
4 Nephi 1:10

Humility and Repentance

Helaman 4:15
Helaman 11:17–19
3 Nephi 10:8–10

Blessing and Prosperity

Helaman 3:25, 32
Helaman 4:15
3 Nephi 6:4–9
4 Nephi 1:20

Destruction and Suffering

Helaman 4:5
Helaman 11:4
3 Nephi 7:1–8
Mormon 4:19–21

Pride

Helaman 3:33–36
Helaman 7:23–24
3 Nephi 6:10–16
4 Nephi 1:24

Wickedness

Helaman 3:33–36
Helaman 10:3
3 Nephi 6:15–18
4 Nephi 1:27

Chart 144

Chart 145

Nephite Cycles
Years 1–49 of the Reign of the Judges (90–40 B.C.)

Key Scripture Alma 1–Helaman 3

Explanation Based on information gleaned from Alma 1–Helaman 3, this chart
plots the general trends of prosperity, political unity, righteousness, and peace of the Nephite people. Notable here is the relative
prosperity and contrasting wickedness of the people, as well as the
fluctuations in peace and political unity. Each trend moves somewhat idiosyncratically, which is what one would expect of authentic politico-historical experience.

Nephite Cycles
Years 1–49 of the Reign of the Judges (90–40 B.C.)

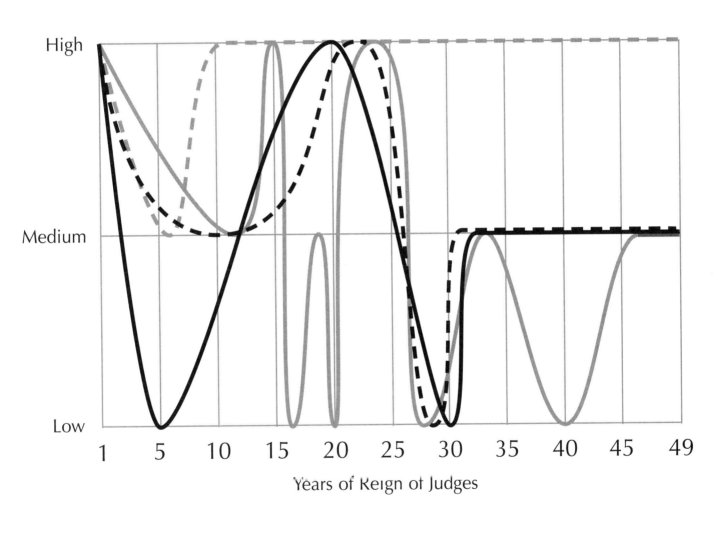

Levels of
Righteousness

High

Medium

Low

1   5   10   15   20   25   30   35   40   45   49

Years of Reign of Judges

Political Unity ———————

Righteousness – – – – – – –

Prosperity – – – – – – –

Peace ———————

Chart 145

Chart 146

Nephite Cycles
Years 50–90 of the Reign of the Judges (39–1 B.C.)

Key Scripture   Helaman 3–16

Explanation   While prosperity fluctuates between medium and high during 39 and 1 B.C., the righteousness of the people dips into major downward trends. Continuous prosperity during these years shows that the dire results of wickedness do not necessarily come immediately. Levels of peace and political unity correlate for a decade as they drop and then recover before political unity stabilizes at a moderate level and peace soars to a twenty-year high, plummets, and increases again.

Nephite Cycles
Years 50–90 of the Reign of the Judges (39–1 B.C.)

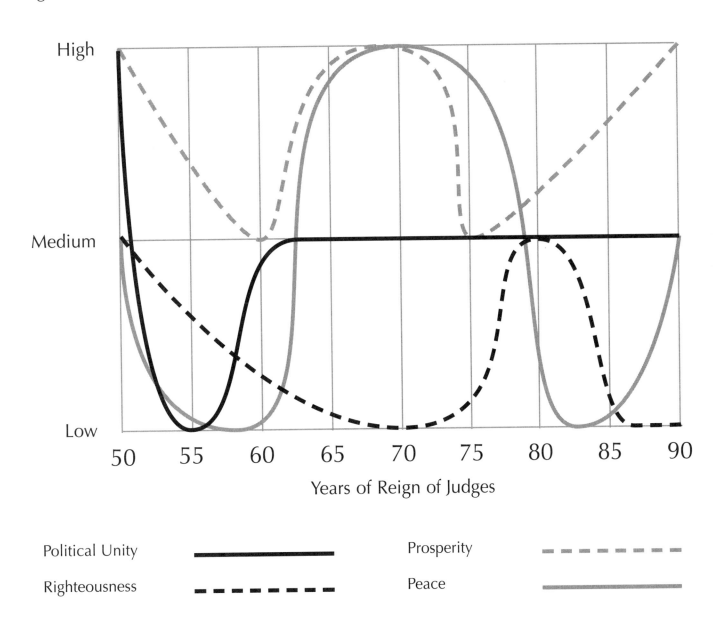

Levels of Righteousness

High

Medium

Low

50   55   60   65   70   75   80   85   90

Years of Reign of Judges

Political Unity ————————

Righteousness ━ ━ ━ ━ ━ ━

Prosperity – – – – – –

Peace ————————

Chart 146

Chart 147

Nephite Cycles
Years A.D. 1–34

Key Scripture   3 Nephi 1–8

Explanation   In this composite chart representing general trends, the first fifteen years following the birth of Jesus Christ show a decline in all areas. Then, with the advent of the wars with the Gadianton robbers, righteousness and political unity increase significantly. Interestingly, between A.D. 20 and 28 prosperity, peace, and political unity increase together while righteousness decreases. It can be argued that the low points of prosperity and political unity are caused by the people's unrighteousness, as the Lord declares would happen in Alma 37:13.

Nephite Cycles
Years A.D. 1–34

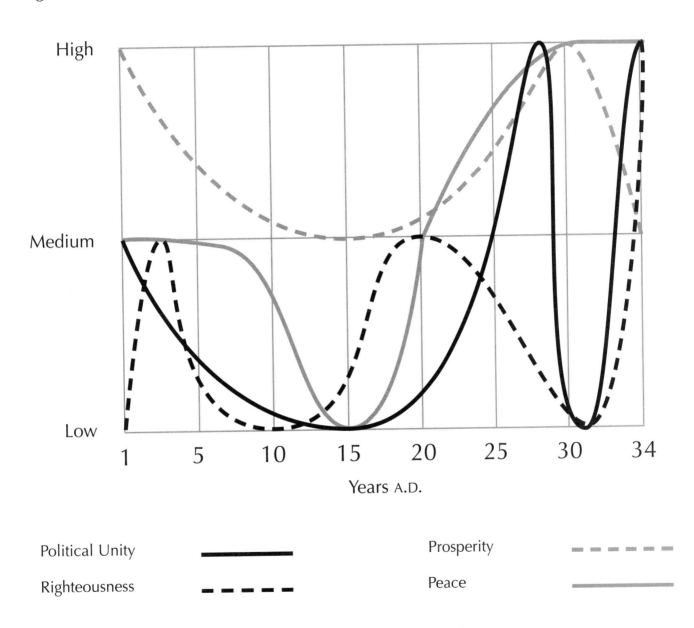

Levels of
Righteousness

High

Medium

Low

1   5   10   15   20   25   30   34

Years A.D.

| Political Unity | ——— | Prosperity | - - - |
| Righteousness | - - - | Peace | ——— |

Chart 147

Geography

in the Book of Mormon

Chart 148

Twelve Requirements for the Land of Bountiful

Key Scripture   1 Nephi 17–18

Explanation   Because the Lehites "exceedingly rejoiced when [they] came to the seashore" at Bountiful (1 Nephi 17:6), Bountiful must have been a fertile area—especially for arid southern Arabia, where they are thought to have journeyed from Jerusalem. Twelve required characteristics of Bountiful, identified by Warren and Michaela Aston, narrow the location of Bountiful to six spots along the Arabian coast. The current-day Wadi Sayq (more specifically Khor Kharfot, a portion of Wadi Sayq, located in Oman) is the most probable location of Bountiful because it is the most fertile coastal location on the Arabian Peninsula. Unless the wadi is reached by traveling through the Arabian interior, as Lehi would have done, Wadi Sayq remains almost completely hidden. Wadi Sayq lies "nearly eastward" of Nehem, Yemen (assumed to be "Nahom"; 1 Nephi 16:34; 17:1), and is the only area in which fruit grows without being cultivated. It also contains the largest freshwater source on the Arabian coast. The twelve required characteristics for the land of Bountiful are listed in this chart.

Source   Warren P. Aston and Michaela Knoth Aston, *In the Footsteps of Lehi: New Evidence for Lehi's Journey across Arabia to Bountiful* (Salt Lake City: Deseret Book, 1994), 28–29. Map used by permission from the Encyclopedia of Mormonism.

Twelve Requirements for the Land of Bountiful

1. Freshwater available year-round

2. Contain "much fruit" and honey (1 Nephi 17:5, 6; 18:6)

3. Both general area (17:5, 8) and specific location where the Lehites camped were fertile (17:6)

4. Permit reasonable access from the interior desert to the coast

5. A mountain prominent enough to justify Nephi's reference to "the mount" (17:7, 18:3) and close enough that he could go there to "pray oft" (18:3)

6. Cliffs from which Nephi's brothers could have thrown him into the depths of the sea (17:48)

7. Shoreline (17:5) suitable for the construction and launching of a ship (18:8)

8. Ore and flint for Nephi's tools (17:9–11, 16)

9. Enough large timber to build a seaworthy ship with (18:1, 2, 6)

10. Suitable winds and ocean currents to take the ship out into the ocean (18:8, 9)

11. No population residing in the area

12. "Nearly eastward of Nahom" (1 Nephi 17:1)

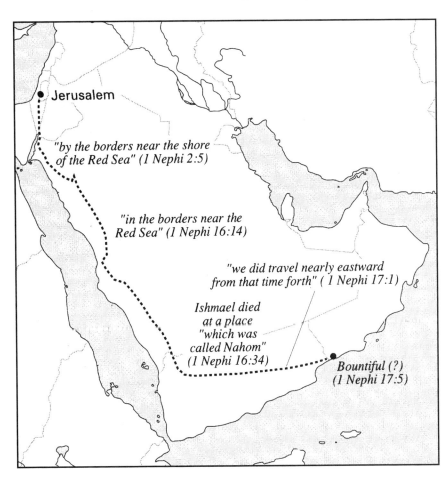

"by the borders near the shore of the Red Sea" (1 Nephi 2:5)

"in the borders near the Red Sea" (1 Nephi 16:14)

"we did travel nearly eastward from that time forth" (1 Nephi 17:1)

Ishmael died at a place "which was called Nahom" (1 Nephi 16:34)

Bountiful (?) (1 Nephi 17:5)

Chart 148

Chart 149

Ten Essential Features
of Book of Mormon Geography

Key Scripture   Alma 22:27–33

Explanation   Many different locations for the setting of the Book of Mormon in the New World have been proposed. While none can be definitively confirmed, some are more probable than others. Archaeologist John Clark has outlined ten essential features that any proposed Nephite geographical location must have in order for it to be consistent with the text of the Book of Mormon. It should be noted that while Nephites do not refer to being located near an isthmus specifically, they do refer to a narrow neck of land that separates the north and south areas (see Alma 22:32). Persons interested in Book of Mormon geography who do not interpret this reference as an isthmus have more difficulty fitting their site to the Book of Mormon than do those who interpret the narrow neck passage as an isthmus. The features listed in this chart are based on the Book of Mormon text.

Source   John Clark, review of *Deciphering the Geography of the Book of Mormon,* by F. Richard Hauck, *Review of Books on the Book of Mormon* 1 (1989): 67–69.

Ten Essential Features of Book of Mormon Geography

1. A narrow neck (isthmus) separated the land northward from the land southward and was flanked by an east sea and a west sea.

2. Nephite and Lamanite lands occupied at least three times as much western coastline as eastern coastline.

3. The eastern wilderness was much wider and lower than the western wilderness but not nearly as wide as the southern wilderness.

4. The city of Nephi was in a highland valley; Zarahemla was in a large river basin.

5. The river Sidon flowed northward through Zarahemla.

6. The Waters of Mormon was probably a highland lake of significant size.

7. Zarahemla was surrounded by Nephite fortifications.

8. The city of Nephi was three weeks' travel south from Zarahemla and near the Waters of Mormon.

9. The city of Bountiful was north of Zarahemla and near the narrow neck; it was about five days' travel from Moroni and guarded the route to the land northward.

10. Cumorah (also called Ramah) was near the eastern sea, not very far north of Bountiful.

Chart 149

Chart 150

Geographical Names
Listed Alphabetically

Key Scripture   Alma 22:27–33

Explanation   The first column of this three-page chart lists geographical names or features found in the Book of Mormon, and corresponding scriptural references appear in the second column. This list may be helpful for a student wishing to search the Book of Mormon for the geographical information found within it. For further information, please refer to the source below.

Source   John L. Sorenson, *The Geography of Book of Mormon Events: A Source Book* (Provo, Utah: FARMS, 1990).

Geographical Names
Listed Alphabetically

Aaron, city/cities of	Alma 8:13; 50:14
Ablom	Ether 9:3
Agosh	Ether 14:15–16
Akish, wilderness of	Ether 14:3–4, 14
Alma, valley of	Mosiah 24:20, 21
Ammonihah, city of	Alma 8:6–13, 16–18; chs. 9–14; 15:1, 15; 16:2–3, 9, 11; 25:2; 49:3, 10–11
Amnihu, hill	Alma 2:15
Amulon, land of	Mosiah 23:31; 24:1
Angola, city of	Mormon 2:4
Ani–Anti	Alma 21:11
Antionum, land of	Alma 31:3; 43:5, 22
Antiparah, city of	Alma 56:14, 31–34; 57:1–4
Antipas, mount	Alma 47:7, 10
Antum, land of	Mormon 1:3
Boaz, city of	Mormon 4:20–21
Bountiful, city/land of	Alma 22:29–33; 27:22; 50:11, 32; 51:28, 30–32; 52:9, 15, 17–18, 39; 53:3–4; 55:26; 63:5; Helaman 1:23, 28; 4:6; 5:14; 3 Nephi 3:23; 11:1
Comnor, hill	Ether 14:28
Corihor, land/valley of	Ether 14:27–28
Cumeni, city of	Alma 56:13–14; 57:7–8, 12, 23, 31, 34
Cumorah, land/hill of	Mormon 6:2–6, 11; 8:2
Desolation, city of	Mormon 3:7; 4:2, 3, 8, 13, 19
Desolation, land of	Alma 50:34; 63:5; 3 Nephi 3:23; Mormon 3:5; 4:1–2, 19; Ether 7:6
Ephraim, hill	Ether 7:9
Gad, city of	3 Nephi 9:10
Gadiani, city of	3 Nephi 9:8
Gadiomnah, city of	3 Nephi 9:8
Gid, city of	Alma 51:26; 55:7–26
Gideon, city/land/valley of	Alma 2:20–26; 6:7–8:1; 13:15; 17:1; 30:21; 61:5; 62:3–6
Gilgal, city/valley of	3 Nephi 9:6; Ether 13:27–30

Chart 150

Gimgimno, city of	3 Nephi 9:8
Helam, city/land of	Mosiah 23:3–4, 19–20, 25–26, 29, 35, 37–39; 27:16
Hermounts, wilderness of	Alma 2:37
Heshlon, plains of	Ether 13:28
Ishmael, land of	Alma 17:19–21; 20:14–15; 21:20–21; 22:4; 23:7–9; 24:5; 25:13
Jacob, city of	3 Nephi 9:8
Jacobugath, city of	3 Nephi 9:9
Jashon, city/land of	Mormon 2:16–17
Jershon, land of	Alma 27:22–24, 26; 28:1, 8; 30:1, 19–21; 35:6, 13–14; 43:4, 15, 18, 25
Jerusalem, city/land	Alma 21:1–4; 24:1; 3 Nephi 9:7
Jordan, city of	Mormon 5:3
Josh, city of	3 Nephi 9:10
Joshua, land of	Mormon 2:6
Judea, city of	Alma 56:9, 15, 18, 57; 57:11
Laman, city of	3 Nephi 9:10
land northward	Alma 22:32
land southward	Alma 22:32
Lehi, city/land of	Alma 50:15, 25–28, 36; 56:24, 26; 62:30; Helaman 6:10
Lehi–Nephi, city/land of	Mosiah 7:1–4, 21; 9:1–6, 8
Lemuel, city of	Alma 23:12–13
Manti, city/land of	Alma 16:6–7; 17:1; 22:27; 43:22, 24–54; 56:14; 58:26–30; 59:6
Melek, land of	Alma 8:3–4; 35:13; 45:18
Middoni, land of	Alma 20:2–3, 4–7, 14–15, 28–30; 21:12–13, 18; 23:10
Midian, land of	Alma 24:5
Minon, land of	Alma 2:24
Mocum, city of	3 Nephi 9:7
Moriancumer, land of	Ether 2:13
Morianton, city/land of	Alma 50:25, 36; 51:26; 55:33; 59:4–5
Moriantum	Moroni 9:9–10
Mormon, place/waters/forest of	Mosiah 18:4–16, 30–35; 25:18; 26:15; Alma 5:3
Moron, land of	Ether 7:5–6, 17; 14:6, 11
Moroni, city/land of	Alma 50:13; 51:22–24; 59:5; 62:25, 32–34; 3 Nephi 8:9; 9:4
Moronihah, city of	3 Nephi 8:10, 25; 9:5
Mulek, city/land of	Alma 51:26; 52:2, 16–26; 53:2, 6; Helaman 6:10
narrow neck of land	Alma 22:32; 63:5
narrow pass	Alma 50:34; 52:9; Mormon 2:29; 3:5
Nehor, city of	Ether 7:9
Nephi, city of	Mosiah 9:15; 21:1, 12; Alma 23:11; 47:20; 47:31

Chart 150

Nephi, land of	2 Nephi 5:8; Omni 1:12, 27–30; Words of Mormon 1:13; Mosiah 7:6–9; chs. 9–22; 28:1–9; 29:3; Alma 2:24; chs. 17–26; 27:1, 20; 28:8; 47:1, 20; 50:8; 53:6; 58:38; Helaman 4:12; 5:20
Nephihah, city/land/plains of	Alma 50:14; 51:24–26, 59:5–11; 62:14, 18–26, 30
Noah, city/land of	Alma 49:12–15
Ogath	Ether 15:10
Omner, city of	Alma 51:26
Onidah	Alma 47:5
Onidah, hill	Alma 32:4
Onihah, city of	3 Nephi 9:7
Ramah, hill	Ether 15:11
Riplah, hill	Alma 43:31, 35
Ripliancum, waters of	Ether 15:8
Sebus, waters of	Alma 17:26, 34; 18:7; 19:20
Shem, city/land of	Mormon 2:20–21
Shemlon, land of	Mosiah 10:7; 11:12; 19:6; 20:1–5; 24:1; Alma 23:12
Sherrizah	Moroni 9:16–17
Sherrizah, tower of	Moroni 9:7
Shilom, city/land of	Mosiah 7:7, 21; 9:6, 8, 14; 10:8, 20; 11:12–13; 22:8–11; 24:1; Alma 23:12
Shim, hill	Mormon 1:3; 4:23; Ether 9:3
Shimnilom, city of	Alma 23:8, 12
Shurr, valley of	Ether 14:28
Sidom, land of	Alma 15:1, 3, 11, 13–17
Sidon, river	Alma 2:15, 34; 4:4; 22:29
Siron, land of	Alma 39:3
Teancum, city of	Mormon 4:3–8, 14
Zarahemla, city of	Alma 2:26; 5:2; 6:1–7; 7:3–5; 8:1; 31:6; 56:25; 60:1; Helaman 1:18–33; 7:10; 13:12; 3 Nephi 8:8, 24; 9:3; 4 Nephi 1:8
Zarahemla, land of	Omni 1:12–13, 24, 28; Mosiah 1:1, 18; 2:4; 7:9, 13–14; 8:1–8, 14; 9:2; 21:24–26; 22:11–13; 24:25; 25:19–23; 27:35; 29:44; Alma 2:15–25; 4:1; 5:1; 15:18; 16:1; 22:32; 27:5–20; 28:1; 35:14; 59:4; 60:30; 62:6–7; Helaman 3:31; 4:5; 5:16–19; 6:4; 7:1; 13:2; 3 Nephi 3:22–23; Mormon 1:6
Zeezrom, city of	Alma 56:13–14
Zerin, mount	Ether 12:30

Chart 150

Chart 151

Geographical Names
Listed by Scripture Reference

Key Scripture   Alma 22:27–33

Explanation   This five-page chart lists, in scriptural order, the place-names that appear in the Book of Mormon. The names of cities, as well as geographical features or places, are all listed. There are well over a hundred named geographical references in the Book of Mormon. Students interested in moving geographically through the texts of the Book of Mormon may find this chart useful. It moves from place to place in the order in which one encounters these places when reading straight through the book. For further information, please refer to the source below.

Source   John L. Sorenson, *The Geography of Book of Mormon Events: A Source Book* (Provo, Utah: FARMS, 1990).

Geographical Names
Listed by Scripture Reference

2 Nephi 5:8	Nephi, land of	Mosiah 11:12	Shemlon, land of
Omni 1:12	Nephi, land of	Mosiah 11:12–13	Shilom, land of
Omni 1:12–13	Zarahemla, land of	Mosiah 18:4–16	Mormon, place, waters of
Omni 1:24	Zarahemla, land of	Mosiah 18:30–35	Mormon, place, waters of
Onmi 1:27–30	Nephi, land of	Mosiah 19:6	Shemlon, land of
Omni 1:28	Zarahemla, land of	Mosiah 20:1–5	Shemlon, land of
W of M 1:13	Nephi, land of	Mosiah 21:1	Nephi, city of
Mosiah 1:1	Zarahemla, land of	Mosiah 21:12	Nephi, city of
Mosiah 1:18	Zarahemla, land of	Mosiah 21:24–26	Zarahemla, land of
Mosiah 2:4	Zarahemla, land of	Mosiah 22:8–11	Shilom, city and land of
Mosiah 7:1–4	Lehi–Nephi, city and land of	Mosiah 22:11–13	Zarahemla, land of
Mosiah 7:6–9	Nephi, land of	Mosiah 23:3–4	Helam, land of
Mosiah 7:7	Shilom, city and land of	Mosiah 23:19–20	Helam, land of
Mosiah 7:9	Zarahemla, land of	Mosiah 23:25–26	Helam, land and city of
Mosiah 7:13–14	Zarahemla, land of	Mosiah 23:29	Helam, land of
Mosiah 7:21	Shilom, city and land of	Mosiah 23:31	Amulon, land of
Mosiah 7:21	Lehi–Nephi, city of	Mosiah 23:35	Helam, land of
Mosiah 8:1–8	Zarahemla, land of	Mosiah 23:37–39	Helam, land of
Mosiah 8:14	Zarahemla, land of	Mosiah 24:1	Amulon, land of
Mosiah 9:1–6	Lehi–Nephi, city and land of	Mosiah 24:1	Shilom, land of
Mosiah 9:2	Zarahemla, land of	Mosiah 24:1	Shemlon, land of
Mosiah 9:6	Shilom, land of	Mosiah 24:20–21	Alma, valley of
Mosiah 9:8	Shilom, city and land of	Mosiah 24:25	Zarahemla, land of
Mosiah 9:8	Lehi–Nephi, city and land of	Mosiah 25:18	Mormon, place, waters of
Mosiah 9:14	Shilom, land of	Mosiah 25:19–23	Zarahemla, land of
Mosiah 9:15	Nephi, city of	Mosiah 26:15	Mormon, place, waters of
Mosiah 9–22	Nephi, land of	Mosiah 27:16	Helam, land and city of
Mosiah 10:7	Shemlon, land of	Mosiah 27:35	Zarahemla, land of
Mosiah 10:8	Shilom, land of	Mosiah 28:1–9	Nephi, land of
Mosiah 10:20	Shilom, land of	Mosiah 29:3	Nephi, land of

Chart 151

Mosiah 29:44	Zarahemla, land of	Alma 16:9	Ammonihah, city of
Alma 2:15	Amnihu, hill	Alma 16:11	Ammonihah, land of
Alma 2:15	Sidon, river	Alma 17:1	Manti, land of
Alma 2:15–25	Zarahemla, land of	Alma 17:1	Gideon, city, land, valley of
Alma 2:20–26	Gideon, city, land, valley of	Alma 17:19–21	Ishmael, land of
Alma 2:24	Nephi, land of	Alma 17:26, 34	Sebus, waters of
Alma 2:24	Minon, land of	Alma 17–26	Nephi, land of
Alma 2:26	Zarahemla, city of	Alma 18:7	Sebus, waters of
Alma 2:34	Sidon, river	Alma 19:20	Sebus, waters of
Alma 2:37	Hermounts, wilderness of	Alma 20:2–7	Middoni, land of
Alma 4:1	Zarahemla, land of	Alma 20:14–15	Middoni, land of
Alma 4:4	Sidon, river	Alma 20;14–15	Ishmael, land of
Alma 5:1	Zarahemla, land of	Alma 20:28–30	Middoni, land of
Alma 5:2	Zarahemla, city of	Alma 21:1–4	Jerusalem, city and land of
Alma 5:3	Mormon, place, waters of	Alma 21:11	Ani–Anti
Alma 6:1–7	Zarahemla, city of	Alma 21:12–13	Middoni, land of
Alma 6:7–8:1	Gideon, city, land, valley of	Alma 21:18	Middoni, land of
Alma 7:3–5	Zarahemla, city of	Alma 21:20–21	Ishmael, land of
Alma 8:1	Zarahemla, land and city of	Alma 22:4	Ishmael, land of
Alma 8:3–4	Melek, land of	Alma 22:27	Manti, land of
Alma 8:6–13	Ammonihah, city of	Alma 22:29	Sidon, river
Alma 8:13	Aaron, city of	Alma 22:29–33	Bountiful, land
Alma 8:16–18	Ammonihah, city of	Alma 22:32	narrow neck of land
Alma 9–14	Ammonihah, city of	Alma 22:32	land northward
Alma 15:1	Ammonihah, land of	Alma 22:32	land southward
Alma 15:1	Sidom, land of	Alma 22:32	Zarahemla, land of
Alma 15:3	Sidom, land of	Alma 23:7–9	Ishmael, land of
Alma 15:10–11	Sidom, land of	Alma 23:8, 12	Shimnilom, city of
Alma 15:13–17	Sidom, land of	Alma 23:10	Middoni, land of
Alma 15:15	Ammonihah, land of	Alma 23:11	Nephi, city of
Alma 15:18	Zarahemla, land of	Alma 23:12	Shemlon, land of
Alma 16:1	Zarahemla, land of	Alma 23:12	Shilom, land of
Alma 16:2–3	Ammonihah, city of	Alma 23:12–13	Lemuel, city of
Alma 16:6–7	Manti, land of	Alma 24:1	Jerusalem, city and land of

Chart 151

Alma 24:5	Ishmael, land of	Alma 47:5	Onidah
Alma 24:5	Midian, land of	Alma 47:7, 10	Antipas, mount
Alma 25:2	Ammonihah, land of	Alma 47:20	Nephi, city and land of
Alma 25:13	Ishmael, land of	Alma 47:31	Nephi, city of
Alma 27:1	Nephi, land of	Alma 49:3	Ammonihah, city of
Alma 27:5–20	Zarahemla, land of	Alma 49:10–11	Ammonihah, city of
Alma 27:20	Nephi, land of	Alma 49:12–15	Noah, city and land of
Alma 27:22	Bountiful, land of	Alma 50:8	Nephi, land of
Alma 27:22–24	Jershon, land of	Alma 50:11	Bountiful, land
Alma 27:26	Jershon, land of	Alma 50:13	Moroni, city of
Alma 28:1	Jershon, land of	Alma 50:14	Nephihah, city and land of
Alma 28:1	Zarahemla, land of	Alma 50:14	Aaron, city of
Alma 28:8	Jershon, land of	Alma 50:15, 25–28, 36	Lehi, city and land of
Alma 30:1	Jershon, land of	Alma 50:25, 36	Morianton, city and land of
Alma 30:19–21	Jershon, land of	Alma 50:32	Bountiful, land
Alma 30:21	Gideon, city, land, valley of	Alma 50:34	narrow pass
Alma 31:3	Antionum, land of	Alma 50:34	Desolation, land of
Alma 31:6	Zarahemla, city of	Alma 51:22–24	Moroni, city and land of
Alma 32:4	Onidah, hill	Alma 51:24	Lehi, city of
Alma 35:6	Jershon, land of	Alma 51:24–26	Nephihah, city of
Alma 35:13	Melek, land of	Alma 51:26	Gid, city of
Alma 35:13–14	Jershon, land of	Alma 51:26	Morianton, city and land of
Alma 35:14	Zarahemla, land of	Alma 51:26	Mulek, city and land of
Alma 39:3	Siron, land of	Alma 51:26	Omner, city of
Alma 43:5, 22	Antionum, land of	Alma 51:28	Bountiful, land
Alma 43:15	Jershon, land of	Alma 51:30–32	Bountiful, land
Alma 43:18	Jershon, land of	Alma 52:2	Mulek, city of
Alma 43:22	Manti, land of	Alma 52:9	narrow pass
Alma 43:24–25	Manti, land of	Alma 52:9	Bountiful, land
Alma 43:25	Jershon, land of	Alma 52:15	Bountiful, land
Alma 43:26–54	Manti, land of	Alma 52:16–26	Mulek, city and land of
Alma 43:31, 35	Riplah, hill	Alma 52:17–18	Bountiful, city and land
Alma 45:18	Melek, land of	Alma 52:39	Bountiful, land
Alma 47:1	Nephi, land of	Alma 53:2	Mulek, city of

Chart 151

Alma 53:3–4	Bountiful, city and land	Alma 62:30	Lehi, city and land of
Alma 53:6	Nephi, land of	Alma 62:32–34	Moroni, land of
Alma 53:6	Mulek, city of	Alma 63:5	narrow neck of land
Alma 55:7–26	Gid, city of	Alma 63:5	Bountiful, land
Alma 55:26	Bountiful, city	Helaman 1:18–27	Zarahemla, city of
Alma 55:33	Morianton, city and land of	Helaman 1:23	Bountiful, city
Alma 56:9, 15, 18, 57	Judea, city of	Helaman 1:27–33	Zarahemla, city of
Alma 56:13–14	Cumeni, city of	Helaman 1:28	Bountiful, land
Alma 56:13–14	Zeezrom, city of	Helaman 3:31	Zarahemla, land of
Alma 56:14	Manti, land of	Helaman 4:5	Zarahemla, land of
Alma 56:14	Antiparah, city of	Helaman 4:6	Bountiful, land
Alma 56:25	Zarahemla, city of	Helaman 4:12	Nephi, land of
Alma 56:24, 26	Lehi, city and land of	Helaman 5:14	Bountiful, city
Alma 56:31–34	Antiparah, city of	Helaman 5:16–19	Zarahemla, land of
Alma 57:1–4	Antiparah, city of	Helaman 5:20	Nephi, land of
Alma 57:7–8, 12	Cumeni, city of	Helaman 6:4	Zarahemla, land of
Alma 57:11	Judea, city of	Helaman 6:10	Lehi, city and land of
Alma 57: 23, 31, 34	Cumeni, city of	Helaman 6:10	Mulek, land of
Alma 58:26–30	Manti, land of	Helaman 7:1	Zarahemla, land of
Alma 58:38	Nephi, land of	Helaman 13:2	Zarahemla, land of
Alma 59:4	Zarahemla, land of	Helaman 13:12	Zarahemla, city of
Alma 59:4–5	Morianton, city and land of	3 Nephi 3:22–23	Zarahemla, land of
Alma 59:5	Moroni, city and land of	3 Nephi 3:23	Bountiful, land
Alma 59:5–11	Nephihah, city and land of	3 Nephi 8:8	Zarahemla, city of
Alma 59:6	Manti, land of	3 Nephi 8:9	Moroni, city of
Alma 60:1	Zarahemla, city of	3 Nephi 8:10, 25	Moronihah, city of
Alma 60:30	Zarahemla, land of	3 Nephi 8:24	Zarahemla, city of
Alma 61:5	Gideon, land of	3 Nephi 9:3	Zarahemla, city of
Alma 62:3–6	Gideon, land of	3 Nephi 9:4	Moroni, city of
Alma 62:6–7	Zarahemla, land of	3 Nephi 9:5	Moronihah, city of
Alma 62:14	Nephihah, city and land of	3 Nephi 9:6	Gilgal, city and valley of
Alma 62:18–26	Nephihah, city and land of	3 Nephi 9:7	Jerusalem, city and land of
Alma 62:25	Moroni, land of	3 Nephi 9:7	Mocum, city of
Alma 62:30	Nephihah, city and land of	3 Nephi 9:7	Onihah, city of

Chart 151

3 Nephi 9:8	Gadiani, city of	Ether 7:9	Nehor, city of
3 Nephi 9:8	Gadiomnah, city of	Ether 7:17	Moron, land of
3 Nephi 9:8	Gimgimno, city of	Ether 9:3	Ablom
3 Nephi 9:8	Jacob, city of	Ether 9:3	Shim, hill
3 Nephi 9:9	Jacobugath, city of	Ether 12:30	Zerin, mount
3 Nephi 9:10	Gad, city of	Ether 13:27–30	Gilgal, city and valley of
3 Nephi 9:10	Josh, city of	Ether 13:28	Heshlon, plains of
3 Nephi 9:10	Laman, city of	Ether 14:3–4, 14	Akish, wilderness of
3 Nephi 11:1	Bountiful, city and land	Ether 14:6	Moron, land of
4 Nephi 1:8	Zarahemla, city of	Ether 14:11	Moron, land of
Mormon 1:3	Antum, land of	Ether 14:15–16	Agosh
Mormon 1:3	Shim, hill	Ether 14:27–28	Corihor, land and valley of
Mormon 1:6	Zarahemla, land of	Ether 14:28	Comnor, hill
Mormon 2:4	Angola, city of	Ether 14:28	Shurr, valley of
Mormon 2:6	Joshua, land of	Ether 15:8	Ripliancum, waters of
Mormon 2:16–17	Jashon, land and city of	Ether 15:10	Ogath
Mormon 2:20–21	Shem, city and land of	Ether 15:11	Ramah, hill
Mormon 2:29	narrow pass	Moroni 9:7	Sherrizah, tower of
Mormon 3:5	narrow pass	Moroni 9:9–10	Moriantum
Mormon 3:7	Desolation, city of	Moroni 9:16–17	Sherrizah
Mormon 4:2–3	Desolation, city and land of		
Mormon 4:3–8, 14	Teancum, city of		
Mormon 4:8	Desolation, city of		
Mormon 4:13	Desolation, city of		
Mormon 4:19	Desolation, city and land of		
Mormon 4:20–21	Boaz, city of		
Mormon 4:23	Shim, hill		
Mormon 5:3	Jordan, city of		
Mormon 6:2–6	Cumorah, land and hill of		
Mormon 6:11	Cumorah, land and hill of		
Mormon 8:2	Cumorah, land and hill of		
Ether 2:13	Moriancumer, land of		
Ether 7:5–6	Moron, land of		
Ether 7:9	Ephraim, hill		

Chart 151

Chart 152

Journeys Indicating Distances

Key Scriptures Mosiah 7; 9; 18; 22; 24

Explanation Many accounts of journeys are found in the Book of Mormon, and approximate distances can be determined from the details in those accounts. For example, Alma's group traveled approximately twenty-one days from the Waters of Mormon (near the city of Nephi) to Zarahemla (see Mosiah 23:3; 24:25). Since the group consisted of men, women, children, and flocks, the journey was probably a relatively slow one. Basing his calculations on the rates of travel for Mormon pioneers and Guatemalan pig herders, John L. Sorenson concludes that Alma's group most likely traveled about eleven miles a day. If we take into account the twists and turns of the wilderness through which they traveled, the journey was probably around 250 miles (180 miles if they traveled in a straight line, as shown on the map). The distances for the other five journeys listed on this map were determined in a similar fashion, although considerable time must be allowed in Ammon's case for the group's losing its way in the wilderness (see Mosiah 7:4).

Source John L. Sorenson, *An Ancient American Setting for the Book of Mormon* (Salt Lake City: Deseret Book and FARMS, 1985), 8–12.

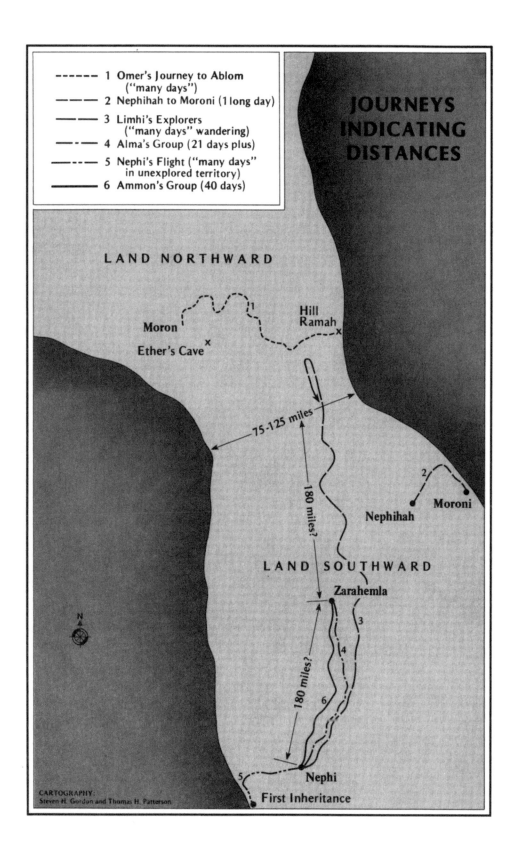

JOURNEYS INDICATING DISTANCES

Legend:

------ 1 Omer's Journey to Ablom ("many days")
— — 2 Nephihah to Moroni (1 long day)
— — 3 Limhi's Explorers ("many days" wandering)
—·— 4 Alma's Group (21 days plus)
—··— 5 Nephi's Flight ("many days" in unexplored territory)
——— 6 Ammon's Group (40 days)

LAND NORTHWARD

Moron
Ether's Cave ×
Hill Ramah ×

75-125 miles

180 miles?

LAND SOUTHWARD

Nephihah
Moroni

Zarahemla

180 miles?

Nephi

First Inheritance

CARTOGRAPHY:
Steven H. Gordon and Thomas H. Patterson

Chart 152

Chart 153

Twelve Journeys between the Cities of Nephi and Zarahemla

Key Scriptures Omni 1; Mosiah 7–8; 24; Alma 17; 27; Helaman 5–6

Explanation This chart lists the twelve recorded journeys between the cities of Nephi and Zarahemla, as well as other pertinent information, such as the dates, purposes, and leaders of the expeditions. The purpose of many of these journeys was to seek safety in another part of the land. Other journeys along this route were made for missionary purposes. Apparently this journey became a common one, and the road became a main thoroughfare, as merchants in 29 B.C. traveled back and forth to sell their wares (see Helaman 6:8).

Twelve Journeys between the Cities of Nephi and Zarahemla

Leader	Reference	Approximate Date	Length of Journey	Direc- tion	Purpose of Journey	Size of Group
Mosiah₁	Omni 1:12	200 B.C.		N	flee Lamanites	all who would hearken to the word of the Lord
"stiffnecked man"	Omni 1:28	195 B.C.		S	reclaim their inheritance	large number
Zeniff?	Omni 1:28	194 B.C.		N	regroup	50 people
Zeniff	Omni 1:29	193 B.C.		S	try again to reclaim their inheritance	considerable number
Limhi	Mosiah 8:7–8	121 B.C.	many days	N	seeking deliverance from bondage	40 people
Ammon	Mosiah 7:1–5	121 B.C.	40 days	S	inquire of their brethren	16 people
Alma the Elder	Mosiah 24	145– 121 B.C.	21 days	N	escape from bondage	205 people with animals
sons of Mosiah	Alma 17	91 B.C.	many days	S	missionary work	4 people
sons of Mosiah	Alma 27:14	77 B.C.		N	flee attackers	many Anti- Nephi-Lehies
Lehi and Nephi	Helaman 5:16	30 B.C.		S	missionary work	2 people
Lehi and Nephi	Helaman 6:7	29 B.C.		N	return home	many people
merchants	Helaman 6:8	29 B.C.		all	to get gain	

Chart 153

Chart 154

Further Details in the Land of Nephi

Key Scripture   Mosiah 7–22

Explanation   This map shows activities in and around the land of Nephi. The city of Nephi was settled by Nephi and his followers when they fled inland many days from the land of their first inheritance around 570 B.C. (see 2 Nephi 5:7). In the second century B.C., the land and city of Nephi (now called the land or city of Lehi-Nephi) was the location of the events reported in Mosiah 7–22. A group of sixteen men, led by Ammon, arrived from Zarahemla, camping at a hill north of the land of Shilom (see Mosiah 7:5). They were taken to King Limhi in the city of Lehi-Nephi, which was then in subjugation to the Lamanite king. Soon Limhi and his people escaped by skirting the land of Shilom (see Mosiah 22:8), not following what would have been the normal path down the valley to Shilom. Earlier, Zeniff had sent spies down to the land of Shemlon, but the Lamanites slipped around to the north side of the land of Shilom and put Zeniff's colony at a distinct disadvantage, which they overcame by trusting in the Lord (see Mosiah 10:8–9, 19–20). This map identifies the Valley of Guatemala as the center of the land of Nephi, which works well in many respects, although any such identification still remains tentative.

Source   John L. Sorenson, *An Ancient American Setting for the Book of Mormon* (Salt Lake City: Deseret Book and FARMS, 1985), 167–75.

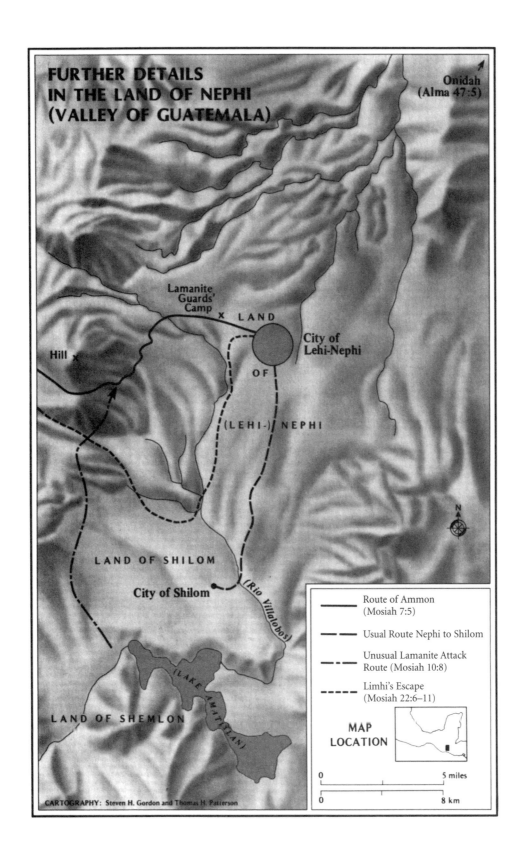

FURTHER DETAILS
IN THE LAND OF NEPHI
(VALLEY OF GUATEMALA)

Onidah
(Alma 47:5)

Lamanite
Guards'
Camp
x LAND

Hill x

City of
Lehi-Nephi

OF

(LEHI-) NEPHI

N

LAND OF SHILOM

City of Shilom

(Rio Villalobos)

(LAKE AMATITLAN)

LAND OF SHEMLON

Route of Ammon
(Mosiah 7:5)

Usual Route Nephi to Shilom

Unusual Lamanite Attack
Route (Mosiah 10:8)

Limhi's Escape
(Mosiah 22:6–11)

MAP
LOCATION

0   5 miles

0   8 km

CARTOGRAPHY: Steven H. Gordon and Thomas H. Patterson

Chart 154

Chart 155

From Nephi to Zarahemla: Alma's Escape

Key Scripture   Mosiah 23–24

Explanation   The flight of Alma and his people, the pursuit of Noah's army, and the flight of Limhi's people are illustrated on this map, which shows a possible location of Helam in relation to the other places mentioned in the Book of Mormon. When Alma was expelled from the court of Noah for pleading with the king to let Abinadi go unpunished (see Mosiah 17:2–3), Alma and his followers went to the Waters of Mormon (see Mosiah 18:7–8). From there they traveled eight days to a place of "pure water" that they named the land of Helam (Mosiah 23:3–4, 19), eventually escaping to Zarahemla through an area they called the valley of Alma (see Mosiah 24:20, 25). Limhi's party apparently went in the same general direction, from the land of Nephi, bending their course, perhaps through the region near the land of Helam, toward Zarahemla (see Mosiah 22:11).

Source   John L. Sorenson, *An Ancient American Setting for the Book of Mormon* (Salt Lake City: Deseret Book and FARMS, 1985), 180–82.

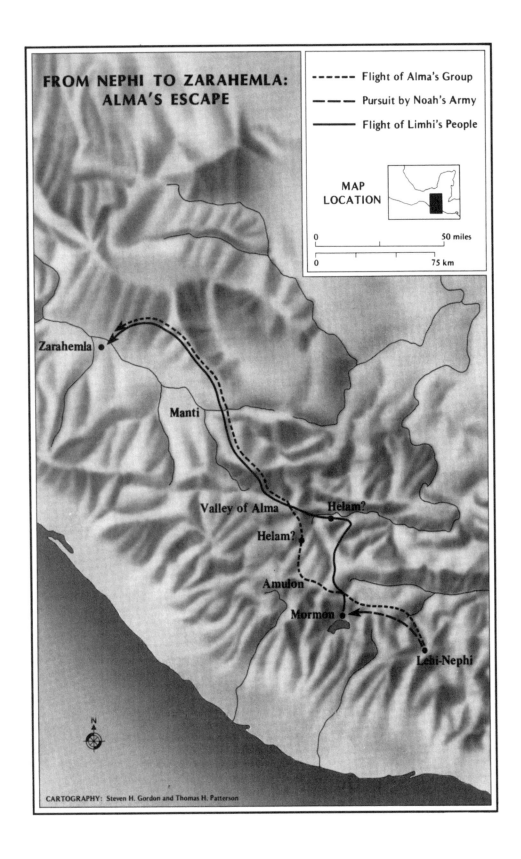

FROM NEPHI TO ZARAHEMLA: ALMA'S ESCAPE

- - - - - Flight of Alma's Group
- — - — Pursuit by Noah's Army
———— Flight of Limhi's People

MAP LOCATION

0   50 miles
0   75 km

Zarahemla

Manti

Valley of Alma   Helam?

Helam?

Amulon

Mormon

Lehi-Nephi

N

CARTOGRAPHY: Steven H. Gordon and Thomas H. Patterson

Chart 155

Chart 156

Proposed Details around Zarahemla

Key Scripture   Alma 2

Explanation   The Nephite war with the Amlicites is graphically illustrated on this map. The Amlicites journeyed southwest near the city of Amnihu and met the Nephites at the Hill Amnihu, across the river Sidon, where they were defeated (see Alma 2:15–18). They retreated past Gideon to the land of Minon and there regrouped and joined forces with the Lamanites, on the road to the land of Nephi, before marching toward Zarahemla (see Alma 2:20, 24). The Nephites, alerted of this attack, cut short their pursuit and returned to protect the city of Zarahemla (see Alma 2:25–26). They met the Amlicites and Lamanites at the ford of the river Sidon and again defeated them after a bloody battle (see Alma 2:27–34). The Nephites pursued the invaders out of the land into the wilderness of Hermounts (see Alma 2:35–38).

The city of Zarahemla, the hub of Nephite government and commerce, is shown here against the topography of the Upper Grijalva Valley. The ancient ruins that correspond best with Zarahemla, called Santa Rosa, are now underwater and cannot be studied in depth; however, what we do know about Santa Rosa is enough to see similarities between it and the city of Zarahemla. Interestingly, Santa Rosa had a dual linguistic and social history, showing that two distinct groups of people most likely lived there. This corresponds with the people of Nephi and the people of Zarahemla under the leadership of Mosiah. Although Santa Rosa cannot be confirmed as Zarahemla, it is an interesting possibility.

Source   John L. Sorenson, *An Ancient American Setting for the Book of Mormon* (Salt Lake City: Deseret Book and FARMS, 1985), 148–61.

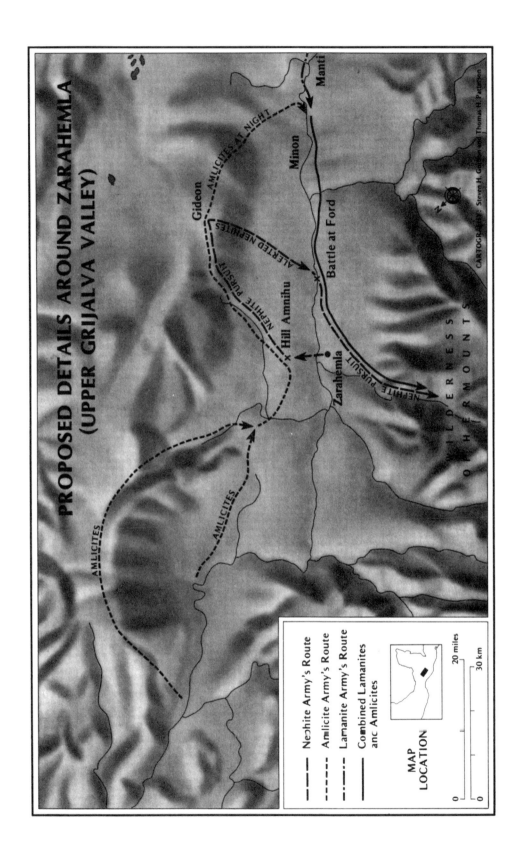

PROPOSED DETAILS AROUND ZARAHEMLA (UPPER GRIJALVA VALLEY)

Manti

AMLICITES AT NIGHT

Minon

Gideon

ALERTED NEPHITES

NEPHITE PURSUIT

Battle at Ford

X Hill Ammihu

Zarahemla

NEPHITE PURSUIT

AMLICITES

AMLICITES

WILDERNESS OF HERMOUNTS

CARTOGRAPHY: Steven H. Golden and Thomas W. Patterson

--- Nephite Army's Route
----- Amlicite Army's Route
---·--- Lamanite Army's Route
——— Combined Lamanites and Amlicites

MAP LOCATION

N

20 miles
30 km

Chart 156

Chart 157

Alma's Journeys in the Land of Zarahemla

Key Scripture   Alma 5–16

Explanation   This map charts out a possible understanding of the travels of Alma the Younger reported in Alma 5–16. He began in Zarahemla by calling the people to repentance in a powerful speech (see Alma 5). The capital city of Zarahemla was located on the river Sidon in the center of the land of Zarahemla. Alma traveled eastward to the city of Gideon (see Alma 6:7), where he preached about the atonement of the coming Christ (see Alma 7). He next had success in the land of Melek, "on the west of the river Sidon, on the west by the borders of the wilderness" (see Alma 8:3), and then traveled three days north to the city of Ammonihah (see Alma 8:6). Rejected, he left Ammonihah but was told to return to that city. There he converted Amulek and his household, preached a major sermon on the holy order of God (see Alma 12–13), yet continued to meet with considerable resistance and imprisonment by the wicked. He and Amulek were eventually delivered from prison, and Ammonihah was destroyed. The city of Noah, not far from Ammonihah (see Alma 49:14–15), may have been on the way to Sidom, where Alma baptized Zeezrom and many others (see Alma 15:1), before returning to Zarahemla.

This map superimposes the travels of Alma on an area in southern Mexico. John Sorenson has proposed geographical locations from Nephite times that may correlate with Alma's journeys. The main purpose of this map, however, is to give only a general idea of the directions and stops in some of Alma's journeys.

Source   John L. Sorenson, *An Ancient American Setting for the Book of Mormon* (Salt Lake City: Deseret Book and FARMS, 1985), 197–207.

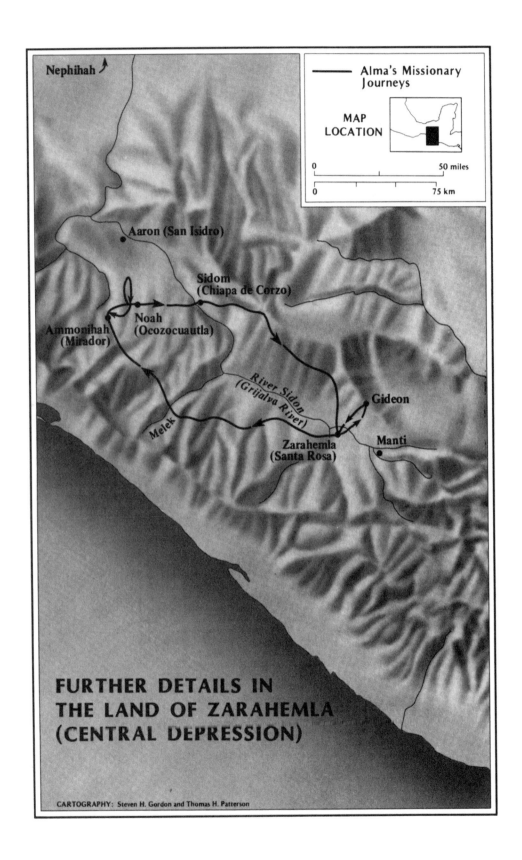

Nephihah

Alma's Missionary
Journeys

MAP
LOCATION

0   50 miles
0   75 km

Aaron (San Isidro)

Sidom
(Chiapa de Corzo)

Noah
(Ocozocuautla)

Ammonihah
(Mirador)

River Sidon
(Grijalva River)

Gideon

Melek

Zarahemla
(Santa Rosa)

Manti

**FURTHER DETAILS IN
THE LAND OF ZARAHEMLA
(CENTRAL DEPRESSION)**

CARTOGRAPHY: Steven H. Gordon and Thomas H. Patterson

Chart 157

Chart 158

From Nephi to Zarahemla:
The Missionary Journeys of Mosiah's Sons

Key Scripture   Alma 17–28

Explanation   During their mission to the Lamanites, Ammon and his brethren journeyed south from Zarahemla to the land of Nephi. Ammon went to the land of Ishmael (see Alma 17:19), where he taught the gospel to King Lamoni and his people. Aaron and his group went to Ani-Anti and down to Middoni (see Alma 21:11–12), where they were cast into prison. Alma and Lamoni later met them in Middoni and delivered them from prison. Later, the people of Ammon journeyed north from Lehi-Nephi to Jershon (see Alma 27:23).

This map places the land of Nephi in highland Guatemala. The place where Ammon and the others separated may be what is now known as Los Encuentros, an ancient meeting point of paths running in four directions (and a highway junction today). The ancient American city of Jerusalem was likely located near some body of water, for Jerusalem was submerged at the time of Christ's crucifixion. Though not proven as of yet, the correlations between certain archaeological ruins and Lamanite cities make this general depiction attractive.

Source   John L. Sorenson, *An Ancient American Setting for the Book of Mormon* (Salt Lake City: Deseret Book and FARMS, 1985), 221–27.

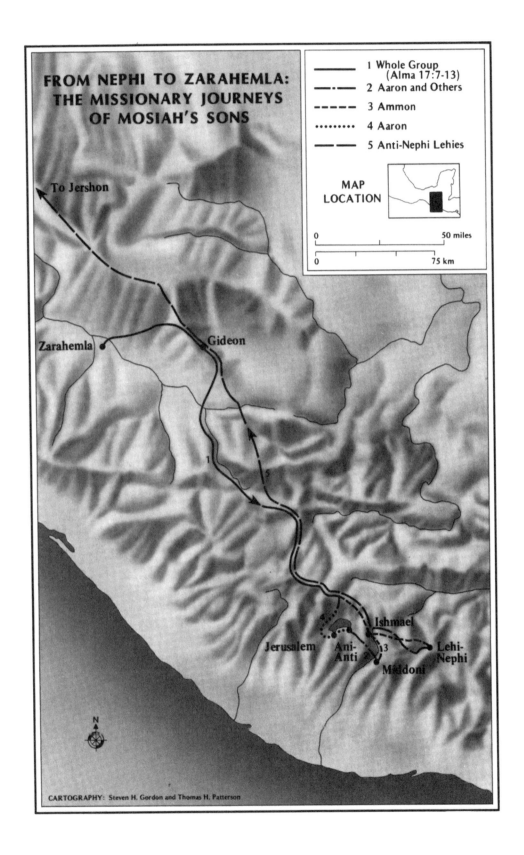

FROM NEPHI TO ZARAHEMLA:
THE MISSIONARY JOURNEYS
OF MOSIAH'S SONS

1 Whole Group
(Alma 17:7-13)
2 Aaron and Others
3 Ammon
4 Aaron
5 Anti-Nephi Lehies

MAP
LOCATION

0   50 miles
0   75 km

To Jershon

Zarahemla   Gideon

Jerusalem   Ani-
             Anti   Ishmael

                    13   Lehi-
                   Maldoni Nephi

N

CARTOGRAPHY: Steven H. Gordon and Thomas H. Patterson

Chart 158

Chart 159

Plausible Locations of the Final Battles

Key Scriptures Mormon 2–6; Ether 9–15

Explanation Though evidence from the Book of Mormon is not conclusive, final battles of the Nephites and the Jaredites probably took place not far north of the narrow neck of land. As shown, the Nephites marched from Angola, through David, and eventually came to the city of Joshua (see Mormon 2:4–6). Nephite defense lines lay in Joshua for fourteen years; finally they collapsed, and Nephites retreated across the narrow neck of land, fleeing to various sites (see Mormon 2:16). The hill Ramah/Cumorah, upon which both the Jaredites and Nephites fought their last battles (see Ether 15:11; Mormon 6:4–6), is shown here on the northwestern edge of the Tuxtla Mountains in Mexico, about ninety miles from a narrow pass (see Mormon 3:5). Other Jaredite locations, including Omer's flight to Ramah (see Ether 9:3), are also shown here. Again, these locations are plausible, but not definite.

Source John L. Sorenson, *An Ancient American Setting for the Book of Mormon* (Salt Lake City: Deseret Book and FARMS, 1985), 335–43.

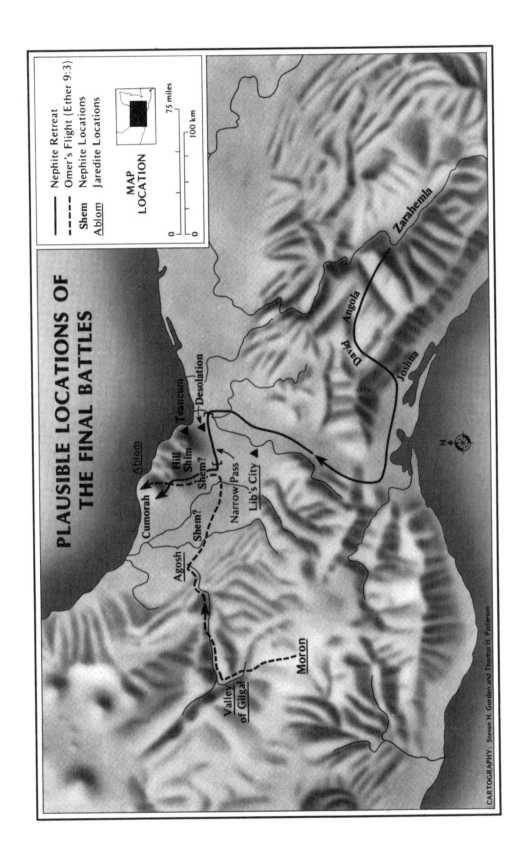

PLAUSIBLE LOCATIONS OF
THE FINAL BATTLES

Nephite Retreat
Omer's Flight (Ether 9:3)
Shem Nephite Locations
Ablom Jaredite Locations

MAP
LOCATION

75 miles
100 km

Zarahemla

Angola

David

Joshua

Desolation

Teancum

Ablom

Hill
Shim

Shem?

Cumorah

Shem?

Narrow Pass

Agosh

Lib's City

Valley
of Gilgal

Moron

CARTOGRAPHY: Steven H. Gordon and Thomas H. Patterson

Chart 159

Chart 160

Plausible Locations in Mesoamerica for Book of Mormon Places

Key Scripture   Alma 22:27–33

Explanation   Many accounts of significant lands and cities are given in the Book of Mormon. The main passage mentions the land of Nephi bordering on the seas, "a narrow strip of wilderness," the land of Zarahemla, and the headwaters of the river Sidon (see Alma 22:27). The land of first inheritance to the west (see Alma 22:28), the land Bountiful to the north, and the land Desolation farther north (see Alma 22:29) are also mentioned. The "land northward" and the "land southward" were divided from each other by a narrow neck of land, whose width was "a day and a half's journey for a Nephite" (see Alma 22:32). Mulek's party first arrived in the land north (see Helaman 6:10) and then moved south into the land of Zarahemla (see Omni 1:16). This map plausibly positions these and other Book of Mormon locations in the general Mesoamerican arena.

Source   John L. Sorenson, *An Ancient American Setting for the Book of Mormon* (Salt Lake City: Deseret Book and FARMS, 1985), 35–37.

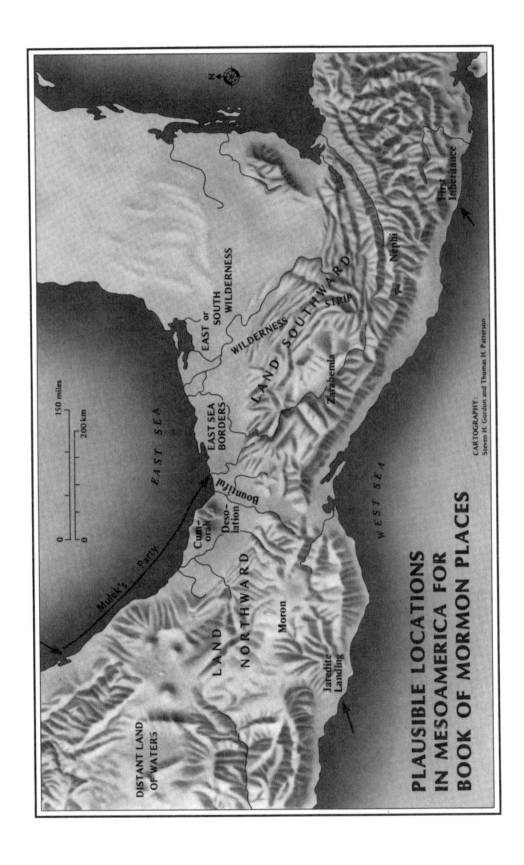

PLAUSIBLE LOCATIONS
IN MESOAMERICA FOR
BOOK OF MORMON PLACES

CARTOGRAPHY:
Steven H. Gordon and Thomas H. Patterson

DISTANT LAND
OF WATERS

LAND
NORTHWARD

Moron

Jaredite
Landing

WEST SEA

Cum-
orah

Deso-
lation

Mulek's
Party

EAST SEA

Bountiful

EAST SEA
BORDERS

WILDERNESS

EAST or
SOUTH
WILDERNESS

LAND SOUTHWARD

STRIP

Zarahemla

Nephi

First
Inheritance

150 miles

200 km

Chart 160

Chart 161

Mesoamerica

Key Scripture Alma 22:27–33

Explanation Archaeological evidence has placed ancient American peoples such as the Olmecs, Teotihuacans, Zapotecs, Mayans, and Chiapas in various general locations in Mesoamerica. The Olmecs are thought to have been contemporaries with the Jaredites, while the Chiapas may possibly have been associated with some of the Nephite peoples. Teotihuacan and Zapotec cultures are seen by John L. Sorenson as survivors or splinter groups of the Jaredite civilization. The Teotihuacans are thought to have been in the land northward where some Nephites resettled about 50 B.C. (see Helaman 3:11), and others in that region may have allied themselves culturally and possibly militarily with the Lamanites near the end of Nephite times.

Source John L. Sorenson, *An Ancient American Setting for the Book of Mormon* (Salt Lake City: Deseret Book and FARMS, 1985), inside front cover.

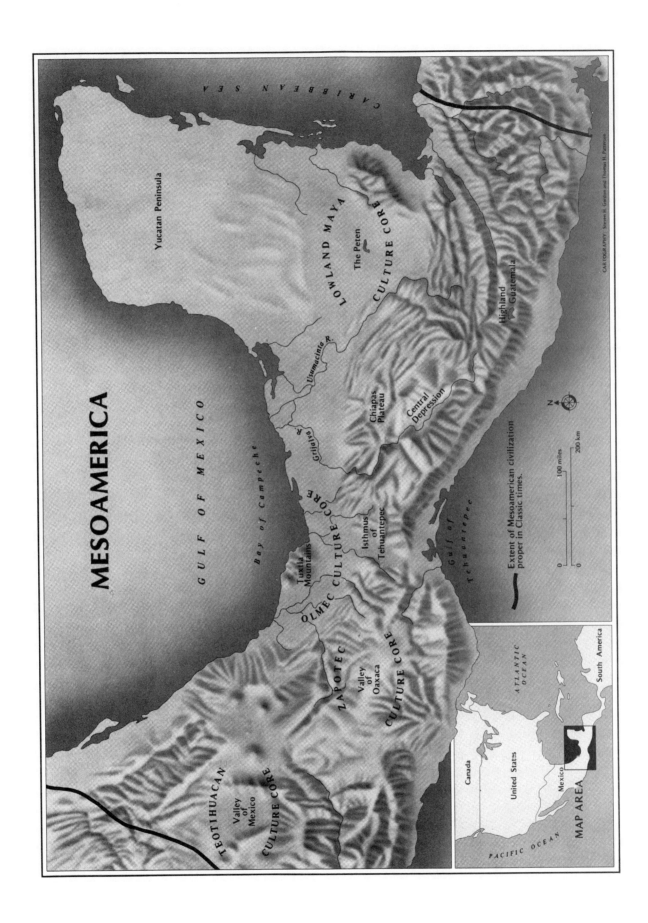

MESOAMERICA

CARIBBEAN SEA

Yucatan Peninsula

GULF OF MEXICO

Bay of Campeche

LOWLAND MAYA

The Peten

CULTURE CORE

Highland
Guatemala

Usumacinta R.

Grijalva R.

Chiapas
Plateau

Central
Depression

Tuxtla
Mountains

OLMEC CULTURE CORE

Isthmus
of
Tehuantepec

Gulf
of
Tehuantepec

ZAPOTEC

Valley
of
Oaxaca

CULTURE CORE

TEOTIHUACAN

Valley
of
Mexico

CULTURE CORE

N

200 km

100 miles

Extent of Mesoamerican civilization
proper in Classic times.

CARTOGRAPHY Steven H. Gardine and Thomas H. Patterson

ATLANTIC
OCEAN

Canada

United States

Mexico

South America

MAP AREA

PACIFIC OCEAN

Chart 161

Chart 162

Archaeological Sites
in Mesoamerica

Key Scripture   Alma 22:27–33

Explanation   Shown here are various archaeological sites in Mesoamerica that may
correspond to Book of Mormon places. Tres Zapotes is close to
where the final Jaredite and Nephite battles are believed to have been
fought. Mirador and Ammonihah/Angola correlate culturally and
chronologically, as do Santa Rosa and Zarahemla. Kaminaljuyu, near
Guatemala city, was occupied at the time of the ancient city of Nephi.
Though definitive answers about Book of Mormon locations cannot
be directly confirmed, some correlations are vivid and significant.

Source   John L. Sorenson, *An Ancient American Setting for the Book of
Mormon* (Salt Lake City: Deseret Book and FARMS, 1985), inside
back cover.

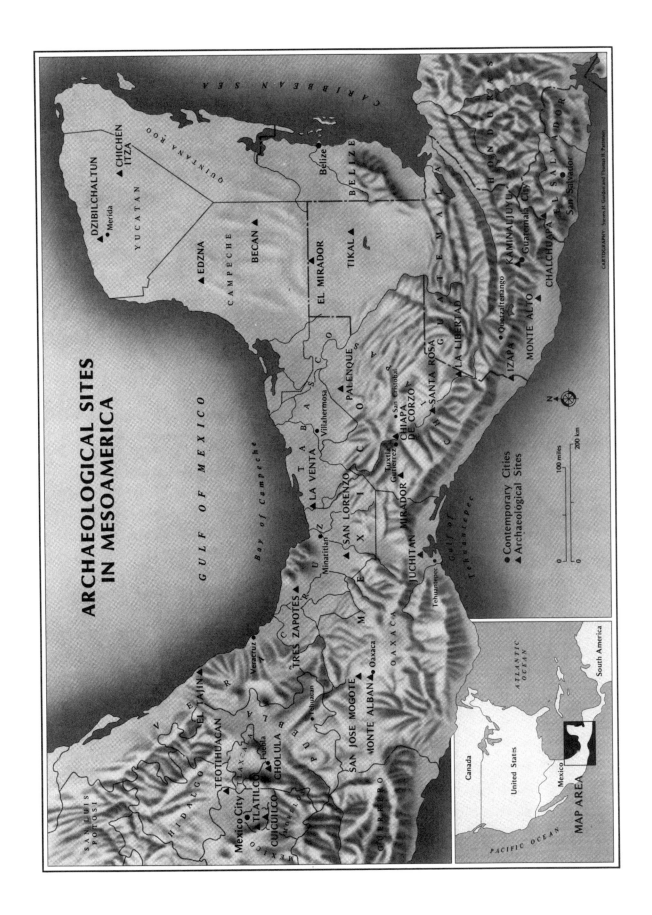

ARCHAEOLOGICAL SITES
IN MESOAMERICA

CARTOGRAPHY: Steven H. Gordon and Thomas H. Patterson

Legend:
- ● Contemporary Cities
- ▲ Archaeological Sites

100 miles
200 km

Labeled features on map:

CARIBBEAN SEA

GULF OF MEXICO

Bay of Campeche

Gulf of Tehuantepec

PACIFIC OCEAN

ATLANTIC OCEAN

QUINTANA ROO

YUCATAN
- ▲ DZIBILCHALTUN
- ● Merida
- ▲ CHICHEN ITZA

CAMPECHE
- ▲ EDZNA
- ▲ BECAN

BELIZE
- ● Belize

- ▲ EL MIRADOR
- ▲ TIKAL

GUATEMALA
- ▲ KAMINALJUYU
- ● Guatemala City
- ● Quezaltenango
- ▲ CHALCHUAPA
- ▲ MONTE ALTO
- ▲ IZAPA

HONDURAS

EL SALVADOR
- ● San Salvador

LA LIBERTAD

SANTA ROSA

TABASCO
- ▲ PALENQUE
- ● Villahermosa

CHIAPAS
- ● San Cristóbal
- ▲ CHIAPA DE CORZO
- ● Tuxtla Gutiérrez

LA VENTA ▲

VERACRUZ
- ● Minatitlán
- ▲ SAN LORENZO
- ▲ MIRADOR
- ▲ JUCHITAN
- ● Tehuantepec
- ● Veracruz
- ▲ TRES ZAPOTES
- ▲ EL TAJIN

OAXACA
- ▲ SAN JOSE MOGOTE
- ▲ MONTE ALBAN
- ● Oaxaca

GUERRERO

PUEBLA
- ● Puebla
- ▲ CHOLULA

TLAXCALA
- ▲ TEOTIHUACAN
- ● Tehuacan

MEXICO
- ● Mexico City
- ▲ TLATILCO
- ▲ CUICUILCO

MORELOS

HIDALGO

SAN LUIS POTOSI

Inset map (MAP AREA):
- Canada
- United States
- Mexico
- South America
- ATLANTIC OCEAN
- PACIFIC OCEAN

Chart 162

Metals in the Book of Mormon

Key Scripture   Ether 10:23

Explanation   Many Book of Mormon texts mention various metals. This chart lists the types of metal that the Nephites, Lamanites, and/or Jaredites knew from their scriptures or found in the Americas. These references are grouped according to the use of the metal in each case. Brass (especially in connection with the plates of brass) is mentioned most often in religious contexts, while gold and silver (often mentioned together) were used largely in commerce or for ornamentation.

Sources   Andrew Holdaway, student of John W. Welch, Book of Mormon 121H, Brigham Young University, fall 1997. See also John L. Sorenson, "Metals and Metallurgy Relating to the Book of Mormon Text" (FARMS, 1992).

Metals in the Book of Mormon

Use	General Reference	Weapons	Religious Artifacts	Currency or Property	Ornamentation or Riches
Gold and Silver	1 Nephi 18:25; 2 Nephi 5:15; 12:7; 23:17; Jacob 1:16; 2:12; Helaman 6:11; 3 Nephi 24:3; Ether 10:23		2 Nephi 12:20; Helaman 6:31	1 Nephi 2:4,11; 3:16, 22, 24; Jarom 1:8; Mosiah 2:12; 4:19; 11:3; 19:15; 22:12; Alma 4:6; 11:3–19; 15:16; Helaman 6:9; 12:2; 3 Nephi 6:2; 4 Nephi 1:46; Ether 9:17	1 Nephi 13:7–8; Mosiah 11:8–9, 11; Alma 1:29; 17:14; 31:24, 28; Helaman 7:21; 13:28; 3 Nephi 27:32; Ether 10:12
Gold	2 Nephi 23:12	1 Nephi 4:9	Mosiah 8:9; 28:11		Mosiah 11:11; Alma 31:28; Ether 10:7
Silver				Alma 11:22	
Iron	2 Nephi 5:15; 20:34; 3 Nephi 20:19; Ether 10:23	Jarom 1:8	1 Nephi 8:19–20, 24, 30; 11:25; 13:5; 15:23	Mosiah 11:3	1 Nephi 20:4; Mosiah 11:8
Brass	3 Nephi 20:19; Ether 10:23	Jarom 1:8; Mosiah 8:10	1 Nephi 3:3, 12, 24; 4:16, 24, 38; 5:10, 14, 18–19; 13:23; 16:10; 19:21–22; 22:1, 30; 2 Nephi 4:2, 15; 5:12, 15; Omni 1:14; Mosiah 1:3, 16; 10:16; 28:11, 20; Alma 37:3; 3 Nephi 1:2; 10:17	Mosiah 11:3	1 Nephi 20:4; Mosiah 11:8, 10
Steel	2 Nephi 5:15	1 Nephi 4:9; 16:18; Ether 7.9, Jarom 1.8			
Copper	1 Nephi 18:25; 2 Nephi 5:15; Ether 10:23	Jarom 1:8; Mosiah 8:10		Mosiah 11:3	
Ziff				Mosiah 11:3	Mosiah 11:8

Chart 163

Chart 164

The Colors of the Scriptures

Key Scripture   1 Nephi 8:11

Explanation   This chart compares the number of times a particular color is referred to in each of the standard works. References to particular colors are most similar between the Old Testament and the Book of Mormon, indirectly tying the Book of Mormon in yet another way to the physical world and culture of the Old Testament. The use of specific colors during ceremonies and rituals under the law of Moses could be one reason for this positive correlation.

Source   Work of a student of John W. Welch, Book of Mormon 121H, Brigham Young University, fall 1997.

The Colors of the Scriptures

Color	OT	NT	BM	D&C	PGP	Total	Notes or Variant Endings
Black	15	3	2	1	1	22	
Black-	6	2	2	4	1	15	-ening, -er, -est, -ish, ness, -ed
Brown	4					4	All refer to conflict between Jacob and Laban
Red	46	6	13	3		68	
Red-	7					7	-dish (Levitical), -ness
Scarlet	46	6				52	Mostly with reference to cloth, priesthood
Scarlets			2			2	Used with reference to cloth
Crimson	5					5	
Yellow	4					4	Mostly Levitical
Green	37	4		1	1	43	Often linked with vegetation
Green-	3					3	-ish (Levitical), -ness
Blue	49					49	Mostly used with reference to cloth, priesthood, temple
Blue-	1					1	-ness (medical, a bruise)
Purple	39	9				48	Mostly cloth, priesthood, temple, kings; once the sea
Gray/Grey	6		1			7	
Gray/Grey-	4					4	-headed, -hound
White	40	26	24	12	2	104	
White-	2	2	4	1	1	10	-ed, -ness, -er
Gold	336	25	55	6	4	426	As a metal
Gold-	48	13	2	1		64	-en
Silver	264	18	47	4	2	335	
Copper	1		8	1		10	
Brass	107	6	37	4	2	156	
Iron	83	7	15	3	1	109	
Amber	3			1		4	D&C 11:2 reads "in color like amber"
Emerald(s)	4	2				6	
Rubies	6					6	
Sapphire(s)	11	1	1			13	
Blood	282	93	135	39	10	559	As in "moon became as blood" (Revelation 6:12)
Bloody	15	1	1			17	

Chart 164

The First Edition

of the Book of Mormon

Charts 165–70

Chart 165

The Original Book of Mormon Title Page

Explanation This photocopy of the title page of the original 1830 edition of the Book of Mormon gives modern readers an idea of how the book first appeared when it was published in Palmyra, New York. The first title page differs from the title page of the current (1981) edition, the most obvious difference being that Joseph Smith is listed as the "author and proprietor" of the Book of Mormon. As the copyright page explains (see chart 167), he named himself the "author and proprietor" consistent with federal law only to secure a copyright for the Book of Mormon, thus making illegal any alteration of text by those who do not hold the copyright.

Sources Joseph Smith Jr., title page of the Book of Mormon, 1830 edition (Palmyra, N.Y.: E. B. Grandin, 1830); and Miriam A. Smith and John W. Welch, "Joseph Smith: Author and Proprietor," in *Reexploring the Book of Mormon,* ed. John W. Welch (Salt Lake City: Deseret Book and FARMS, 1992), 154–57.

THE

BOOK OF MORMON:

AN ACCOUNT WRITTEN BY THE HAND OF MORMON, UPON PLATES TAKEN FROM THE PLATES OF NEPHI.

Wherefore it is an abridgment of the Record of the People of Nephi; and also of the Lamanites; written to the Lamanites, which are a remnant of the House of Israel; and also to Jew and Gentile; written by way of commandment, and also by the spirit of Prophesy and of Revelation. Written, and sealed up, and hid up unto the LORD, that they might not be destroyed; to come forth by the gift and power of GOD unto the interpretation thereof; sealed by the hand of Moroni, and hid up unto the LORD, to come forth in due time by the way of Gentile; the interpretation thereof by the gift of GOD; an abridgment taken from the Book of Ether.

Also, which is a Record of the People of Jared, which were scattered at the time the LORD confounded the language of the people when they were building a tower to get to Heaven; which is to shew unto the remnant of the House of Israel how great things the LORD hath done for their fathers; and that they may know the covenants of the LORD, that they are not cast off forever; and also to the convincing of the Jew and Gentile that JESUS is the CHRIST, the ETERNAL GOD, manifesting Himself unto all nations. And now if there be fault, it be the mistake of men; wherefore condemn not the things of GOD, that ye may be found spotless at the judgment seat of CHRIST.

BY JOSEPH SMITH, JUNIOR,
AUTHOR AND PROPRIETOR.

PALMYRA:
PRINTED BY E. B. GRANDIN, FOR THE AUTHOR.

1830.

Chart 165

Chart 166

Preface to the Book of Mormon

Explanation Written by the Prophet Joseph Smith, the preface to the 1830 edition of the Book of Mormon is not included in the current edition, for the preface already served its purpose. At the time he wrote it, Joseph needed to explain the 116 lost manuscript pages and why the book of Lehi was not retranslated. This preface also served to dissuade enemies of the Book of Mormon from their evil designs. Most important, the preface contains Joseph Smith's personal attestation that he translated the book "by the gift and power of God."

Source Joseph Smith Jr., preface to the Book of Mormon, 1830 edition (Palmyra, N.Y.: E. B. Grandin, 1830).

PREFACE.

To the Reader—

As many false reports have been circulated respecting the following work, and also many unlawful measures taken by evil designing persons to destroy me, and also the work, I would inform you that I translated, by the gift and power of God, and caused to be written, one hundred and sixteen pages, the which I took from the Book of Lehi, which was an account abridged from the plates of Lehi, by the hand of Mormon; which said account, some person or persons have stolen and kept from me, notwithstanding my utmost exertions to recover it again—and being commanded of the Lord that I should not translate the same over again, for Satan had put it into their hearts to tempt the Lord their God, by altering the words, that they did read contrary from that which I translated and caused to be written; and if I should bring forth the same words again, or, in other words, if I should translate the same over again, they would publish that which they had stolen, and Satan would stir up the hearts of this generation, that they might not receive this work: but behold, the Lord said unto me, I will not suffer that Satan shall accomplish his evil design in this thing : therefore thou shalt translate from the plates of Nephi, until ye come to that which ye have translated, which ye have retained; and

1*

behold ye shall publish it as the record of Nephi; and thus I will confound those who have altered my words. I will not suffer that they shall destroy my work; yea, I will shew unto them that my wisdom is greater than the cunning of the Devil. Wherefore, to be obedient unto the commandments of God, I have, through his grace and mercy, accomplished that which he hath commanded me respecting this thing. I would also inform you that the plates of which hath been spoken, were found in the township of Manchester, Ontario county, New-York.

The Author.

Chart 166

Chart 167

Copyright Page of the Book of Mormon

Explanation   This chart shows the copyright page of the 1830 edition of the
Book of Mormon. It is of historical interest and is not included in
the 1981 edition. As this photocopy shows, the copyright was
secured on 11 June 1829. The copyright application used the language of the title page as the book's description. At the bottom of
this page, the text of the federal copyright statute appears, author-
izing "authors and proprietors" to secure copyrights for books. To
protect the integrity of this sacred scripture, the Prophet Joseph
Smith took all available steps to ensure its safety.

Source   Joseph Smith Jr., copyright page of the Book of Mormon, 1830
edition (Palmyra, N.Y.: E. B. Grandin, 1830).

Northern District of New-York, to wit: **B**E IT REMEMBERED, That on the eleventh day of June, in the fifty-third year of the Independence of the United States of America, A. D. 1829, Joseph Smith, Jun. of the said District, hath deposited in this office the title of a Book, the right whereof he claims as author, in the words following, to wit: "The Book of Mormon: an account written by the hand of Mormon, upon plates taken from the plates of Nephi. Wherefore it is an abridgment of the Record of the People of Nephi; and also of the Lamanites; written to the Lamanites, who are a remnant of the House of Israel; and also to Jew and Gentile; written by way of commandment, and also by the spirit of Prophesy and of Revelation. Written, and sealed up, and hid up unto the Lord, that they might not be destroyed; to come forth by the gift and power of God, unto the interpretation thereof; sealed by the hand of Moroni, and hid up unto the Lord, to come forth in due time by the way of Gentile; the interpretation thereof by the gift of God; an abridgment taken from the Book of Ether. Also, which is a Record of the People of Jared, which were scattered at the time the Lord confounded the language of the people when they were building a tower to get to Heaven: which is to shew unto the remnant of the House of Israel, how great things the Lord hath done for their fathers; and that they may know the covenants of the Lord, that they are not cast off forever: and also to the convincing of the Jew and Gentile, that Jesus is the Christ, the Eternal God, manifesting Himself unto all nations. And now if there be fault, it be the mistake of men; wherefore condemn not the things of God, that ye may be found spotless at the judgment seat of Christ.—By Joseph Smith, Jun. Author and Proprietor."

In conformity to the act of the Congress of the United States, entitled, "An act for the encouragement of learning, by securing the copies of Maps, Charts, and Books, to the authors and proprietors of such copies, during the times therein mentioned;" and also the act, entitled, "An act supplementary to an act, entitled, 'An act for the encouragement of learning, by securing the copies of Maps, Charts, and Books, to the authors and proprietors of such copies, during the times therein mentioned, and extending the benefits thereof to the arts of designing, engraving, and etching historical and other prints." R. R. LANSING,
Clerk of the Northern District of New-York.

Chart 167

Testimony of the Three Witnesses

Explanation The Testimony of Three Witnesses in the 1830 edition of the Book of Mormon was originally included at the end of the book, as a final seal of its veracity. These witnesses—Oliver Cowdery, David Whitmer, and Martin Harris—testified that they had heard God's voice declare that the book had been translated by the gift and power of God, and also that they had seen the engravings on the plates, shown to them by an angel of God. Ancient documents often needed the signatures of witnesses in order to be considered authentic or legally binding. By providing the testimonies of witnesses and including them at the end of the Book of Mormon, Joseph Smith was following not only the ancient pattern called for by Nephi, but also the guidance and inspiration of the Lord.

Source Joseph Smith Jr., appendix to the Book of Mormon, 1830 edition (N.Y.: E. B. Grandin, 1830).

THE TESTIMONY OF THREE WITNESSES.

BE it known unto all nations, kindreds, tongues, and people, unto whom this work shall come, that we, through the grace of God the Father, and our Lord Jesus Christ, have seen the plates which contain this record, which is a record of the people of Nephi, and also of the Lamanites, his brethren, and also of the people of Jared, which came from the tower of which hath been spoken; and we also know that they have been translated by the gift and power of God, for his voice hath declared it unto us; wherefore we know of a surety, that the work is true. And we also testify that we have seen the engravings which are upon the plates; and they have been shewn unto us by the power of God, and not of man. And we declare with words of soberness, that an Angel of God came down from heaven, and he brought and laid before our eyes, that we beheld and saw the plates, and the engravings thereon; and we know that it is by the grace of God the Father, and our Lord Jesus Christ, that we beheld and bear record that these things are true; and it is marvellous in our eyes: Nevertheless, the voice of the Lord commanded us that we should bear record of it; wherefore, to be obedient unto the commandments of God, we bear testimony of these things.— And we know that if we are faithful in Christ, we shall rid our garments of the blood of all men, and be found spotless before the judgement seat of Christ, and shall dwell with him eternally in the heavens. And the honor be to the Father, and to the Son, and to the Holy Ghost, which is one God. Amen.

OLIVER COWDERY,
DAVID WHITMER,
MARTIN HARRIS.

Chart 168

Chart 169

Testimony of the Eight Witnesses

Explanation This chart is a photocopy of the first printed Testimony of the Eight Witnesses. The punctuation and spelling are slightly different from that of the 1981 edition, although the words themselves remain unchanged. As was true for the Testimony of Three Witnesses, these names were included at the end of the Book of Mormon to place this seal of testimony upon the published record. The Eight Witnesses were shown the plates by Joseph Smith. They handled the plates and saw the engravings. Despite hardships and difficulties, the Book of Mormon witnesses remained true to their testimonies of this book throughout their lives.

Source Joseph Smith Jr., appendix to the Book of Mormon, 1830 edition (Palmyra, N.Y.: E. B. Grandin, 1830).

AND ALSO THE TESTIMONY OF EIGHT WITNESSES.

Be it known unto all nations, kindreds, tongues, and people, unto whom this work shall come, that Joseph Smith, Jr. the Author and Proprietor of this work, has shewn unto us the plates of which hath been spoken, which have the appearance of gold; and as many of the leaves as the said Smith has translated, we did handle with our hands; and we also saw the engravings thereon, all of which has the appearance of ancient work, and of curious workmanship. And this we bear record, with words of soberness, that the said Smith has shewn unto us, for we have seen and hefted, and know of a surety, that the said Smith has got the plates of which we have spoken. And we give our names unto the world, to witness unto the world that which we have seen: and we lie not, God bearing witness of it.

CHRISTIAN WHITMER,
JACOB WHITMER,
PETER WHITMER, Jr.
JOHN WHITMER,
HIRAM PAGE,
JOSEPH SMITH, Sen.
HYRUM SMITH,
SAMUEL H. SMITH.

Chart 169

Chart 170

Comparison of Chapter Divisions: 1830 and 1981 Editions

Explanation   The differences in the chapter divisions between the first edition of the Book of Mormon and the 1981 edition are listed in this three-page chart. Chapters in the 1830 edition were longer, in part because the Book of Mormon was printed in narrative rather than verse form—what we would expect from a historical record. The text was first arranged into its present verses in the 1879 edition to facilitate the location of particular passages. Modern readers may be interested to see how the sections of the Book of Mormon were divided in the 1830 edition, which are divided along broad conceptual lines. For example, all of Jacob's speech in Jacob 2–3 and all of Alma's blessing to his son Corianton in Alma 39–42 were single chapters.

Comparison of Chapter Divisions
1830 and 1981 Editions

1830 Edition Chapters	Pages	1981 Edition Chapters	Pages
FIRST NEPHI			
I	5–16	1–5	1–11
II	16–21	6–9	11–17
III	21–35	10–14	17–30
IV	35–38	15	30–33
V	38–52	16:1–19:21	33–46
VI	52–56	19:22–21:26	46–50
VII	56–59	22	50–53
SECOND NEPHI			
I	59–66	1–2	53–60
II	66–68	3	60–62
III	68–71	4	62–65
IV	71–73	5	65–67
V	74–78	6–8	67–72
VI	78–83	9	72–77
VII	83–85	10	78–80
VIII	86–91	11–15	80–86
IX	91–99	16–22	86–93
X	99–102	23–24	94–96
XI	102–112	25–27	96–106
XII	112–118	28–30	106–112
XIII	118–120	31	112–115
XIV	120–121	32	115–116
XV	121–122	33	116–117
JACOB			
I	123–124	1	117–119
II	124–129	2–3	119–123
III	129–139	4–5	123–132
IV	139–140	6	132–133
V	140–143	7	133–135

Chart 170

1830 Edition		1981 Edition	
Chapters	**Pages**	**Chapters**	**Pages**
ENOS			
I	143–145	1	136–138
JAROM			
I	146–147	1	138–140
OMNI			
I	148–151	1	140–143
WORDS OF MORMON			
I	151–153	1	143–145
MOSIAH			
I	153–162	1–3	145–154
II	162–165	4	154–157
III	166–167	5	157–159
IV	167–168	6	159
V	168–173	7–8	159–164
VI	173–177	9–10	164–167
VII	177–184	11:1–13:24	167–173
VIII	184–189	13:25–16:15	173–179
IX	190–201	17–21	179–189
X	201–202	22	189–190
XI	202–215	23–27	190–202
XII	215–216	28:1–19	202–203
XIII	217–221	28:20–29:47	203–207
ALMA			
I	221–230	1–3	207–215
II	230–232	4	215–217
III	232–238	5	217–223
IV	238–239	6	223
V	239–242	7	223–226
VI	242–245	8	226–228
VII	245–248	9	228–231

Chart 170

1830 Edition		1981 Edition	
Chapters	**Pages**	**Chapters**	**Pages**
VIII	248–254	10–11	231–237
IX	254–259	12:1–13:9	237–242
X	259–266	13:10–15:19	242–248
XI	266–268	16	248–250
XII	269–282	17–20	250–261
XIII	282–289	21–22	261–266
XIV	289–299	23–26	266–275
XV	299–304	27–29	275–280
XVI	304–323	30–35	280–297
XVII	323–330	36–37	297–304
XVIII	330–332	38	304–305
XIX	332–340	39–42	305–313
XX	340–347	43–44	313–320
XXI	348–362	45–49	320–332
XXII	362–366	50	333–336
XXIII	366–370	51	336–339
XXIV	370–377	52–53	339–344
XXV	377–381	54–55	344–348
XXVI	382–393	56–58	348–357
XXVII	393–398	59–60	357–361
XXVIII	398–400	61	361–362
XXIX	400–405	62	363–366
XXX	405–407	63	366–368

HELAMAN

1830 Edition		1981 Edition	
I	407–411	1–2	368–372
II	412–426	3–6	372–384
III	426–436	7–10	384–392
IV	436–441	11–12	392–397
V	441–451	13–16	397–406

THIRD NEPHI

1830 Edition		1981 Edition	
I	452–456	1–2	406–410
II	457–465	3–5	410–417
III	465–470	6–7	417–422

Chart 170

1830 Edition		1981 Edition	
Chapters	**Pages**	**Chapters**	**Pages**
IV	470–476	8–10	422–427
V	476–483	11–13:24	427–434
VI	483–485	13:25–14:27	434–435
VII	485–488	15–16	435–440
VIII	488–493	17–18	440–444
IX	493–500	19:1–21:21	444–452
X	501–503	21:22–23:13	452–454
XI	503–505	23:14–26:5	454–457
XII	506–508	26:6–27:22	457–460
XIII	509–513	27:23–29:9	460–464
XIV	513–514	30	464

Fourth Nephi

I	514–518	1	465–468

Mormon

I	518–524	1–3	469–474
II	524–528	4–5	474–478
III	529–531	6–7	478–481
IV	531–538	8–9	481–487

Ether

I	538–547	1–4	487–496
II	547–548	5	496
II	548–555	6–8	496–502
IV	555–562	9–11	502–508
V	562–566	12	508–512
VI	566–573	13–15	512–518

Moroni

I	574	1	518
II	574	2	518–519
III	575	3	519
IV	575	4	519
V	575–576	5	519–520
VI	576	6	520
VII	577–580	7	521–525
VIII	581–583	8	525–527
IX	583–585	9	527–529
X	585–588	10	529–531

Chart 170

Invitations

of the Book of Mormon

Invitations

Key Scriptures 2 Nephi 26:33; 33:10; Mosiah 4:10; 3 Nephi 27:20; Moroni 7:13; 10:4, 32

Explanation The Book of Mormon is a very inviting book. The following charts present only a few of the verses in the Book of Mormon that invite all people everywhere to come unto Christ (see 2 Nephi 26:33), to believe in him and his words (see 2 Nephi 33:10), to forsake sin and be forgiven by the Lord Omnipotent (see Mosiah 4:10), to become sanctified and spotless before God (see 3 Nephi 27:20), to do good and to love God and serve him (see Moroni 7:13), to ask God for a witness of the truthfulness of the Book of Mormon (see Moroni 10:4), and to become perfected in him (see Moroni 10:32). These heartfelt invitations, universally extended by Nephi, Benjamin, Mormon, Moroni, and Jesus Christ himself, consistently greet all people with open arms, inviting them to come and partake of the fulness of God's joy. Through invitations such as these, readers everywhere feel included in God's saving love. They accept these invitations in faith by forsaking their sins, being baptized, and going forth to do good under the Lord's inspired direction.

[The Lord] doeth nothing save it be plain unto the children of men; and he inviteth them all to come unto him and partake of his goodness; and he denieth none that come unto him, black and white, bond and free, male and female; and he remembereth the heathen; and all are alike unto God, both Jew and Gentile.

—2 Nephi 26:33

Chart 171

Hearken unto these words and believe in Christ; and if ye believe not in these words believe in Christ. And if ye shall believe in Christ ye will believe in these words, for they are the words of Christ.

—2 Nephi 33:10

Chart 172

Believe in God; believe that he is, and that he created all things, both in heaven and in earth; believe that he has all wisdom, and all power, both in heaven and in earth; believe that man doth not comprehend all the things which the Lord can comprehend. And again, believe that ye must repent of your sins and forsake them, and humble yourselves before God; and ask in sincerity of heart that he would forgive you; and now, if you believe all these things see that ye do them.

—Mosiah 4:9–10

Chart 173

Repent, all ye ends of the earth, and come unto me and be baptized in my name, that ye may be sanctified by the reception of the Holy Ghost, that ye may stand spotless before me at the last day.

—3 Nephi 27:20

Chart 174

Behold, that which is of God inviteth and enticeth to do good continually; wherefore, every thing which inviteth and enticeth to do good, and to love God, and to serve him, is inspired of God.

—Moroni 7:13

Chart 175

Chart 176

Moroni's Promise

Key Scripture   Moroni 10:4

Explanation   Moroni was the last to write on the plates of Mormon. He sealed the record with his testimony and called upon God as his primary witness of the truth of the records he was sealing up. He exhorted his brethren, the Lamanites (see Moroni 10:1–23). He admonished readers to ponder the words of the Book of Mormon in their hearts (see Moroni 10:3) and then to ask God with real intent, having faith in Christ, "if these things are not true." He testified that God will manifest the truth of the Book of Mormon by the power of the Holy Ghost and that "by the power of the Holy Ghost ye may know the truth of all things" (see Moroni 10:4–5).

And when ye shall receive these things, I would exhort you that ye would ask God, the Eternal Father, in the name of Christ, if these things are not true; and if ye shall ask with a sincere heart, with real intent, having faith in Christ, he will manifest the truth of it unto you, by the power of the Holy Ghost.

—Moroni 10:4

Chart 176

Chart 177

Moroni's Invitation

Key Scripture Moroni 10:32

Explanation Moroni concluded his record by addressing "all the ends of the earth" (see Moroni 10:24–34). He invited all to come unto Christ, to lay hold upon every good gift, to avoid all ungodliness, and to love God. Thus, through the grace of God, all may become "perfected," or complete, in Christ. The structure of this passage shows that becoming perfected in Christ calls for a double emphasis on shunning evil, together with a double measure of the grace of God.

Come unto Christ,

and be perfected in him,

and deny yourselves of all ungodliness; and if ye shall deny yourselves of all ungodliness,

and love God with all your might, mind and strength,

then is his grace sufficient for you, that by his grace

ye may be perfect

in Christ

—Moroni 10:32

Chart 177

Scripture Index

Subject Index